Dedication
This book is dedicated to Mags, our sons Guy and Greg, his wife Kristen and their two lovely sons Andrew and Austin. And to all our wonderful family and dear friends.

Published in March 2018

ISBN 978-1-910505-31-1

Published by Evro Publishing
Westrow House, Holwell, Sherborne, Dorset DT9 5LF

Edited by Mark Hughes
Designed by Richard Parsons

Printed and bound in Slovenia by GPS Group

Every effort has been made to trace and acknowledge holders of copyright in photographs and to obtain their permission for the use of photographs. The publisher apologises for any errors or omissions in the credits given throughout this book and would be grateful to be notified of any corrections that should be incorporated in future reprints or editions.

www.evropublishing.com

Co-author
Andrew Marriott has spent his career in motorsport journalism, broadcasting and sports marketing. He covered his first Formula 1 race for *Motoring News*, the British weekly newspaper, at the age of 19 and over 50 years later he still reports from the Le Mans pitlane for US TV channel Fox Sports. He has often crossed paths with David Hobbs, reporting some of his early Lotus Elite races, documenting his Grand Prix and sports car exploits, and working on the same US broadcast team. He lives in West Sussex in the UK.

Jacket illustrations
The main image on the front cover shows the Ford GT40 that David Hobbs drove with Paul Hawkins in the 1968 Le Mans 24 Hours (*The Revs Institute for Automotive Research/Eric della Faille*). On the back cover, in chronological order, are 12 highlights from David's career: 1961 Lotus Elite (*Ben Cox*), 1963 Lola Mk6 (*Getty Images/GP Library*), 1968 Ford GT40 (*Bill Warner*), 1971 Ferrari 512M (*LAT Images*), 1971 Formula 5000 McLaren M10B (*Jim Culp*), 1973 Can-Am McLaren M20 (*Bill Warner*), 1973 Indycar McLaren M16C/D (*Getty Images/The Enthusiast Network*), 1974 Formula 1 McLaren M23 (*LAT Images*), 1977 BMW 320i Turbo (*Bill Warner*), 1983 Trans-Am Chevrolet Camaro (*The Revs Institute for Automotive Research/Geoffrey Hewitt*), 1984 Porsche 956B (*Bill Warner*) and 2017 Monaco Grand Prix television broadcast (*NBC*).

HOBBO

MOTOR RACER, MOTOR MOUTH
THE AUTOBIOGRAPHY OF DAVID HOBBS

DAVID HOBBS WITH **ANDREW MARRIOTT**

FOREWORD BY **SAM POSEY**

CONTENTS

FOREWORD
Sam Posey

When I heard that the much-overdue Hobbs book was in the works I feared, as a friend, that to make it at all interesting he would have to rely on fabrications and exaggerations — after all, people like to read about success. I envisioned a slim book with large print.

Instead, the only large print is on the cover, and inside *Hobbo* bulges with stories from David's two careers — racing and TV. As it happens, I was a rival of his in racing and I've worked with him in TV for almost 20 years, so I can tell you a couple of things about David that his innate modesty prevented him from writing about.

For example, he's a natural entertainer — the funniest in racing. You get a sense of it in his TV commentary, but obviously he's restrained, somewhat, when he's on the air. Given a congenial after-dinner atmosphere where everyone, especially David, has had some drinks, he becomes inspired. The next thing you know he's strutting around doing his German impressions or on his knees fondling imaginary breasts in the twenty-quid joke. I've been his straight man for many of his performances and he has never, ever disappointed.

As for TV, the intimacy of it — you're right there in someone's living room — eventually weeds out people who aren't genuine. David

has been at it for over 40 years, so I guess we can agree he has passed that test. A commentator also has to know what he's talking about and David brings to the booth a racer's feel for the flow of a race, what's going to matter and what isn't. He didn't compete for Emmys, which is too bad because by now David could have had a whole shelf full of them.

As a driver, David stands out because he almost never had a bad day. Roger Penske liked him because he used common sense and always brought the car back in one piece. BMW liked him because he talked the same language as their engineers — and he won races. I liked racing against him because I could trust his skill and in the wheel-to-wheel stuff we gave each other room — not a lot, just enough.

Best of all is the privilege of being able to call him a friend, and I think that as you read this book you will come to feel you know him, too.

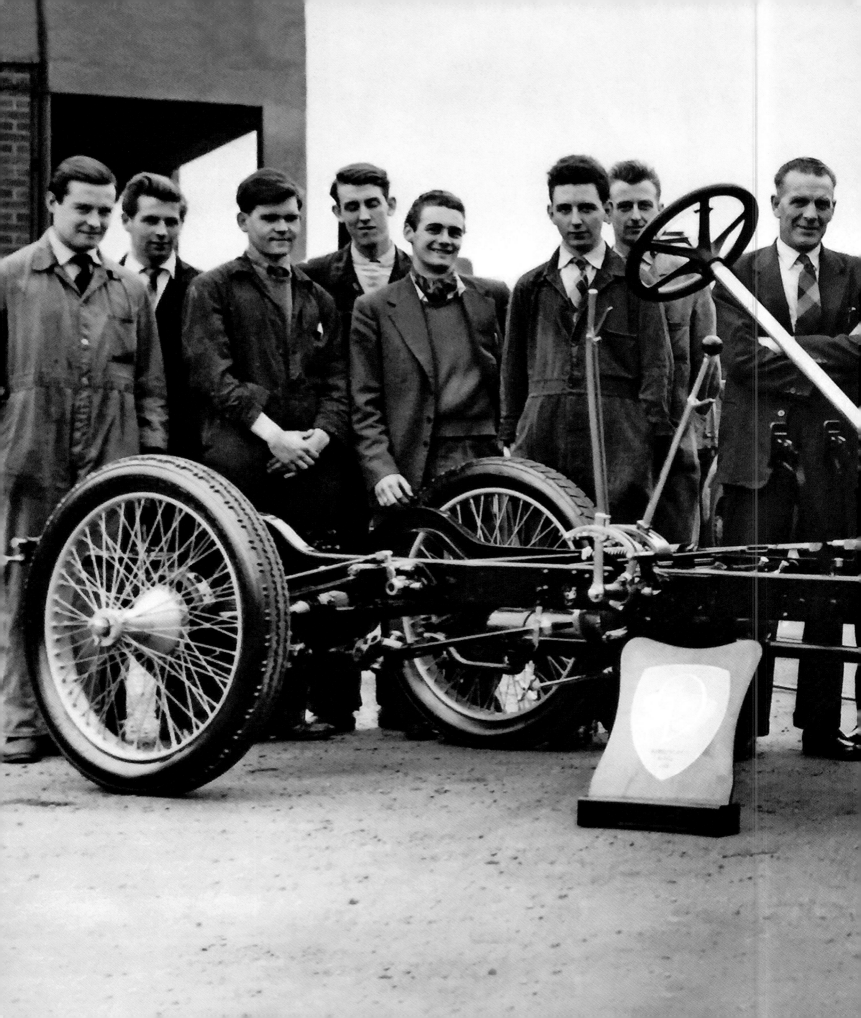

CHAPTER 1
1939–59
ALMOST AUSTRALIAN

Most people think of me as very British, but my parents, Howard and Phyllis, were Australian and came to Britain because of my father's work. Phyllis, my mother, was from a large family, the Reids, fairly new settlers in Australia as her father, a bridge engineer, had emigrated from Scotland. Dad was the son of an orange grower who was already the third generation working the Hobbs family's large grove on the outskirts of Adelaide, capital of South Australia.

The first representatives of the Hobbs family arrived in Australia from Wiltshire in the mid-1800s and, just in case you are wondering about my ancestry, Adelaide was never a convict town. Laid out by Colonel William Light in a grid pattern, with very wide streets and boulevards, Adelaide is one of the prettiest cities in Australia. On one of my trips to the Adelaide Grand Prix in the 1980s, I visited the church on Payneham Road attended by my ancestors and one of the windows there is dedicated to my grandfather, who was a fairly important figure in Adelaide in the early 1900s.

Dad went to the best boys' school in the city, Prince Alfred College, where he excelled particularly in mathematics and physics. He certainly had a mechanical bent because he started to invent things at a very early age. One thing he made was an orange grader, which

LEFT Daimler apprentices check out the chassis of a 1917 car that we restored. I am fourth from the left, eyeing up the rear suspension.
David Hobbs collection

shook the oranges around and sorted them so they could be packed by size. In about 1916, when he was 15, he even built an aeroplane, a monoplane with only one wing at a time when most aircraft were biplanes. He was a long way ahead of his time with that, but luckily for him he never managed to take off with it as he would have most likely crashed and killed himself. It was powered by an old motorcycle engine, probably a Villiers V-twin, and he just taxied around as he had no strip for getting into the air.

Dad became a self-taught engineer and inventor. Car gearboxes in those days were 'crash boxes', absolute pigs to handle with straight-cut gears and no synchromesh, and Dad was convinced that automatic transmissions were the way to go. He made various prototypes and his ideas attracted the interest of a consortium of Australian businessmen who sent him to Britain in 1929 to develop them further. There was a good reason for this choice of destination because the motor industry had become huge in Britain, which exported vast numbers of cars of numerous makes. In all parts of the British Empire, including Australia, practically the only cars you could buy were British, so companies like Austin, Morris, Jaguar, Rover, Hillman, Humber and Riley had become big manufacturers. So if Dad wanted to go into production with his automatic gearboxes, this was the place to go. The idea was to get his transmission into production and then return to Australia.

When my parents arrived in Britain they had an introduction from Dad's Australian backers to meet a Major C.J.P. Ball, who lived in Hampshire. Today he would probably be called a venture capitalist. He was pretty wealthy and sat on various boards including that of Alcan, the aluminium company. Major Ball supported Dad for nearly 30 years as his patron and took a gamble. Despite producing the best automatic transmission available at the time, however, the venture never paid off for either of them.

By the time war came in 1939, the British government wanted Dad to help with the war effort using his engineering expertise. He did some prototype testing for the War Office —

problem solving, engineering, inventions and ideas — and this work stopped him and my mother from returning to Australia.

I am the youngest of three children. My sister Barbara, 12 years older than me, was born in Australia. Soon after my parents came to Britain my brother John arrived and six years later I followed, on 9 June 1939, just three months before the war started. I was named David Wishart Hobbs — 'Wishart' you ask? Wishart is a family name on my Scottish maternal grandfather's side, descended from Admiral James Wishart, a British Admiral and Member of Parliament who died in 1723. So, next time you see me, pipe me aboard ye landlubbers.

Wartime

My earliest memories are of the Second World War when I was three or four years old. The first recollection is more of a sound than anything else, the shriek of air-raid warning sirens. Our home was a typical little British pre-war house, brick-built with a tiled roof and an attached garage, in Woodcote Road in Royal Leamington Spa, to give the place its full title. Mentioned in the Domesday Book of 1086, it is pretty much in the centre of England and became famous in the 17th century for the healing effects of its water. Queen Victoria visited and enjoyed the place so much that it was given the Royal Charter. After one of those air-raid warnings the Germans dropped a bomb — luckily a rare occurrence for Leamington Spa — right by a statue of Queen Victoria. It took a bit of a beating but only moved an inch on its plinth. The statue still stands in its modified resting place to this day.

With a population at that time of about 35,000, Leamington Spa was really a dormitory town to the big industrial centre of Coventry, about nine miles north. Coventry, the epicentre of car production in Britain, turned to manufacturing armaments during the war and so became a major target for the Luftwaffe. When Dad took me on test drives there were all sorts of dramatic things to see, like anti-aircraft guns heavily camouflaged with painted netting, barrage balloons to deter low-flying aircraft, and lots of big searchlights. Also nearby was the town of Warwick, and where the racecourse is now was the aerodrome, a fighter base, with Spitfires lined up against the fence. They all looked huge to me back then, although of course they seem so small when you see them now.

Between Leamington Spa and Coventry was Stoneleigh Park, the grounds of Stoneleigh Abbey, family home of Sir Thomas Leigh, a Lord Mayor of London. The beautiful house and its hundreds of acres were requisitioned for the Americans, who turned it into a huge base housing hundreds of soldiers. Occasionally my parents would host one or two American soldiers and they would stay in our spare bedroom. Naturally my teenage sister thought this was a very cool gesture of kindness to our allied friends and I am sure she enjoyed their visits immensely. To me they seemed nearly as old as my parents but of course they were probably only about 18 or 19. I vividly remember that one of them, a Texan named Jimmy, had a gun, the first I had ever seen. Long after the war, Stoneleigh became the site of Britain's biggest agricultural showground, where the Royal Show, always attended by Her Majesty The Queen, was held for many years. Today it is the home of the big classic motorsports exhibition Race Retro, held every February.

There are other things I remember about wartime. As all modern transport was used for the war effort, rubbish was collected by an ancient steam lorry or even a wagon drawn by a rather doleful horse. The domed top of the red postbox on the corner of our street was painted yellow to serve as a gas detector; the paint would change colour in the event of a gas attack, although by the time the gas was strong enough to do that we would probably all have been dead on the floor anyway. Everyone, including children, had a gas mask. I remember the lantern-shaped streetlights were gas in those days, with a mantle, not a flame, and in wartime the glass was painted blue, very dark at the top and lighter at the bottom, to provide just a bit of illumination during the blackout. Cars also had headlight guards, a bit like the head piece of

a suit of armour, and with them you could see next to nothing.

At the end of our street was a gigantic water tank, about 30 feet long, and it used to fascinate me. There were tanks like this everywhere to fight fires in case the water mains were damaged by bombing. Occasionally children must have drowned in them, because not only were they about five feet deep but they were also slab-sided, so if someone fell in there was no way of getting out without help.

Later there was some irony in my interest in these tanks. The Lotus Elite I raced early in my career had a Coventry Climax engine, which

ABOVE Every racing driver's book has to contain a photograph like this — on my soapbox 'racer' in the garden at Woodcote Road in Leamington Spa.
David Hobbs collection

RIGHT This is Mum and Dad, happy parents on the day of our marriage, in 1961. Despite coming from Australia, they look very much the 1950s British couple.
David Hobbs collection

was designed specifically to drive the high-pressure water pumps used with the tanks. Coventry Climax made thousands of these high-performance engines during the war and there were lots of little grey lorries made by Bedford (a division of GM) running around with trailers, each carrying a Coventry Climax engine and pump. This four-cylinder engine was very advanced for the day, with a single overhead camshaft and lightweight aluminium construction, and went on in much-developed form to power many race cars, including the Formula 1 World Championship winners of Jack Brabham and Jim Clark. The Coventry Climax engine was designed by Walter Hassan, whose sons went to school with my brother John. Later I got to know them too, and a generation later my two kids were at school with Hassan children — which is a round-about way of observing that there are many links, connections and happenstances that lead you through life.

Allotments were a big part of the war effort. Many sports fields, large gardens and even sections of parks were dug up and replaced by allotments, and anybody could have a patch of land to cultivate. Of course, the English have always been pretty keen on their gardening anyway and so hundreds of these allotment sites sprang up all over the country, and many still exist to this day on the same little fertile tracts of land. With Dad's family background, he knew about growing fruit and vegetables and dug up our small lawn, turning it into a very productive garden in which I was always so helpful with my own little wheelbarrow.

Compared with lots of children, my war years were rather fortunate, because Leamington Spa was definitely not a bomb target. Although the sirens were always going off, nothing much ever happened there, unlike Coventry, where on the night of 14 November 1940 almost 5,000 homes were destroyed with major loss of life and a third of the city's factories were damaged or destroyed. In Leamington Spa the only bomb damage I remember was to the town's one big department store, which was a beautiful old Regency building with a great big gap in it

that Dad used to delight in showing me.

Our main shelter against bombs involved the table that still sits in our kitchen. It was a wedding present for Mum and Dad when they married in 1925, so it came from Australia. When the sirens went off at night we would all trot downstairs and huddle under it. I was just a toddler and Mum would pop me into a thing we called a 'siren suit', which was like a one-piece, zip-up fleece, with legs and arms all part of it; such things seemed to come back into fashion recently as 'onesies' or something weird like that.

At the back of our garden was a playing field that fortunately had not been turned into allotments. I had plenty of space to play there, often with another little boy, Peter Robinson, who lived about four houses away. Of course, there were kids in cities who suffered real deprivation during the war, especially if they lived where bombs fell, perhaps even with their parents killed, but we were so relatively unaffected in Leamington Spa. I really did not notice that food was rationed, only one egg a week and rarely any meat, because that was just what life was like and any small child like me had never known anything different.

When I was about five, some Nissen huts — pre-fabricated buildings made from a half-cylindrical skin of corrugated steel — were erected on the outskirts of the town, not far from home, in an area that is now part of the grounds of a big comprehensive school. Housed there was a bunch of Italian prisoners of war and these guys were just as happy as Larry, living in Leamington Spa and out of the war. My brother and I used to go through a hole in the fence and visit them. John, being so much older than me, must have thought this was the bee's knees because they gave him cigarettes, and I have no doubt they must have tried to get me to smoke too. I remember being fascinated by the brown coveralls they had to wear, with a great big red splodge on their backs, which, years later, I realised was a target. However, I think escape would have been the last thing on the minds of most of these men because the camp was a good place for them to be.

Special boxes

Dad was always part of my childhood because he did all his work at home. Even though petrol was severely rationed, he received a bit extra to test cars with his automatic transmissions. His workshop was our single-car garage, with a dirt floor, a small treadle-operated lathe, a drill and a minimum of tools. He made a lot of smaller parts himself and was always experimenting with different hydraulic valves for his transmissions. He would make adjustments to a transmission, scrabbling about on the floor under a car on some old steel ramps, then drive off to assess the result. Very often I would accompany him on these test drives on very quiet, almost deserted roads. The only other vehicles were military — including the occasional tank — and public transport, plus bicycles and pedestrians.

These days children are such a part of our daily lives all the time, constantly with us. But when 'The Major' came to town to have a meeting, followed by dinner at our home, John and I were banished to the kitchen for our meal. We were expected to meet him very briefly and politely — 'Good evening, Major Ball, how are you, sir?' — and then go back to the kitchen. When I see kids now talking back to their parents, even their parents' friends, I think back to how strict things were in those days, although it was perfectly normal to me.

Dad's company produced prototype gearboxes for almost every vehicle manufacturer and fleet user you can name: Austin, Morris, Ford, Fiat and BMW, Bedford cars and trucks, Midland Red buses, Sheffield buses, and even railway trains. There was one prototype after another, but he could never get anybody to commit to putting it into production. I think if Dad had had a bit of entrepreneurship in him it would have been a different story. As a designer, as an inventor, he was unique, and obviously incredibly gifted, but then he ran into the problem that, despite his innate talent and knowledge, he had no real technical qualifications. He could have gone to university and easily obtained an engineering degree, but I expect his father, and Dad himself, always thought that he would follow his

After the war, our great wartime Prime Minister, Winston Churchill, came to Leamington Spa. We all trooped up to the main Kenilworth Road and watched him drive by in his Daimler car, giving us his famous 'V' for victory sign.

I was pretty spoiled by my mother. She knew hardly anyone in England and she became stir-crazy. She wanted to get back to Australia, to all her family, and decent weather. She and Dad both came from big families: she had eight brothers and sisters, all older, and he had five, four of them brothers. When I came along Mum used to say that I was her saviour and I was very much the apple of her eye. She insisted that my brother had to let me play with him and his pals and, of course, he thought I was a complete pest. By the time John was 11 or 12, the last thing he wanted was this five-year-old dragging along, so he and his friend John Sidwell used to tease me horribly, doing things like climbing trees with me but leaving me at the top unable to get down on my own. But by and large I do not remember any unhappiness during my childhood.

forebears into the orange-growing business. When Dad had meetings with senior engineers in car companies to interest them in his automatic transmission, often they could not get their heads around the fact that this untrained Aussie had developed something so far ahead of its time. Dad fought that sort of establishment resistance throughout his life.

Dad did all his design work using a slide rule and writing out his calculations in long hand. To me and my son Greg, it seems quite uncanny how he managed this, especially as that genius missed our two generations, and now it looks like it is missing the third one too. Dad even used his traditional, self-taught methods to design the incredible planetary gear train in his final four-speed Mecha-Matic gearbox, the one that nearly made it.

Fortunately by this stage Dad had a relationship with Daimler Cars in Coventry. Daimler was part of the Birmingham Small Arms group, BSA, which made motorcycles as well as Daimler and Lanchester cars. The company had a number of prototypes running around and was very pleased with them. So pleased that in 1954 BSA purchased 50 per cent of Dad's company, Hobbs Transmission, but without a controlling interest. Lanchester, one of the oldest car companies in the country, intended to produce a car called the Sprite, which was going to be the world's first automatic small car. Besides its Hobbs automatic transmission mated to a 1.4-litre engine, the Sprite had a ground-breaking monocoque structure — with integral body and chassis — at a time when almost all cars were built on separate chassis with bolt-on bodies. There was a big unveiling of the car at the 1955 Earls Court Motor Show, then by far the biggest such exhibition in the world, but unfortunately the Sprite was stillborn as BSA was falling on hard times and lacked the capital to go into production.

One of BSA's problems was that it was run by a flamboyant individual called Sir Bernard Docker. Sir Bernard and Lady Docker were the Donald and Melania Trump of their day,

ABOVE Can you spot me in this photo from my time at Feldon School for Boys in Leamington Spa? Next to me, to my left, is my mate Paul Young, whose sister, Margaret, became my wife.
David Hobbs collection

ABOVE One of Dad's biggest disappointments, the Lanchester Sprite of 1955, was well ahead of its time, complete with Hobbs Mecha-Matic gearbox. Here, some years later, Dad, brother John and I are standing with the car at the Jaguar factory.
David Hobbs collection

always in the newspapers and spending money like there was no tomorrow. Lady Docker wore outrageously expensive clothes and her spending was very conspicuous at a time when petrol remained scarce and foods like eggs, sugar, jam and meat were still rationed. They had a large yacht, a rare thing in those days, a fleet of Daimler limousines and numerous houses. Unfortunately their extravagance with BSA's money — including the creation of a string of lavish Daimler show cars made available for Lady Docker's personal use — took the company to the brink, and the Lanchester Sprite was one of the victims. Daimler Cars, along with Lanchester, was purchased by Jaguar Cars, just across town, while the Westinghouse Brake and Signal Company Ltd purchased the shares held by BSA in Hobbs Transmission.

When I left school in 1956, my astonishing record meant that university was out of the

question and I became a Daimler apprentice, very much as a result of Dad's connections with the company. Apprenticeship is a marvellous training and should be more actively pursued today, in both Britain and the US. Apprentices went through every department of the company — machine shops, assembly and experimental, and then the offices for design, sales and administration — and for one day and one evening a week we went to the technical college. The end result was supposed to be at least an Ordinary National Certificate (ONC) but preferably a Higher National Certificate (HNC), which was equivalent to a university degree. Don't even ask which I got… somehow I managed to evade both of these objectives. Anyway, two years into my five-year apprenticeship I became a Jaguar apprentice, not a Daimler one.

Dad and his company Hobbs Transmission, now with help from Westinghouse, continued

LEFT Stirling Moss takes a special interest in our exhibit at the Earls Court Motor Show. After Jimmy Clark raced my Lotus Elite at Daytona equipped with Mecha-Matic transmission, both he and Stirling had their personal Elites fitted with it as well.
David Hobbs collection

BELOW This is the Hobbs Mecha-Matic transmission in all its glory. When Michael Tee of *Motor Sport* tried it in a converted Ford Cortina in 1963, he described it as 'the best clutchless transmission we have used'.
The Revs Institute for Automotive Research/ Karl Ludvigsen

HOBBS TRANSMISSION, LTD.
78 Russell Terrace, Leamington Spa.

HOBBS Vehicle-type Transmission. The unit comprises a planetary gear train, plate clutches, and plate brakes carried by different elements of the gear train so that engagement of suitable combinations of clutches and brakes provides the required forward and reverse ratios. The clutches are used as main clutches for starting and stopping the vehicle. The transmission can be changed from one ratio to another without loss of traction. The clutches and brakes are actuated hydraulically by oil pressure acting on a synthetic rubber-faced diaphragm of relatively large area. The hydraulic pressure in the clutches is controlled by centrifugally actuated valves which provide an automatic action for starting and stopping. The change from one ratio to another is automatically controlled. The transmission is built up with a number of standard units, and may be readily adapted to various installations.

The Automatic Control Unit provides fully automatic changes in ratio according to road speed. The speeds at which changes occur are normally greater for "up" than for "down" changes, but are influenced by engine throttle opening and by movement of the throttle pedal beyond the full throttle position. Changes may be made at maximum or minimum predetermined engine speeds at will, according to the position of the pedal. An overriding hand control is also provided.

Assemblies and Diagrams showing the construction and operaion of the gearbox and automatic control.

the stable block but now had garage space for eight cars.

The gardener, Mr Gilkes, lived in the gatehouse. When he and Dad first met, Mr Gilkes said, 'It's a funny thing but I have worked before for a Mr Hobbs.' When Dad asked where, Mr Gilkes replied that there was obviously no connection because it was on an orange farm near Adelaide in Australia. At which point Dad struggled to contain his astonishment. Talk about a small world.

That year of 1955 continued to be a banner year. For my 16th birthday Dad bought me a Lambretta scooter and, rather more importantly, in the summer I met Margaret Young, the sister of one of my best school friends. So began my relationship with 'Mags' that continues to this day.

That Christmas, Dad took the whole family to Australia, including my sister Barbara, by then married, and her husband Alan. Mum bitterly regretted that she had not been able to return to Australia to live, and she had not visited since 1937, the year of her one and only previous return trip, when she took my brother and sister with her, by sea. Of course, being younger, I had never been and knew none of my relatives.

We flew around the world, first class, out via America and back via the Far East. We crossed the Atlantic with BOAC (British Overseas Airways Corporation) on a Boeing Stratocruiser, which took 19 hours to get to New York, in three legs, from London to Shannon in Ireland, then to Gander in Newfoundland, and finally to New York, where we stayed at the Taft Hotel. Then we flew to San Francisco in a Douglas DC-7, which, as the piston-engine forerunner of the DC-8 jet, was by far the noisiest thing I had ever travelled on. Finally we crossed the Pacific, landing at Honolulu and Fiji, and reached our destination, where I met so many relatives for the first time. My granny and grandpa on Dad's side were still alive, as were most of Mum's and Dad's sisters and brothers, and there were lots of cousins lurking, and of course they are still there. Some of them I met again when I took part in the Tasman Series in 1972 and there were new relatives to meet when, with Bob Varsha, I covered the Australian

to develop his automatic gearbox for other manufacturers, including Borgward, the German car company that built the very pretty Isabella, as raced successfully in British saloon car racing by Bill Blydenstein. Like Lanchester before it, Borgward decided to become the first manufacturer to produce a mid-sized car with an automatic gearbox. Almost unbelievably, Borgward also bit the dust and so Dad's dreams were squashed a second time, although his company did still have much-needed financial security from Westinghouse.

In the spring of 1955 Dad used some of the proceeds from the sale of half of his company to BSA to buy a beautiful home called Bericote House on the outskirts of Leamington Spa, just a mile or so from where the prisoner of war camp had been. A gorgeous house with nine acres of garden, it cost £12,000, but today would probably be worth at least £6 million. It had a beautiful winding drive with a gatehouse, a large walled kitchen garden with greenhouses, and a cobbled stone courtyard with a clock tower that had been

Grand Prix for television when it was held in Adelaide, from 1985 to 1995.

When the family returned from Australia, and I was reunited with Mags, her brother Paul came up with the idea of having a dance in the massive room, once a hay loft, above our garage block. We invited some friends and acquaintances, bought a leatherette-covered Pye record player, made some sandwiches with Heinz Sandwich Spread, opened the door and put on Cliff Richard and Elvis Presley. It was a success. The following weekend we had another go and even more people showed up. The whole thing just took off and soon the place was packed every week. Part of our popularity was probably that it only cost two shillings to get in, to help defray the cost of the Sandwich Spread. At first my parents were not too concerned, although the tenants in the flat under the clock tower were not very impressed. Down in the garage one night, however, I became aware of the ceiling throbbing up and down to the beat of Bill Haley and I realised our venture was getting out of control. Some pretty odd people were also turning up by now, no doubt eyeing up our rather grand home, checking out the window fastenings. It seems that Mags, her brother Paul and I had some impresario tendencies in us, but we had to let it go, fun as it had been.

In the meantime, in the real world Hobbs Transmission and Westinghouse thought they were going to get a very big order. Ford had purchased a large number of prototype transmissions and fitted them to the vehicles driven by the company's district sales managers. The response was incredibly positive: the reps loved them and so did the dealers they visited. The gearbox was to go into the new Ford Cortina, which became a bestseller in Britain. Once again it would have been the smallest automatic car in the world — and yet again the deal fell through. It seems hard to believe that a business as substantial as Westinghouse would not have had its i's dotted and t's crossed, but obviously something went badly wrong at a late stage because the company built a brand-new factory just outside Manchester to make 500

transmissions a day but in the end produced only a handful there.

Dad never gave up designing and drawing. His last endeavour was an infinitely variable gearbox and again he was ahead of the curve as nowadays thousands of cars a day are built with similar transmissions. He always compared himself to Dr Rudolf Diesel, who fell off a boat in 1913 before the value of his invention, the diesel engine, was recognised.

Dad was a pioneer and a mechanical genius. My sister Barbara and brother John were blessed with the same sort of brain power. I wanna know wot 'appened in my case.

ABOVE My mother and me on my 21st birthday, at the Manor House Hotel in Leamington Spa. Mags and I had our wedding reception there too.
David Hobbs collection

CHAPTER 2

1959–61
FAMILY RACING

I was lucky to acquire my first motorised transport, the Lambretta scooter, when I was 16 and I soon went everywhere on it flat out, including when Mags, my girlfriend, was on the pillion seat. When I say 'flat out', that was only about 50mph, so within just a few months I exchanged it for an older but much faster motorcycle, a 1952 500cc Triumph Speed Twin. Then we really did hurtle around the countryside.

Back then, of course, there was so little traffic, which made for more speed and in my opinion a lot less danger, although my sister Barbara, who by then was a qualified doctor, got quite upset with me and used to read me the riot act: 'If you could see some of the injuries I see every day in hospital, etc, etc, etc.' But that was water off a duck's back. I just loved going fast, judging the speed of other people on the road and swooping through corners. I hardly ever fell off, which was a good sign, whereas one of my friends who also had a bike often ended up on the ground. So I felt I had some natural balance and speed, and I considered racing the Speed Twin.

Then Mags and I went on the bike to a car race at the little 1.3-mile Mallory Park circuit, which was quite a short journey from home. There I watched a guy called Tony Lanfranchi driving an Elva Courier in one race. I thought to myself that cars might be a better racing option. So I decided to race Mum's car, a seven-year-old Morris

LEFT At Oulton Park in 1960, in front of big crowds and television cameras, I had an inauspicious start to my first race in my father's Jaguar XK140 drophead coupé, equipped with his Mecha-Matic automatic gearbox.
John Holroyd

Oxford. That idea would be absolutely ludicrous nowadays. The Morris's registration number was MOL 44 and the car became known as 'Mol'.

Mum's Morris Oxford

At this stage Dad had his own factory and it was quite well equipped, with a number of lathes, milling machines and drillers, and a pit for working under vehicles. We thought it was a big place but actually it was only 5,000sq ft. Dad had done some prototype work for BMC, the British Motor Corporation, formed from the merger of Austin and Morris, and in this workshop he had a B-series engine attached to a Mecha-Matic gearbox. The B-series was an overhead-valve design that in due course replaced the side-valve engine for later models of the Morris Oxford and the Austin A70, classic British family saloons of the time, as well as being fitted to the MGA and MGB sports cars. So we put this B-series engine into my potential race car, which remained Mum's daily driver, and of course it was still attached to the Hobbs automatic gearbox. I fitted an MGB inlet manifold and a pair of SU carburettors that I managed to buy for a couple of quid from Daimler, where there were rooms full of these carbs, thousands of them, that were not needed and were probably going to be scrapped. So now I had a much-uprated engine in the Morris.

In my apprenticeship I was working through all aspects of the machine shops at Daimler and I had a stint at balancing the two halves of a fluid flywheel. This involved filling each half with hot wax and when it solidified we skimmed the surface down to the vanes and put it on a balance wheel. Then we drilled small indents that we filled with lead until we got a balance. As you can imagine, this shop looked like some Stygian hole with big vats of boiling wax, filled with smoke and with its walls and ceiling covered in soot.

Now for me the exhaust note was very important: 'Mol' had to sound like a Triumph TR3 or a Jaguar XK120, even if she would only do about 90mph downhill with a tail wind. Working in this balancing area at Daimler was Bill, the pipe bender, who had been around for so long that he must have made up a set of exhaust pipes

for every Daimler ever made. Dotted around those vats of boiling wax were coke braziers with glowing coals and various lengths of pipe. So I suggested to Bill that we make a sporty manifold and set of pipes for 'Mol', which we duly did, and they fitted perfectly. There was no silencer, just an open four-into-one exhaust system with the tail pipe under the driver's door, and noise-wise it was most satisfactory. What Mum must have thought on her way to the hairdressers I cannot imagine but she was a good sport and never mentioned it. So now I had a rorty racer of sorts.

To go racing I had to join a club, of which there were several options. The famous British Racing Drivers' Club (BRDC) was out of the question as membership was by strict invitation only. You had to have won international races to join and have the committee reckon you were a decent chap too. But there were groups such as the British Automobile Racing Club (BARC), the British Racing & Sports Car Club (BRSCC), the Nottingham Sports Car Club (NSCC), and so on. You only had to be a member of one of these because most of them invited the other clubs to their events and to join you merely had to pay a subscription fee of about £5 a year.

The very first race I entered was at Snetterton in eastern England, near where the Lotus factory is now situated. The date was 24 April 1959, not long before my 20th birthday. The idea was to drive the car to the races and then drive it back afterwards. We did the first bit right: I got it there, driving with my old school chum Tony Barrett, who remains a close friend today even though we now have the Atlantic between us. I was entered, naturally, in the saloon category, but when I checked in they said, 'Oh, goodness, you've got an automatic gearbox in there. This is not homologated; this car does not come with an automatic. So we're going to have to put you in the sports car category.'

Suddenly I was mixing it with Austin-Healeys, Triumph TR2s, Lotus Elites and Jaguar XK120s, and all I had was this big four-door saloon. Besides, I was racing on Michelin X road tyres, not knowing all the ramifications of racing tyres, lowered suspension settings, and all of that. My

car even had a bench seat, not buckets. So I just dragged around at the back and, of course, blew up the engine, running the big ends. I had seen a movie where the hero had put the silver lining papers from a cigarette packet underneath the bearing shells and went on to win his big race. I tried that but it did not work. So we had to leave 'Mol' at Snetterton and got a lift home. A few days later another friend persuaded his father to drive me the 120 miles back to the track and then tow the Morris all the way home cross-country, on a dreadful route with no decent roads. This was my first experience of a long-distance tow, a very sedate one behind the Rover of a responsible middle-aged father.

My next tow home was rather more exhilarating. I had been to Goodwood for a test day with the BARC. The idea was to lap the track while various strategically placed observers would judge how well they thought you were driving. Points were awarded at the end of the day and these were vital to get your full racing licence. I wobbled around the circuit in 'Mol' on my

ABOVE Three snapshots from my scrapbook recording my first-ever race meeting, with 'Mol', Mum's seven-year-old Morris Oxford, at Snetterton on 24 April 1959. With me is Tony Barrett, my first racing helper.
David Hobbs collection

ABOVE Exploring the limits with 'Mol' at Silverstone during 1959. I removed the bumpers and the straight-through exhaust can be seen. I think the ride height could have been usefully lowered.
David Hobbs collection

BELOW My first visit to Goodwood with 'Mol', seen in the paddock between the Healey Silverstones of Bill Pinckney and Ben Cox.
Ben Cox

Michelin X road tyres and eventually the engine went 'bang' — but I did get my points. Meanwhile, I made a new racing buddy, Bill Pinckney, whom I met through Tony Barrett, and he rushed around picking up his points too in his Healey Silverstone, a pretty potent car on Dunlop R5 racing tyres.

Bill, being a resourceful chap, had a tow rope, so we hooked up my blown-up Morris racer behind his Healey Silverstone and set off for home at a fair clip, again on a tortuous route with lots of narrow country lanes and villages. To keep the rope taut, I tried to anticipate Bill's braking and it worked well, although the rope broke a couple of times and by the time we reached Banbury, about 20 miles from home, it was pretty short. Our cars were so close together for that last leg of the journey that I could barely see the back of Bill's car, just his head. It was also pitch dark by now and as I was so close behind I turned off my headlights, relying on Bill's to see as far ahead as possible. Those 20 miles took us just over 20 minutes — a real white-knuckle ride.

At Goodwood Bill introduced me to another

rookie racer, Bill Postins, and we all became firm friends. When I come to Britain I still see Bill Postins and his wife Joan as well as Bill Pinckney's widow Evy — so through racing I made friends for life. Joan has good motoring connections as her father owned Abbey Panels, the famous company that made the steel monocoque chassis for the Jaguar D-type and E-type and also the Ford GT40, among many other cars.

Despite these somewhat ignominious experiences, my first season was a lot of fun. Mags and I would drive to the races in the Morris with a picnic basket and it seemed very exciting and glamorous. Sometimes her friend Jane Hutt, who would later become our bridesmaid, would come along too, and my mate Tony might bring a couple of pals as well. It was all very sociable, and if we did well we would all go off to a pub afterwards and have a few drinks to celebrate. It was very happy-go-lucky.

As well as competing, I took Mags, her brother Paul, her friend Jane and another Jaguar apprentice called Dickie Stewart to spectate at the *Daily Express* International Trophy meeting at Silverstone. This was an important fixture, a non-championship Formula 1 race, and all the big teams including Ferrari took part. We set off in 'Mol' with me at the wheel in very racy mood, the five of us packed in like sardines in a can. I knew a neat back route on winding lanes with hedges and ditches on both sides, but for a big race like this my quiet roads were suddenly full of traffic, most of which I overtook in pretty hairy situations, egged on by my passengers.

Just after the village of Preston Capes was a very nice right/left 'S' bend but such was my speed that I lost grip, spun 180 degrees and slid into a ditch. 'Mol' ended up facing the wrong way and on her side. We all had to climb out of the two doors that were not trapped by the ditch while our earlier 'victims' passed us gesturing the famous two-fingered salute. Fortunately a farmer came along and pulled us out and a small amount of money changed hands. There was no damage to the car, or us, and off we set again. Many years later a man came up to me and said:

BELOW PUSH! This is the famous occasion when I put 'Mol' into a ditch in the village of Preston Capes on the way to Silverstone. At the back is Mags's brother Paul. A local tractor driver was quickly on the scene to pull us back on the road. *David Hobbs collection*

'I remember you. You overtook me on the back road to Silverstone, then I passed you on your side in a ditch thinking what a daft pillock you were. Before I got to Silverstone, you passed me again!'

Dad's Jaguar XK140

For my second season, 1960, I managed to persuade Dad to let me race his Jaguar XK140, which was a drophead coupé dating from 1955, quite luxurious with wind-up windows, wood veneer on the doors, and a beautifully plush convertible top. Initially I also raced this car on its regular Michelin X road tyres and just said to people that I was still learning, although obviously rather slowly.

The season opener was at Oulton Park in April and on the last lap I turned the car on its roof. Oddly enough, some of the races were televised in those days, including this one, so by the time I called home Dad already knew what had happened. He said, 'Well, you broke it, so you fix it.' The flip did quite a bit of damage, all fairly

THIS PAGE Disaster at Oulton Park. After racing Mum's Morris Oxford in my first season, I moved up to Dad's Jaguar XK140 drophead coupé for 1960 — and did this to it in my first race. I was unhurt but chastened as I watched from the nearby commentary box while marshals dealt with the clear-up.
John Holroyd

superficial, but it was quite expensive to repair. Even more damage occurred on the way home with Mags when the bonnet suddenly flew up, folded itself over the windscreen and completely blocked the view forwards — that was more scary than the shunt itself. Somehow I managed to force the bonnet closed, tied it down and we continued on our way.

A guy from the paint shop at Daimler resprayed the car in his small garage at home. He had to do the job after work, in the late evening when the air was rather cool, and this caused the finish to go matt. What with that, and my use of a piece of old canvas to replace the plush roof, Dad's poor Jaguar never looked the same again. Thankfully, however, he was fairly laid back about this, and indeed about my racing — he neither particularly encouraged me nor discouraged me. As with Mum's Morris, I paid all the racing costs from my wages at Jaguar, by that time about £8 a week.

After that initial setback, I modified the XK140 quite a bit and, significantly, finally purchased

some Dunlop R5 racing tyres. I must admit that some of the parts I needed came out of the stores at Jaguar, where I was now serving my apprenticeship because Jaguar had taken over the ailing Daimler. I managed to acquire a triple carburettor set-up and some disc brakes appeared as if by magic to replace the original drums. I was lucky that Len Lucas, one of Jaguar's top engine builders who had put together a lot of the racing engines for the C-types and D-types, got enthusiastic about my racing and prepared a strong engine for me, again hooked up to a Mecha-Matic gearbox. Len and I would knock off from work at Jaguar at 5pm and drive to Dad's factory in Leamington Spa to work on the car and then I would take him back to Coventry — all for no charge. Len's one requirement was that he had to be at his favourite pub, The White Lion at Allesley, no later than 10pm, so that he had half an hour before 'last orders' — Britain's licensing laws at that time meant no alcohol could be served after 10.30pm.

By the end of a Friday the XK140 would be

LEARNING FAST : At the beginning of the day's racing at the Eight Clubs Silverstone meeting, D. Hobbs looked a trifle wild in his XK140 with Hobbs automatic transmission, but by the end of the day he had won a race and finished fifth in the " Motor Sport " Silverstone Trophy handicap

ABOVE This is the first colour shot I have of my racing. Here, at Mallory Park in the XK140, I sweep down from Devil's Elbow, with a bit of elbow showing in my short-sleeved shirt. As you can see the Jaguar was an unusual sky-blue colour.
David Hobbs collection

BELOW The Mallory Park paddock with the Jaguar XK140 parked alongside someone's Lotus Elite on a bright day early in 1960. I had a good look at that car and made a mental note that it might be a sensible choice for the following season.
David Hobbs collection

ready for Sunday's racing, and Mags and I, with Len, would head off for places like Snetterton, Silverstone, Oulton Park, Brands Hatch or Goodwood, leaving at an excruciatingly early hour because we always seemed to be the first to be scrutineered, at about 8am. There was no question of travelling to the track the night before, partly because Len had to have his session in The White Lion the previous evening. He had an amazing constitution: without trying he could put away 12 pints of beer a night and still show up for work the next day none the worse for wear. On a Saturday evening he would certainly have drunk that much, on top of six or seven pints at lunchtime, but every Sunday morning at about 5.30am when Mags and I arrived at his house in Coventry there would be Len, standing on the doorstep, tapping his foot. Mags would fold herself up in what passed as back seats and off we would go.

At that time Jaguar's managing director was F.R.W. 'Lofty' England, who was very well known and influential in racing circles as he had been

LEFT The Jaguar XK140 had a very strong engine thanks to some expertise from the factory. Here I am checking out the three SU carburettors with Derek Callender, a chum who used to help me out.
David Hobbs collection

BELOW Another Mallory Park paddock view, complete with the lake behind, and my mother and father with my brother John and his wife Jenny.
David Hobbs collection

team manager when Jaguar had so much success at Le Mans with the C-types and D-types. He lived near us so I vaguely knew him and we even used the same route to work. There were times when I came across him, sometimes driving a pre-production E type, and raced him on my big Triumph motorbike, although there was the slight problem that I was supposed to be at work an hour earlier than him.

When I started to race Dad's XK140, 'Lofty' showed quite a bit of interest. He must have realised that a lot of factory parts mysteriously found their way onto my car, but he never said anything. He was a clerk of the course (the term for 'race director' in that era) at Silverstone and one day he strolled by and looked over my car on the grid, sitting on pole position. Remember, it looked horrible after that paint job on that the cold night, and it also had one headlight missing so that I could create a primitive duct to the carburettors using an old inner tube from a tyre. 'Lofty' finished his examination and said sarcastically, 'Smart turn-out.' But apparently

he liked the way I drove and thought I was a promising racer.

By the end of my second season I was really starting to learn the racing game and I had won the occasional club race. My best memory is a hell of a race against an Aston Martin DB4, a car that was four or five years younger than my Jaguar, but I beat it and won the race. By now a few influential people were starting to take notice.

Getting serious with a Lotus Elite

For the 1961 season I switched from the Jaguar to one of Colin Chapman's beautiful little Lotus Elite cars complete with that fire-pump-derived Coventry Climax engine and, of course, the Hobbs Mecha-Matic transmission. It seemed a good move because Elites were already being raced successfully in the GT category. One of the most successful was the famous car with the number plate DAD 10 as raced by Les Leston, who ran a motor accessory business and virtually invented fire-proof racing overalls and specialist pit boards. There was also Graham Warner, who

ABOVE The Aintree paddock, with the Jaguar XK140 and my friend Bill Pinckney's Lotus Eleven behind.
David Hobbs collection

BELOW I did acquire a Lotus Elite for the 1961 season. With a Lotus Eleven chasing, this is Silverstone early in the season, before I painted a big stripe on the car.
David Hobbs collection

LEFT The Elite in Dad's workshop in Leamington Spa on its trailer ready for my most important race yet — the sports car race supporting the Formula 1 International Trophy race at Silverstone on 6 May 1961. Many of these early colour photos were taken by my friend Ben Cox.
Ben Cox

BELOW Loaded up behind the faithful Ford Zephyr tow car ready for the Silverstone International Trophy meeting. In the back is Henry Lee, the ex-Lotus mechanic who helped develop my Elite into a race winner.
Ben Cox

RIGHT In the Silverstone paddock. I think this is the day the back window broke, as several chaps seem to be scrutinising it. We lightened the car considerably following suggestions from Henry Lee.
Ben Cox

LEFT Looking very apprehensive before the start of a race in the Elite.
David Hobbs collection

ran the big sports car sales outfit in London called The Chequered Flag and his car had the registration LOV 1. My car's number plate was rather less memorable — 5649 UE.

My early races in Britain went well, particularly after an ex-Lotus man called Henry Lee joined us. He saw me race at Mallory Park and offered his expertise in setting up the car — and I was able to win with it. As things were going well I decided to be more adventurous and enter my first race abroad. This was the Nürburgring 1,000Km in May 1961 and with that kind of distance I needed a co-driver, so I invited my friend Bill Pinckney. He had switched to a Lotus Eleven sports racer at the same time as I moved up to the Elite and he was very quick in that car and also winning races, so we were quite a good combination.

We found ourselves at the Nürburgring, learning the incredible 14.2 miles of the Nordschleife amid the mist and pine trees of the Eifel region, and after some trials and tribulations we were decently fast. But then we had a major

setback when we were thrown out of our class, GTs up to 1,300cc, after being protested by a fellow competitor for having my Dad's automatic gearbox in the car. This same driver had told me some time earlier that I must be mad to use an automatic, but I blew him off at Brands Hatch a week before the Nürburgring race and when we got to Germany he decided to protest.

I had to go to the clerk of the course's office where I was told, 'Herr Hobbs, your car is not homologated because of your automatic gearbox. So we are going to put you in the 1,600cc sports car class.' This left us with little chance of a good result because there were faster Porsches in that class with some good drivers. Well, to cut a long story short, we won the class. Standing on the podium with Bill was a wonderful experience, sharing an absolutely massive laurel wreath covered with golden leaves and having the British national anthem played. I must admit, too, that back in 1961 there was the slight lingering feeling of still being part of the Allied powers when winning a race in Germany. Another big plus

RIGHT My first race abroad was the Nürburgring 1,000Km, a round of the World Sports Car Championship, on 28 May 1961, with my friend Bill Pinckney co-driving. Here, with Bill before practice, I am a picture of sartorial elegance in my go-faster jacket.
David Hobbs collection

BELOW We had to run to our cars at the echelon start of the Nürburgring 1,000Km and, as shown by this view with my Elite still stationary in the foreground, I was one of the slowest away in the field of 64 cars.
The Revs Institute for Automotive Research

VII. Internationales
ADAC **1000km** RENNEN
28. Mai 1961 NÜRBURGRING   Weltmeisterschaftslauf für Sportwagen

Das offizielle Ergebnis nach Klassen:
==================================
(44 Runden = 1003,64 km)

Sportwagen bis 3000 ccm:
1.StNr.1 Gregory/Casner   USA   Maserati   44 Rd. 7:51.39,2=127,6
2.StNr.5 P.u.R.Rodriguez   Mexiko Ferrari   43 "   7:52.32,4=124,5
3.StNr.4 Trips/Ph.Hill   D/USA   Ferrari   43 "   7:54.59,3=123,9
4.StNr.7 Trintignant/Maglioli F/I Maserati   39 "   7.12.16,5=123,8
Weitere Zieldurchfahrten: StNr.3 Hill/Trips, Ferrari, 24 Rd; StNr.11
McLaren/Clark, NZ/GB, Aston Martin, 23 Rd; StNr.6 Trintignant/Maglioli,
F/I, Maserati, 7 Rd; StNr.10 Dixon/Halford, GB, Cooper, 7 Rd;
Ausgeschieden: StNr.12 Gachnang/Caillet, Ch, Ferrari.
Schnellste Runde: StNr.3, Graf Trips/Ph.Hill, D/USA, Ferrari 9.15,8=
147,7 km/h (neuer Rundenrekord für Sportwagen).
Von 9 Gestarteten 4 gewertet.

Sportwagen bis 2000 ccm:
1.StNr.22 Linge/Greger   D   Porsche   43 Rd. 8:02.07,5=122,0
          Moss/G.Hill   GB
2.StNr.21 Bonnier/Gurney   S/USA   Porsche   41 Rd. 7:52.37,1=118,6
3.StNr.25 Siffert/Liebl   Ch/D   Ferrari   40 "   7:52.32,8=115,8
Weitere Zieldurchfahrten: StNr.27 Graham/Martyn, GB, Lotus, 35 Rd.;
StNr.20 Moss/Hill, GB, Porsche, 21 Rd; StNr.24 G.u.H.de Bandeira, P,
Ferrari, 7 Rd; StNr.26 Wicky/de Siebenthal, CH, Maserati, 6 Rd; StNr.23
Barth/Herrmann, D, Porsche, 2 Rd.
Schnellste Runde: StNr.20, Moss/G.Hill, GB, Porsche, 9.42,1=141,0 km/h.
Von 8 Gestarteten 3 gewertet.

Sportwagen bis 1600 ccm:
1.StNr.92 Hobbs/Pinckney   GB   Lotus   40 Rd. 8:01.06,4=113,6
2.StNr.36 Bislas/v.Saucken D   Porsche   40 "   8:01.42,8=113,6
3.StNr.33 Runte/Lindemann   D   Porsche   39 "   8:00.48,7=111,0
4.StNr.32 Kräft/Nyffeler   D   Porsche   39 "   8:01.09,8=110,9
Weitere Zieldurchfahrt: StNr.31 H.Walter/H.Müller, CH, Porsche, 27 Rd;
Schnellste Runde: StNr.31 H.Walter/H.Müller, CH, Porsche, 10.00,5=136,8.
Von 5 Gestarteten 4 gewertet.

Sportwagen bis 1150 ccm:
1.StNr.43 Kerrison/Sargent GB   Lola   41 Rd. 8:02.15,8=116,3
2.StNr.42 Bekaert/de Selincourt GB Lola   40 "   7:53.24,0=115,6
3.StNr.41 Vögele/Ashdown   CH/GB Lola   40 "   7:59.22,2=114,2
4.StNr.47 McCowen/Hedges   GB   Austin H. 38 "   7:57.26,7=108,9
5.StNr.51 Laureau/Armagnac F   DB   37 "   7:51.47,9=107,4
6.StNr.52 Moynet/Caillaud   F   DB   37 "   8:01.37,0=105,1
Weitere Zieldurchfahrten: StNr.45 Hawkins/Simson, AU/GB, Austin Healey,
21 Rd; StNr.44 Hitches/Hicks, GB, Lola, 11 Rd.
Schnellste Runde: StNr.43 Kerrison/Sargent, GB, Lola, 10.25,3=131,4
Von 8 Gestarteten 6 gewertet.
Der Stand der Sportwagen-Weltmeisterschaft: Ferrari 22 Pkt.; Maserati
11 Pkt.; Porsche 8 Pkt.

ABOVE On the way to our amazing class win at the Nürburgring. It came after we had been removed from the GT class and put in with the sports racers because of my Elite's automatic gearbox.
David Hobbs collection

FAR LEFT Both Bill Pinckney and I are taking our Nürburgring 1,000Km class victory ceremony pretty seriously.
David Hobbs collection

LEFT Here's the proof — winners of 'Sportwagen bis 1600 ccm' in the 1961 Nürburgring 1,000Km.
David Hobbs collection

ABOVE My second foray abroad with the Elite in 1961 was for another World Sports Car Championship race, at Pescara in Italy. Here the Hobbs équipe — the Ford Zephyr estate with the Elite on the trailer and Dad's Borgward Isabella as support vehicle — stops for fuel. It was a long way to drive, over 1,250 miles each way.
Ben Cox

was the prize money: the Germans, being very methodical people, had a structured prize money scale, so the smallest GT cars got the least and the big sports cars the most. Our class transfer meant that we won about ten times as much dough. All in all it was a good day and the cash bonus came thanks to a whingeing rival.

That night we attended our first international prize-giving, held in the Sporthotel. A very impressive building, this was a huge hotel and conference centre that also comprised the main grandstand across the track from the pits. All the speeches were in German and Alice 'Baby' Caracciola, widow of the great racing driver Rudolf Caracciola, presented the prizes. It seemed to us that every Porsche in the race received a prize… the first blue Porsche, the slowest Porsche… you get the drift. Anyway Frau Caracciola started off perfectly well but as the evening wore on she waxed ever more lyrical about her late husband, who had died prematurely through illness only 18 months earlier, and became increasingly emotional, so

that by evening's end she was a mass of tears.

I carried on racing and winning in the car in Britain and then Bill and I went abroad again to another incredible track. This was the 15.9-mile road circuit of Pescara in Italy. The circuit was roughly triangular, with two long straights between villages and a twisty bit through hills forming the third side of the triangle. There was a demanding section in the seaside town of Pescara, including a railway crossing, and parts of the track were very narrow and bumpy too. It was a big challenge, and even included a couple of errant cows on the road at one point. We qualified well but had a rare engine failure on the opening lap, with Bill at the wheel. So we packed up our pit, a trestle table in the main street alongside the track, and went off to a wonderful beach while Lorenzo Bandini won the race in a Ferrari. It turned out that this was the last-ever race at this historic circuit.

As Bill Pinckney was my very first team-mate, he was obviously significant in my racing career although we did not actually drive together very

often because the opportunities were quite few. He was also a great friend and Mags and I had a wonderful time with him and his wife Evy for many years, until poor old Bill was killed.

Bill was a gung-ho character who did all sorts of outrageous things. He started flying his own aeroplane and on one occasion left the house, without mentioning a thing to Evy, and disappeared for several days. At first she thought he had just gone to the pub but eventually she received a cable from South Africa. He had flown there in his single-engine aeroplane, down the entire length of darkest Africa and over hundreds of miles of jungle, where he would never have been found if he had gone down. He had started off with a friend who quit when they got to Cairo so Bill continued on his own. Over one of the central African countries the authorities ordered him to land, while he was flying over dense jungle, but after about 20 minutes of discourse a German voice from about 20,000 feet above Bill, the captain of a Lufthansa 747, said, 'Vehr do you sink he is going to land? On ze treetops?' Silence

ABOVE The first race lap at the 15.9-mile Pescara circuit, on the twisty section through the Abruzzi mountains, with Bill Pinckney at the wheel behind a group that includes Nino Vaccarella in a Maserati (number 2). Unfortunately for us, the engine blew up before the end of the lap.
David Hobbs collection

BELOW Pieces from a broken Coventry Climax engine. This is the damage that occurred at Pescara, where the circuit's two long straights, each of around four miles, meant sustained running at maximum revs.
Ben Cox

RIGHT After our early departure from the four-hour race at Pescara, we went to the beach. Here I am with Mags and my brother John.
David Hobbs collection

BELOW Back at Silverstone in July 1961, I line up to pass John Chatham in his famous and very fast Austin-Healey 3000 in the British Empire Trophy race. That car is still racing today, but I have no idea what happened to the Elite.
David Hobbs collection

followed. Of course, once Bill got to South Africa he had to fly back again.

Bill also got to know my great friend John Sadiq, whose brother Johnny was senior captain for Pakistan International Airways. One day on a whim Bill thought he would 'pop' over to Pakistan and visit Johnny. He flew over some dodgy countries and right at the end of the trip ran out of fuel and was forced to land on a dusty street in a Pakistani town. The police must have thought he was some kind of drug runner and put him in jail, so Johnny had to get him out.

In the end Bill's craziness caught up with him. After a short but successful racing career he turned his hand to pig farming and did extremely well. As a pilot he belonged to the Flying Farmers' Association and he flew with a couple of friends to the Hebrides. After checking out the pigs on a farm somewhere in the Western Isles, he attempted a take-off from a short downhill grass strip and clipped a fence with the plane's undercarriage. That was it. Bill was gone, about 20 years after we had raced

together at the 'Ring. It was a very stern message that we really are here today and gone tomorrow. Mags and I still miss him.

My third season racing had gone well and I had recorded 14 wins from 18 starts — not a bad record. I had a learned a good deal about motor racing and proved I had the requisite talents and speed, and I was becoming more widely noticed. At the end of the year the prestigious *Motor Racing Annual* wrote: 'Another notable GT competitor in an Elite was David Hobbs, whose car was equipped with the Hobbs Mecha-Matic four-speed automatic transmission — a seemingly unlikely device for a race car, but one which has proved effective during a busy competition programme.'

Not only had I won a lot of races but those successes had further impressed my boss at Jaguar. That was very useful and 'Lofty' England proved to be a helpful ally in more ways than one.

One day during 1961 the apprentice supervisor at Jaguar called me into his office and proceeded to give me a severe dressing down.

ABOVE A very pleasing victory came in the Astley Trophy race at Aintree on August Bank Holiday Monday. That was an impressive garland and I still have the trophy, awarded by Sir Stanley Bell.
John Holroyd

ABOVE During 1961,
as I was reaching the
end of my Jaguar
apprenticeship, a
fabulous opportunity
came my way when
'Lofty' England invited
me to do a Silverstone
test in this experimental
car, E2A, a sort of 'halfway
house' between the
D-type and the E-type.
*The Revs Institute for
Automotive Research/
George Phillips*

'You are without doubt the worst boy we have ever had through the programme. Your work ethic is non-existent, your school work at the technical college is a complete failure' — I regret to state that he had a very valid point there — 'and in my opinion you will never make anything of your life. You will be a complete failure. I hope you never darken my doorstep again and I never have the misfortune to interact with you in any way. Good day, and don't let the door hit you on the arse on the way out.'

Phew! Why not give it to me straight, Mr Barker? Even I was a bit subdued at this onslaught, but life works in mysterious ways.

Not long after this, I was working — well, lurking — in the Experimental Department when the shop supervisor came to me and said, 'Mr England wants to see you, mate.' Now I was really worried. Was the managing director himself going to work me over? On arrival in his office, though, a very different climate prevailed.

'Ah, David,' said 'Lofty', 'we have an experimental car on the premises which we would like to test at Silverstone. Rather than have Norman do it, we would like you to drive it as you have experience in other race cars.'

To say I was relieved would be an understatement. It was like a dream come true — the opportunity to test a factory Jaguar racer! The car, known simply as E2A, was something of a cross between the D-type and the newly launched E-type road car. The 'Norman' referred to by 'Lofty' was Norman Dewis, Jaguar's long-time chief test driver. E2A had raced a few times, starting in the previous year's Le Mans 24 Hours, driven by Dan Gurney and Walt Hansgen until the engine suffered head-gasket problems.

To brief me, 'Lofty' called a meeting and I found myself, in my green apprentice overalls, walking through the main office block with

Jaguar's four most senior men: managing director F.R.W. 'Lofty' England, chief engineer Bill Heynes, competition manager Mike MacDowel and chief engine designer Wally Hassan. Our group passed the office of Mr Joe Barker, apprentice supervisor, who, to my very great satisfaction, looked at me with a mixture of puzzlement and disapproval as I gave him a cheery wave and a gracious nod of the head. That was an extremely satisfying moment.

The test at Silverstone took place on a rather grey day. In those days all such activity was based at Abbey Curve, then a very fast, almost flat left-hander, and teams set themselves up on the outside of the bend. We had one mechanic and the engineer in charge was Mike Parkes, an early racing hero of mine who drove some terrific saloon and GT races, including Le Mans, and eventually ended up as a works Ferrari driver in sports cars and Formula 1. Compared

with my tiny Elite, E2A was much larger and more powerful, and I took a few laps to settle in. Then I started to give it some wellie — and lost control. The car went into a long, lurid slide, a giant arc, leaving tyre marks that lasted for a couple of years. It came to rest at the feet of Parkes, who looked down on me with the same sort of gaze I had received from Mr Barker. Unfortunately, all four tyres were flat-spotted and we had no spares, so that was it.

Soon after that 'Lofty' pulled a few strings and set me up with a professional drive for the 1962 season with team owner Peter Berry, who was running two Jaguars, an E-type and a 3.8 Mark II saloon. So with my apprenticeship concluded, I had a paid-for drive for 1962 — I was going to be a Professional Racing Driver. Even more importantly, I married my childhood sweetheart Mags on 16 December 1961. So all in all it was a very good year.

ABOVE By the time I drove Jaguar's E2A, it had been retired from its brief racing career. Here it is on its début, in the Le Mans 24 Hours of 1960 driven by Dan Gurney and Walt Hansgen.
The Revs Institute for Automotive Research/ George Phillips

CHAPTER 3

1962—63
GOING INTERNATIONAL

The first day of 1962 was a bit of a low point. Mags and I had only been married for just over two weeks when we went to the Saxon Mill restaurant between Warwick and Kenilworth, definitely the 'in' spot for some years, with my brother John, his wife Jenny and some friends. We decided after I had recovered that it was the oysters, not the large amounts of red wine. Anyway, for poor Mags, sleeping alongside me daily for the first time, it all came as a bit of a shock, definitely some of the worse as in 'for better or worse'.

After this unfortunate start, the year ahead looked rosy. I had my contract with Peter Berry to drive both his E-type and his 3.8 Mark II saloon in British events and I decided to continue running the Elite in selected races, helped by £500 sponsorship from Castrol. What could possibly go wrong?

E-type endeavours

My first race for Peter Berry was a new event on the calendar, the Continental Three Hours at Daytona International Speedway in Florida — a bit of a step up from Mallory Park. About three months before the Daytona race, which took place in February, I received a call from Colin Chapman at Lotus asking if he could borrow my Elite for Jimmy Clark to drive there, which was perfect as I was already down to drive the E-type. I am sure

LEFT This shot of the Formula Junior Lola Mk5A I raced in 1963 clearly shows its unusual front suspension with trailing links. I am on my way to third place in the support race for the British Grand Prix at Silverstone.
David Hobbs collection

PRESTOLITE AT THE "DAYTONA CONTINENTAL"

Everyone knew that Prestolite was at the "Daytona Continental."

Of course Miss Universe created quite a stir. Everywhere she went in her "Prestolite" blouse and sweater she called attention to the new symbol. In addition Prestolite racing caps were on the heads of drivers, mechanics and some spectators.

But even more important of the first 34 cars finishing the race, 26 had Prestolite equipment aboard . . . including that of the winner Dan Gurney.

Let's take a look at some of the activities of Miss Universe as well as others at the track.

Marlene and the Winner, Dan Gurney of COSTA MESA, CALIFORNIA.

Happy David Hobbs of LEAMINGTON SPA, ENGLAND, grins broadly for the camera.

"What's it like out there," Marlene asks of Joakim Bonnier of STOCKHOLM, SWEDEN.

Marlene watches Jimmy Clark of BERWICKSHIRE, SCOTLAND, make some adjustments to a part.

Young Pat Ryan of MONTREAL, CANADA was a little bashful—but a hot driver. That's W. W. Taylor, President, Prestolite Batteries of Canada Ltd. right.

"You mean you're Miss Universe?" Mauro Brenna, VENEZUELAN driver, seems to ask.

ABOVE This Prestolite 'advertorial' from the Daytona Continental has some wonderful period photos. I made the beauty parade together with Miss Universe, who appears to be in every shot.
David Hobbs collection

that Chapman, a design genius, was particularly interested in the car's automatic transmission and I have often wondered if he was thinking about trying it in Formula 1.

I had been watching Jimmy right from the start of his career because he also raced an Elite, but mainly in northern England and Scotland. Over that winter, like a lot of Formula 1 drivers, he took part in the very popular jaunt to South Africa for the Springbok series and there he twice beat Stirling Moss. This really got my attention because Stirling was my hero but now Jimmy was coming up fast.

Anyway Jimmy, Peter Berry and I all met up at Heathrow and flew to New York as there were no direct flights to anywhere in Florida in those

days. On arrival in New York we were met by some of Briggs Cunningham's people — Briggs had started running E-types at that time — and they provided a car for us to drive down to Florida and arranged the freight-forwarding of our racers. The 1,000-mile drive was quite a performance then, before Interstate highways, with lots of towns to go through and many speeding tickets to be picked up. Jimmy and I were fascinated by law-enforcement dress — shirts with crisp creases that you could cut your finger on and Smokey the Bear hats — although the order 'Hands on the roof' became a bit tiresome. When we finally arrived, Jimmy and I shared a room at the Carousel Motel on the way up to Ormond Beach. I remember one day we looked out of the window and saw a bloke drive his car straight down the beach and into the sea, whereupon the thing got stuck and gradually disappeared under the waves — which Jimmy thought was hilariously funny. During our stay he also commented on the size of my belly — which I thought a trifle unfair as I was built like a rail.

In the race itself I dropped out early with fuel-pump failure on the E-type but Jimmy built up an absolutely massive class lead in my Elite. Unfortunately when he came in for his single fuel stop, the car refused to restart, so he did not finish either. Later Jimmy had his road-going Elite fitted with one of Dad's automatic gearboxes and loved it. Stirling Moss also had one installed in a car and he liked it too.

While at Daytona I met Bill France. I must say Bill Sr was a real promoter who pulled out all the stops and welcomed the Europeans in a big way with parties and functions almost every night. There was always something going on and he got to know us all very well. After the race Bill Sr arranged for Jimmy and I to try a Holman & Moody Ford Galaxie, potentially to take part in the upcoming Daytona 500 NASCAR race. I managed to average about 150mph, not too far off the pace at the time, and it was terrifying. I had never even driven at 150mph let alone do laps at that speed, and the car was very unresponsive to steering and would not stop at all. Luckily Dan

Gurney, who won our three-hour race, was on hand and drove the car in the 500. Phew, close call. I did stay on to watch the race, though, and what a spectacle it was. For some reason the newly married Mrs Hobbs did not share this feeling of wonderment.

Bill Sr was probably about 50 at the time and now we have his grandson Brian at a similar age, so it meant something special to me in January 2014 when I was invited to be the Grand Marshal of the Rolex 24 Hours at Daytona — 52 years after first racing at the track.

Back in England I was looking forward to my races with Peter Berry, the first being Oulton Park in April, but it was clear from the outset that we were outclassed by the competition, with Graham Hill driving for John Coombs and Mike Parkes and Jack Sears for Equipe Endeavour. Bruce McLaren had driven for Berry the previous year and at Daytona and I soon realised why he had quit the team. Berry's cars were way behind in terms of preparation and specification, tended by a friend of Peter's who was only a weekend

ABOVE While I had a disappointing run in Peter Berry's Jaguar E-type in the Daytona Continental, Lotus's Colin Chapman borrowed my Lotus Elite for my hero Jimmy Clark.
David Hobbs collection

BELOW Seen low on the Daytona banking while a big Chevy Corvette passes, Jimmy Clark led his class by miles in my Elite until the engine refused to fire after a pit stop.
Getty Images/RacingOne

ABOVE With the
E-type at Oulton Park
in April 1962, holding
off Tony Maggs in his
Aston Martin DB4GT
Zagato. Maggs got past
eventually to finish
third, while I had to
settle for fifth place.
John Holroyd

mechanic, and there was no attempt to make them competitive. Unfortunately, instead of improving, the whole thing came to a grinding halt in early June when Peter discovered the joys of flying. He dropped everything to take up his new love and with it the promise of a good 1962 season took a serious hit.

Ironically, in 2013 I became the green Jaguar E-type known as David Hobbscap in the Disney movie *Cars 2*. Just like me, Hobbscap had done the Le Mans 24 Hours 20 times and retired to become a broadcaster, who along with Brent Mustangburger and Darrell Cartrip provided commentary on the World Grand Prix.

My first Le Mans

After the shock of losing my Jaguar drives, I was luckily saved by Castrol, who put me in one of the factory-backed Team Elite entries for the Le Mans 24 Hours.

Meanwhile, two weeks before Le Mans I decided to do the Nürburgring 1,000Km again with my own Elite, this time with fellow Jaguar

apprentice Richard Attwood. Jimmy Clark also entered in a Lotus 23, a rear-engined sports car in which he had been incredibly quick in some races in England and was now making its international début. The car was unbelievable around the 'Ring and Jimmy led the entire field, including plenty of larger-engined Ferraris, Maseratis and Porsches, by three or four minutes until the exhaust manifold cracked, causing him to inhale some noxious fumes, lose consciousness and go off the road, thankfully without hurting himself. The gauntlet had been well and truly thrown down. As for Richard and me, we retired just after half distance with overheating.

At the Le Mans 24 Hours I shared one of the two Team Elite cars with Frank Gardner. Frank, an Aussie, was always a laugh, one-liners one after another. The other car was driven by team principal Clive Hunt with John 'Mac' Wyllie. After Clark's sensational performance at the Nürburgring, there were also two factory Lotus 23s on the entry list. It was a very hot weekend with a lot of intrigue.

ABOVE This time at the Nürburgring I drove with fellow Jaguar apprentice Richard Attwood, who salutes our arrival at the main gate.
David Hobbs collection

LEFT Preparing to insert myself into the little Elite at the start of the Nürburgring 1,000Km. Richard Attwood and I were unable to repeat the previous year's class win as the engine overheated just after the halfway point of the race.
David Hobbs collection

ABOVE **The two Team Elite entries at Le Mans in 1962. The car I shared with Frank Gardner is the one in the background. Clive Hunt and John 'Mac' Wyllie drove the sister car.**
The Revs Institute for Automotive Research/ George Phillips

In those days the scrutineers at Le Mans were the butcher, the baker and the candlestick maker from town, and the procedure was done in a field behind the pits. They threw all sorts of difficulties in the way of the Lotus 23s, including the requirement for the car to carry a spare wheel. They said, 'You have six-stud fixings for the back wheels but four studs for the front — your spare wheel can't fit both.' So Mike Costin, later of Cosworth fame but at that time a Lotus engineer, flew back to England in Colin Chapman's plane, had a set of four-stud fixings made for the rear wheels, and returned with them. When he got back, the French officials then judged the four-stud rear wheels to be unsafe, despite Costin giving them all sorts of supporting evidence, including stress calculations. To this Colin Chapman responded, 'I'll never darken your doorstep again', with plenty of swearing added for good measure. So Clark and fellow Grand Prix driver Trevor Taylor were on the sidelines.

The reason the French tipped out the Lotus 23 was because it was such a threat to the little blue French DB-Panhards in the Index of Thermal Efficiency, a category based on fuel consumption, time, weight and so on. There was also the Index of Performance, another category designed for home-grown machinery, because at that stage there were no front-running French cars.

So Frank and I went out in our Lotus Elite and did an absolutely sterling job, if I do say so myself. We finished eighth overall, won our class and also won the precious Index of Thermal Efficiency, adding third place in the Index of Performance for good measure. So Lotus was well and truly vindicated, and Frank was really good fun to drive with. We were both completely knackered at the finish as it was in the 90s all day on Sunday.

Unfortunately I never drove with Frank again but I did do another race with Richard Attwood that year, sharing my Elite with him in the Trophée d'Auvergne at the tortuous French track of Clermont-Ferrand. This was another classic old course, five miles long, with lots of elevation change as it weaved its way around a large hill overlooking the city. During practice I

was starting the long, winding climb up the hill, going through some fast sweepers, when I saw Paul Hawkins, another quick Aussie, gaining on me in a Lotus 23B. We were about to go into a long, fast left-hander, so I eased over as far as I could to let him through and he swept by, then pulled back to the right-hand side of the road to set himself up for the left-hander.

At this point a Simca saloon car containing four very portly French farmers came down the hill. *Mon Dieu! Sacré Bleu!* Paul and I both pulled into the pits at the top of the hill where a number of ashen-faced drivers were all asking, 'Did I just see what I thought I saw?' If I had held up Paul for another second he would have gone head-on into that Simca. It turned out that the farmers were on their way to the Friday market in town and the gendarme patrolling their gate had somehow missed them, probably because he was having a massive coughing fit from a Gitanes cigarette. Later that afternoon I had an 'off' going down the hill and damaged the car enough to prevent us from starting the race.

Seduced by single-seaters

Part of the deal for Richard to drive my Elite at the Nürburgring and Clermont-Ferrand was that I got to race his Formula Junior Cooper back in England later in the season. Richard and I had quite a lot in common because, as I mentioned earlier, he was also a Jaguar apprentice and his family lived relatively close to me, in a large mansion in a gorgeous parkland setting. His father owned a chain of car dealerships and Richard went to Harrow School, which, with Eton College, was one of the two top schools in England. He even had his school colours on his crash helmet, like Eton-educated Piers Courage. When Richard wanted to go racing, his father bought him a single-seater and he became part of a team called the Midland Racing Partnership (MRP), based in Wolverhampton. There were four other drivers in the team — David Baker, Bill Bradley, Jeremy Cottrell and Alan Evans — and they all had the latest Cooper Formula Junior cars, this category being just one step down from Formula 1 at that time. They had a smart-looking transporter, full-time mechanics and workshop space next door to one of the Attwood garages. It was a pretty big set-up.

My chance to become an MRP driver came on 11 August 1962 at Oulton Park, the swooping parkland circuit near Manchester. The team told me that I might get into the top four but would not be able to beat quick guys like local heroes Keith Francis and John Fenning. Well, I won my first-ever open-wheel race by over ten seconds, with Francis second and Fenning third. I absolutely loved it: I thought that these were the kind of cars I wanted to race. On one lap I did have a massive slide at the notorious Knickerbrook, a fast right-hand sweep, and the track commentator stationed there became so hysterical about it that Richard, in the pits, thought I had crashed his car until I came past again. By the way, if you want to know why Knickerbrook got its name, 'Blaster' Bates, a demolition expert who worked on the construction of Oulton Park and later became a stand-up comic, used to tell a great story that you can see on YouTube — it is hilarious.

The following weekend we were at Snetterton but this time I retired with a mechanical failure and my team-mate Bill Bradley won the race. Yes, tin-top racing was out! This single-seater stuff was the way to go!

I did race my Elite a few more times that year, but my plans for 1963 were now focused on single-seaters. The chances I got in 1962 were probably way beyond what most aspiring racers could achieve at that time, although I think there were more opportunities at that time than there are now.

The 1963 Formula Junior season

This was going to be an important year for me. My win at Oulton Park in Richard Attwood's Cooper had impressed the MRP gang and for 1963 I was offered a full season with them in a brand-new car. The team had done a deal with Lola boss Eric Broadley to race his factory Formula Juniors and the new Lola Mk5A was a very nice little car, maybe not quite as good as the Brabham BT6 that Denny Hulme, Frank Gardner and Paul Hawkins all drove, but certainly promising. Our cars gave about 102–103bhp, a really good engine maybe 105bhp.

One of MRP's existing drivers, David Baker, a successful businessman who was a good bit older than the rest of us, decided to hang up his helmet to become the team manager, so I took over his seat in effect and received payment of £25 a race. There was a bit of a catch, however, as all the hangers-on at MRP were major fans of Richard Attwood and that became increasingly apparent as the year unfolded.

One thing I remember about MRP was the chief mechanic, a distinctive fellow called Harry Curzon with a square jaw, white hair and a very high-pitched voice. He also drove the transporter and one time managed to tip it on its side after weaving around to wake up some slumbering

BELOW **Making the newspapers for the wrong reasons. This cutting records how I demolished a wall in Greville Road, Warwick, in my Ford Zephyr estate car. Although I was concussed, I was otherwise uninjured, and the Zephyr came off better than the wall.**
David Hobbs collection

Workmen removing the base of the wrecked metal lamp standard in Greville Road, Warwick, today. In the foreground are the demolished garden walls of Nos. 70 and 68, Greville Road.

RACING DRIVER'S CAR DEMOLISHES WALLS IN CRASH

Injured at Warwick

DAVID HOBBS, 23 years old sports car racing driver, of 58, Blacklow Road, Warwick, was taken to Warwick Hospital with concussion after a spectacular road accident at Warwick early today.

mechanics. He had competed in the Isle of Man TT motorcycle races and fancied himself as a driver. His standard of preparation was top class.

For our first race of the new season we were back at Oulton Park for the Spring Cup. Having won there the previous year, I was pretty confident but this time a lot of the big names were on hand. I managed to finish second behind Pete Arundell, driving the factory Lotus 27, the first monocoque design in Formula Junior, entered by Ron Harris Racing. Paul Hawkins was third with the MRP cars of Richard and Bill Bradley fourth and fifth. Instead of being happy, people in the team made remarks that had an undercurrent of, 'Er, well that was very good, David. Um, well done, ahem, yes', as if to say, 'Hell, he's not going to beat Richard regularly, is he?'

Our next race was at Aintree, the track near Liverpool that was interwoven with the horse racecourse where the famous Grand National steeplechase is held. This time I started fourth but retired with electrical problems, while Richard spun off and Bill finished fourth. The race was

won by a young New Zealander by the name of Denny Hulme in the official Brabham entry, although he had to do most of the work on the car himself. This was Denny's first win of the year on the way to winning the championship. He went on to become the 1967 Formula 1 World Champion, still driving for Brabham, and became very well known in the USA driving in the Can-Am series.

Next stop was Silverstone for the International Trophy meeting, where our event was one of those supporting the non-championship Formula 1 contest. Once again our race had a star-studded entry, including Frank Gardner, Pete Arundell and Mike Spence. It was one of the best races of my life. From the start Denny and I just cleared off, leaving a madly dicing field in our dust. We were glued together and passed and repassed a couple of times. I worked out Denny's weak spots and knew I could beat him, but the old black cloud appeared with about five laps to go when the knob fell off the gear lever, leaving just a very short stub. I quickly sussed out how to

ABOVE Although I had competed in a couple of Formula Junior races at the end of 1962 in a Cooper, for the following season I became a full member of the Midland Racing Partnership team. In this new Lola Mk5A at the opening Oulton Park meeting I finished second to Pete Arundell in the factory Lotus. Here I am leading Paul Hawkins. *David Hobbs collection*

change up with my finger crooked around the stub and used my thumb to downshift, but it was somewhat dodgy. While I sorted this out, I fell back a bit but then started to close up again. We crossed the finish line together and I set a new lap record on the last lap, but Denny beat me by a few inches. Richard was fourth and Bill fifth.

After the race, still feeling pretty euphoric, I was walking through the paddock when to my astonishment Dan Gurney, who was there for the main Formula 1 event, stopped to speak to me. I cannot think how he even knew who I was. I was completely stupefied, shuffling from foot to foot and mumbling. He wanted to congratulate me on a terrific race and added words of wisdom and advice. He was very encouraging, wishing me well in my racing endeavours. The encounter lasted just a minute or two but has always remained a treasured memory.

After those single-seater races, I got the chance to drive for Team Elite again for my third attempt at the Nürburgring 1,000Km. I was paired with Trevor Taylor, who by now was in Formula 1 as

Jimmy Clark's team-mate at Lotus. We had a brilliant race, finishing ninth overall, with only seven Ferraris and a factory Porsche in front of us. We won our class for up to 1,300cc GT cars and even beat the Porsche that won the 1,300–1,600cc GT category.

The season was going well and my next event, back in the Formula Junior Lola, was a big one — the support race for the Monaco Grand Prix. The bumper entry of over 40 cars meant that this contest was split into two heats and a final. Both Richard and I were in the first heat and while he finished second, right behind Pete Arundell, I had a problem and was only classified 13th, five laps down, which meant that I did not even make the final.

MRP honour was more than saved, however, because the crankshaft in Arundell's engine broke and Richard went on to win by far the most important Formula Junior race of the year ahead of Frank Gardner and Jo Schlesser, while Bill Bradley came home fifth. There must have been something about Monaco for Richard because he was always fantastic there and five years later had his best-ever Grand Prix result when he finished second and set a new lap record driving a works BRM. We celebrated in a well-known watering hole — I think it may have been the Tip-Top bar — and Mags danced the night away with Jimmy Clark to all the latest hits, including Little Richard's 'Let's Twist Again'.

With his terrific win at Monaco, Richard's MRP fans were more than vindicated, and it did not get any better for me a couple of weeks later at Mallory Park, where Richard was second behind Arundell and I came in third. As at Monaco, Mallory had a very tight hairpin and Richard was the ace through corners like that.

By now Le Mans was on the horizon but before going over to France we visited another tight little racing venue, Crystal Palace in south London, a tricky track that was only used occasionally but always attracted a big crowd as it was readily accessible by underground train from all over the city. Again there were two heats and a final and in my heat I only managed sixth place

MONACO WINNER TO RACE AT MALLORY

THE former Jaguar apprentice, Richard Attwood, who won the Monaco Junior Grand Prix in a Lola four days ago, is to compete in the Whit Sunday race meeting at Mallory Park.

Attwood's win at Monaco surprised many experts for he was up against the top Formula Junior

SPOTLIGHT ON MOTORING

drivers, not only from Britain but from France, Germany, Austria, Italy and Switzerland.

Even more important was the impressive manner in which he drove to victory. He must start a firm favourite to win at Mallory.

Main Event

Once again Attwood will be driving a Lola for the Midland Racing Partnership. He will have the backing of Bill Bradley and David Hobbs, of Leamington.

Other leading Formula Junior drivers entered for the event, include Peter Arundell, who was favourite at Monaco, and Paul Hawkins, driving a Brabham.

The main event of the meeting, organised by the British Racing and Sports Car Club, is the 20 laps Midlands Trophy event for Formula Libre and sports cars.

This has attracted Reg Parnell's 2.7 litre Lola which will be driven by the young New Zealander, Chris Amon, who was robbed of a drive in the Monaco Grand Prix Formula I race through mechanical trouble.

Larger Class

David Hobbs of Leamington on the starting grid at Monaco with the Lola he is to race at Mallory Park.

in his new two-litre Climax-powered Attila.

The last race is a 10-lap handicap for Grand Touring and sports cars of unlimited capacity.

Ken Baker (E-type Jaguar), Jack Pearce (Lotus Twenty Three) and John Dangerfield (Morgan Plus Four) are among a varied and highly competitive field.

Judging from the entry list, this promises to be one of the best meetings staged at Mallory Park and the race organisers tell me they are confident that lap records will go if the track remains dry. The first race begins at 2.15.

Ledbrook to Attack Shelsley Climb Time

MIKE LEDBROOK, of Coventry, and Chris Summers, of Ansty, are among the large list of entries accepted for the Shelsley Walsh national open hill climb on June 9.

Ledbrook is to drive his modified Cooper in the class for racing cars up to 500 c.c. He will be all out

Dick James, at 39.33sec.

Summers will have two Cooper cars running. One is fitted with

Vespa

VESPAGRAMS No. 9

Don't ask how much it costs—ask how little it costs and how much you save. Betta Getta Vespa from your main dealers

FRETTONS

SMITHFORD WAY and 112, STONEY STANTON ROAD, Coventry.

Advertiser's Announcement

Keen's Kolumn. No. 2, 3rd Series

PENNY WISE!

With the holiday season just around the corner, quite a few motorists are considering the problem of what type of roof rack to buy and they will obviously be shopping around for prices, etc. Although there are some very cheap ones on the market, don't, for the sake of those few extra shillings, buy a rack which could, in the long run, prove a lot more expensive, especially when at some future date you try to get spares for it. The Eversure Victor, which is available for most makes of car, is only a little more expensive than one which is sold by a large multiple store, but it is far more robust and those fittings, which, during the winter, tend to be mislaid, are readily available from most accessory shops. So don't be "Penny wise" and go for quality at the right price.

Cheerio. Safe and Happy Motoring.

KEEN'S, City Arcade.

ABOVE **Tyres smoking as we blast off the line at Crystal Palace. I am in the middle in the Lola between the Tyrrell-run Cooper T67 of Chris Amon in the foreground and Mike Spence's factory Lotus 27 run by Ron Harris.**
David Hobbs collection

while Richard was third. In the final his clutch went and I came home fourth in a race again commanded by Hulme and Gardner in their Brabhams, probably the best of the eight different makes of chassis that were out there.

Lola at Le Mans

As a result of our success in his Formula Junior cars, Eric Broadley asked Richard and I to drive his new GT, the Lola Mk6, in the Le Mans 24 Hours that year. It was the forerunner of the GT40, a monocoque sports car, very swoopy-looking, with a big 4.6-litre Ford V8 engine mid-mounted. But it was also far behind schedule.

Eric was an egghead, a geek, the same age as Colin Chapman and similar to him in many ways. Like Chapman, Broadley had designed and raced his own sports car, the Lola-Climax Mk1, which was similar to the Lotus Eleven. Both men were very capable racing drivers, as I saw first hand at Silverstone with Chapman when I watched him race a Jaguar 3.8 Mark II saloon in which he was very spectacular, and both knew

RIGHT **Following my early Formula Junior success, Lola boss Eric Broadley asked me to share his new GT car, the Mk6, with Richard Attwood in the 1963 Le Mans 24 Hours. The car did not get to Le Mans until the last minute, driven there on the road by Eric.**
Getty Images/GP Library

ABOVE At Le Mans the
Lola certainly had plenty
of speed but it was
just too new, its Colotti
gearbox in particular
giving us a lot of trouble.
LAT Images

no fear when driving on public roads. Both also
decided they were even better at building their
own cars than racing them.

The Lola factory at the time was in Bromley, a
suburb south of London, and the place was tiny
by modern standards, hardly bigger than a small
apartment. Eric was the designer, the brains,
while Rob Rushbrook ran the workshop as Eric's
partner and was in charge of building the cars.
Whenever I drove a Lotus, Rob, a lovely guy,
would say to me, 'Cor, you be careful in those
Lotuses… you know that Colin Chapman…'
Of course, Lolas broke about as often as Lotuses
did back then.

Preparation of the Lola Mk6 was running so
late that Richard and I found ourselves at the
workshop on the Monday before the 24 Hours,
just two days before the first practice session,
with the car nowhere near ready. Finally, Eric told
us to go on ahead to Le Mans, sign on and get our
medical checks done, so off we drove to Dover to
catch the cross-channel ferry. We were booked
into this dreadful little hotel in Le Mans itself

called Le Bon Laboureur — the good labourer. It
was a complete dive.

On the Wednesday Eric himself delivered
the Lola Mk6 to Le Mans, driving it over at such
speed that I would not have liked to have been
a passenger on that ride. Someone followed him
down with a van and trailer to take the car back
home again afterwards.

Scrutineering was as farcical as it had been
the previous year. These amateur officials,
people who seemed to have very little technical
knowledge, took a hard look at our new car with
its engine at the rear and tiny obligatory luggage
compartment at the front, squeezed behind the
radiators. They would measure dimensions
with boxes and when one box would not fit we
would hammer the area, cut holes and so on.
Then the officials decided that the rear-view
mirror, which looked through a large Plexiglas
sheet covering the engine, did not provide good
enough rearward vision. We offered to mount
side mirrors, but, no, they insisted that we had
to have a regular mirror. So Eric cut a hole in the

roof and put a mirror up there with a view over the top of the car.

The paddock was terrible back then and the lavatories were grotesque, with an unforgettably appalling smell. In charge of them was a toothless old crone who sat literally at the door of the men's facilities doing her knitting. Everyone had to give a franc to pass but I doubt whether she ever actually went inside, judging by the state of the place. She was there for years.

Despite the lack of running, that Lola was immediately quick, and in the race we got it up to eighth position by around midnight. During the middle of the night I did the second fastest lap of the race, with only the Phil Hill/Willy Mairesse Ferrari quicker, But the car's difficult Italian Colotti gearbox was a weak link and continually troublesome. Soon after midnight it went wrong, and of course you could not replace it as the big teams do today. You had to fix it. Malcolm Malone, the chief mechanic, was our saviour. Malcolm had a big gap in his front teeth, and when working intently with both hands,

changing brakes or whatever, he would stick his cigarette in the gap. With cars screaming past flat out a few feet away and no pit wall, Malcolm scrambled around under the car with the gearbox in pieces on bits of rag on the ground. Eventually, after nearly two hours, he got it back together, but now we were down to three gears.

Unfortunately, the gearbox jammed a couple of hours later, at around 5am, as I was going down to the Esses and the car spun, putting us out of the race. When I arrived back at the pits poor Eric was almost in tears, after so much effort, and I certainly did not feel much better myself although the circumstances were out of my hands. I went on to race at Le Mans 20 times and that was my only significant 'off'. Only 14 cars finished that year and the Elite I had raced at the Nürburgring was 10th overall. But it was our Le Mans performance that led to Lola being selected to create the car that would become the Ford GT40, although Ford took the project from poor Eric and gave it to Carroll Shelby, Holman & Moody and John Wyer.

ABOVE This is how my race at Le Mans in the Lola Mk6 ended. The Colotti gearbox jammed as I changed down before the Esses and I could do nothing about the resultant spin into the barrier. *LAT Images*

More French adventures

After Le Mans we stayed in France for three Formula Junior races on consecutive weekends, all on circuits using closed public roads. The first was at the daunting and dangerous Rouen-Les-Essarts for a round of the French Formula Junior Championship. All my usual rivals attended and there were nearly 40 entries. This time Richard was in the first heat and he finished third while I was in the other heat and came home in second place, so we were in a good position for the final. Come the final, however, Paul Hawkins won in his Brabham with Richard just inches behind, on yet another track with a very tight hairpin, this one with a cobblestone surface. I had to be content with sixth place.

For our next French adventure we moved on to the incredibly fast circuit at Reims, famous for its champagne, for a support race at the 12 Hours sports car event. The track was outside the city on country roads through wheat fields. Soon after the start there were very fast left- and right-handers where the road was higher than the

fields, so if you went off you rolled down a slope. Our cars, with their tubular spaceframe chassis, were pretty flimsy so you certainly did not want to do that. After those sweepers you arrived at the first hairpin, a very sharp right-hander, followed by a steep uphill straight to a brow, and then the road was like an arrow for another mile. From the brow there was an amazing view, if you had time to look, of the city with its magnificent cathedral, and after that we charged gently downhill towards Thillois, another tight right-hander that led back to the pits and another mile up another long straight.

Our race was mayhem, with awesome slipstreaming. You could go into Thillois in a massive bunch — all dust, tyre smoke and the smell of brake pads — in 16th place and pass the pits in the lead, and then after the second hairpin you could be back in the middle of the field. I finished sixth again and Richard was third.

Hotel accommodation at Reims was scarce and Richard and I finished up in the attic room of some small farmhouse on the outskirts of the city. This room was so hot that it was impossible to get a decent night's sleep, so Richard and I fixed that. There was an amazing champagne reception organised by Moët et Chandon at their cellars and to this day I have to say it is one of the most impressive functions I have ever attended. Together with Graham Hill, Phil Hill, Dan Gurney and others, Richard and I helped dispose of the champagne and afterwards went to a bar where all the top drivers hung out. We did not stagger into bed until about 2am — and practice was the next day albeit not until late afternoon. Jeremy Cottrell, who was one of Richard's big supporters, was absolutely furious with me, accusing me of leading Richard astray, although I reckoned he was old enough to look after himself. I think this was probably the moment when my fate as an MRP driver was sealed.

The last race of our French sojourn was at Clermont-Ferrand, which Richard and I knew from our trip there the year before. This time there were two 12-lap races and the times were combined to give an aggregate result. I remember little of what happened but I was classified sixth

BELOW The start of the Formula Junior final at Rouen, with me nearest the camera and Mike Spence alongside. I finished sixth.

David Hobbs collection

yet again and Richard was one spot in front of me.

For the rest of the season my Formula Junior racing was back in Britain on familiar ground at Silverstone, Goodwood, Brands Hatch and Snetterton. The Silverstone race supported the British Grand Prix and I was determined to do well there. This time I did not come sixth and instead made it to third place, but Richard finished ahead of me in a race won yet again by Pete Arundell. The Goodwood race supported the famous RAC Tourist Trophy race and here the order was Arundell, Attwood, Hulme and me. Brands Hatch a few weeks later was a disaster for me as I got involved in a first-lap accident that also took out my team-mate Bill Bradley. The season ended with a second place behind Denny at Snetterton.

In the final points standings for the *Express & Star* Formula Junior Championship, sponsored by the evening newspaper in Wolverhampton, I was fourth equal with none other than Richard, who for some reason missed the last two races, while Pete Arundell was the champion with

Denny Hulme second and Frank Gardner third.

During the time Richard and I were on the road together in 1963 we sometimes joked with each other, 'There's another one we got through!' We were laughing on the outside but inside we knew we were flirting with disaster. Mags also started worrying about the danger when I transferred to single-seaters. She had known me since before I started racing and had never in any way tried to deter me, believing that it is pointless to seek to change how people are because you only make them resentful, and they do not change anyway.

With the racing, and by now working for Dad after the end of my apprenticeship at Jaguar, that year I earned about £1,500, which was quite good money for someone my age, so we stuck it out. Over the years that followed, she must have been terribly worried whenever I went off to race, especially to dangerous places like Rouen or Reims. When she and, later, our two boys waved me off, she must have wondered if she would ever see me again. I know I wondered as well when I looked in the rear-view mirror.

ABOVE As with the Monaco Grand Prix, the Formula Junior support race at the British Grand Prix was a great opportunity to impress Formula 1 bosses. I finished third behind Pete Arundell and Richard Attwood.
David Hobbs collection

CHAPTER 4
1964–65
ALL SORTS

The start of 1964 was rather bleak. At the end of 1963 a lifetime of work and inventive genius by my father came to a close as Hobbs Transmission Ltd went under. In spite of great hopes that his fabulous Mecha-Matic transmission would be used in the Ford Cortina, everything fell apart at the last minute and Ford settled for a very inferior alternative. This put Mags and I in a very sticky situation as I had been working for Dad at his factory earning about £900 a year, supplemented by income from my driving. We had one small child, Greg, and another on the way.

Mags and I had some pretty serious discussions regarding my future. Should I forget the racing and go back into the car business, or could/should I turn into a professional racing driver, with all the uncertainty of A) getting drives, B) surviving in a dangerous sport and C) making enough money at it. Mags proved to be an incredible support and urged me to stick with what I loved and to have a go, even though she must have been worried sick with fear. To add to our woes, I had been sacked by the Midland Racing Partnership, who instead wanted to run Tony Maggs, a young Rhodesian driver with some Formula 1 experience.

Once Mags and I had come to a decision regarding our future, I had to get cracking and find some drives. As I had performed well in 1963, my resumé was fairly strong, and my brother John helped in the search.

LEFT In 1964 I moved up to Formula 2, driving this works Merlyn Mk7 for the most part. This is my second race for the team, the Grovewood Trophy at Mallory Park, where I finished seventh. Bearing down on me are Tony Hegbourne (15) and Alan Rees, who were fifth and fourth respectively.
The Revs Institute for Automotive Research/ Max LeGrand

Not a wizard Merlyn

In the end I wound up driving for a bloke called
Selwyn Hayward and his outfit Colchester
Racing Developments, which built cars called
Merlyns. Selwyn had been going for about three
years and for 1964 his new models were the Mk6
sports racer and the Mk7 single-seater, which was
designed for the new Formula 2 and Formula 3
categories that replaced Formula Junior that year.
I was unsure how wizard the Merlyn would be
and Selwyn was short of money. His little factory,
in the Essex town that gave its name to his
company, was a long haul from Leamington Spa,
especially in those days before much of Britain's
motorway system existed.

My first race with the team, the Aintree 200,
was strange because it was actually a non-
championship Formula 1 event. There were
about 18 Formula 1 cars and the field was padded
out with Formula 2 cars. I lined up on the same
grid as Graham Hill, who was on pole, Jimmy
Clark, Phil Hill and Jack Brabham, but I was on
the ninth row. Brabham went on to win the race

while I was an early retirement after my Mk7's
little 1-litre Ford-based SCA engine started
overheating.

My next race was back with MRP, for reasons
lost in the mists of time, in a Lola fitted with a
BMC engine, not the more powerful SCA. This
was the Eifelrennen at the Nürburgring, held not
on the usual Nordschleife but on the Südschleife,
which had a 4.8-mile lap and used the same pits.
Although this circuit was much shorter, it was
nonetheless very tricky. One memory is that the
track was bordered by barbed wire, which would
have taken your head off in a crash. Jimmy Clark
won the race and Richard Attwood, still driving
for MRP, was second, while I was the last finisher
in eighth place.

For the next event, the Grovewood Trophy at
Mallory Park, I returned to the Merlyn and led
people like Frank Gardner and Paul Hawkins
on my way to seventh place, right behind Denny
Hulme and in front of Tony Maggs. As it was
Tony who had taken my place at MRP, that put
a smile on my face. This was the race where an

unknown Austrian with a broken nose appeared from nowhere and finished third in a Brabham. His name was Jochen Rindt. The very next day, Whit Monday, a public holiday, we were at Crystal Palace and Rindt showed the uncanny skills he possessed by winning both his heat and the final, beating Graham Hill. A star had been born but unfortunately not me. I came home in eighth place, just behind Richard.

Just a week later I had a one-off Formula 2 outing at the AVUS track in Berlin driving for Ron Harris's works-supported Lotus alongside regular driver Peter Proctor. Ron was a strange guy whose main business was, if I recall, distributing smutty films with names like *Diary of the Half Virgin*. He was a very unlikely-looking team owner, with baggy trousers, a cigarette hanging out of his mouth, and his hands in his pockets. AVUS had been used for racing since 1921 and comprised the two parallel carriageways of the *autobahn* out of town with a loop at both ends. For many years there had been a massive 180-degree banked corner at one end, but that had

gone by the time I raced there. I retired after one lap of the race with suspension damage. It is odd how things break when you slam into the back of the car in front.

Back with the Merlyn, I guess you could say that my Formula 2 season around Europe continued in somewhat mediocre fashion. I usually qualified about 11th or 12th, and my best finishes were eighth at Reims and Karlskoga, then a very good fourth at Zolder. I finished the season with two British races, at Oulton Park for the Gold Cup and at Snetterton, but retired from both with engine problems.

The most memorable of these events was the one that rejoiced in the name of Kanonloppet at Karlskoga in Sweden. To save money, I travelled there by road (and car ferry across the North Sea) in a Cortina driven by Mike Beckwith and Tony Hegbourne, a very successful duo with the Normand Racing Team in Coopers in Formula 2 and Lotus 23s in sports car events. Both, it turned out, were suicidal road drivers. I sat in the back seat as far as possible from the likely point of impact as both of them seemed to believe in some sort of divine intervention. Flat out at 90mph, even 100mph, they would pass trucks, cars and tractors around the outside of blind corners and over blind brows. I was very relieved to arrive at the track without calamity.

Karlskoga is an armaments town and there seemed to be security fencing everywhere. Alcohol was quite difficult to obtain and could only be bought at government-run outlets, but the Swedes seemed to consume plenty of it. At that latitude in the summer it stayed light until very late. One evening we had to stay at the track until quite a late hour but the place was still full of spectators, all drunk. When it got dark the police just locked them in for the night behind the fencing and left them there. It was most peculiar. After my eighth place, which I was quite happy with considering the calibre of the field, I had to steel myself for the hair-raising trip back to the ferry.

Selwyn Hayward was obviously a pretty good engineer, because a few years later Tim Schenken drove for him in Formula Ford and absolutely cleaned up, and later still Jody Scheckter also made his name in a Merlyn. So Selwyn came good in the end, but when I joined him he was still pretty new and getting a feel for things.

Lotus Cortinas

Away from single-seater racing, I picked up occasional drives for Colin Chapman in a works Lotus Cortina. My first race in this touring car was at Roskilde Ring in Denmark, a strange, very short track built in a quarry pit, and apparently now the site of a supermarket and housing development. Team Lotus's chief mechanic on the Lotus Cortinas was Bob Dance, the long-time fixture who was still at it decades later, working for the likes of Ayrton Senna. He was a genial chap who liked a bit of fun and we had a very amusing evening in a bar while we were in Denmark. There were two cars entered, the other for Mike Spence, who was just starting as number two to Jim Clark in Lotus's Formula 1 team. I beat Mike in the first race and that was obviously not in his calculations at all, but he

won the second race with me second. So between us we stitched up both races against what must have been a poor field.

My other two races in Lotus Cortinas that year were in America. As Lotus was embarking on distribution of production cars in the US, Colin Chapman wanted to raise his company's profile in this new market and sent over factory cars for these Sports Car Club of America (SCCA) events, at Marlboro and Road America.

Marlboro, also now a housing development (there seems to be a trend here), is in Maryland, not far from Washington DC, and held this important 12-hour touring car race every August. I drove with Dave Clark, an American bloke, not the singer who had hits with his band the *Dave Clark Five*. In the second car Jackie Stewart was paired with Mike Beckwith, while the third car was shared by Tony Hegbourne and Sir John Whitmore, a saloon racing star who famously let Steve McQueen race his Mini at Brands Hatch.

In the race my front suspension broke and I stopped the car on the outside of a left-hand sweeper. Somehow I jacked the car up and propped the offending corner on a couple of bricks. As the mechanics were not allowed to work on the car away from the pits, they shouted instructions to me through the fence; no guard rail, just a fence. I could not see what was happening on track because I was lying under the car on the other side, hearing all this frenzied tyre-squealing while fiddling with the suspension and desperately hoping the whole thing would not fall on top of me. I eventually got the car back to the pits for proper repairs and we did get to the finish, in eighth place, while the other two Lotus Cortinas stayed in command with first and second places.

Then, the following month, I returned to the USA for a 500-mile race at Road America in Wisconsin. This time I was paired with Chris Craft, a good British driver who later drove a lot for Alain de Cadenet. The Lotus secretary who made our hotel booking had obviously looked at a very large-scale map of America because she decided that the best place for us to stay

would be in Madison, nearly 100 miles from the track. We tried a different route every day to get to this unfamiliar circuit and got lost every time. When you go off into those Wisconsin counties you find roads called simply 'County A', 'County AA', 'County B', 'County BB' and so on. But between Madison and Road America there are several different counties and much potential for confusion. When we asked locals for directions, they would say something like, 'Well, you go down here until you get to A, then you take A until you get to CC, then take CC north.' What they would forget to tell you was that between the two towns there are about four different roads all with the same identification — and Americans tease the Brits about our 'funny addresses'!

Other than that we finished the race in 14th place, I have little recollection of what happened at Road America, but I certainly loved the track and in due course it became one of my great favourites and, as time went on, a very special place for the Hobbs family.

In addition to Formula 2 and Lotus Cortinas,

I also did some sports car races. The first was a return to the Nürburgring 1,000Km, where I raced a Porsche for the first time, a 904 GTS owned by SMART, the Stirling Moss Automobile Racing Team, and painted a very strange shade of green. I was paired with the American Lloyd 'Lucky' Casner and we finished ninth overall and fourth in the class. With Stirling, 'Lucky', an airline pilot and racing enthusiast, had won the Nürburgring 1,000Km, the high point of his career, three years earlier in one of his own factory-backed Team Camoradi 'Birdcage' Maseratis. Unfortunately, a year after our race together his luck ran out at the Le Mans test weekend and he was killed at the end of the main straight in one of his Team Camoradi Maseratis.

Our race weekend at the Nürburgring also involved more scary road driving, this time as passenger to my hero and team boss for the weekend. The team was staying some miles from the track and on race day the traffic jams were huge. Completely unconcerned, Stirling just drove for many miles on the wrong side of

ABOVE By 1964 I was an old hand at the Nürburgring, this being my fourth outing in the 1,000Km. This time my entrant was one of my heroes, Stirling Moss, in the Porsche 904 GTS he was running that year. Driving with Lloyd 'Lucky' Casner, I finished ninth overall and fourth in class. *The Revs Institute for Automotive Research/ Eric della Faille*

the road, causing apoplexy among people in the stationary cars we were passing. Many pulled out of line as we approached in an attempt to stop us but Stirling just took to the grass, going the wrong side of trees to pass them, and we finally got to the 'Ring with minutes to spare — and me a nervous wreck. It was terrifying and did not get the day off to a good start.

Triumph at Le Mans

Just two weeks later I had a seat in the Le Mans 24 Hours again but in a rather slower car than the Lola I raced the year before with Richard Attwood. Triumph asked me to drive one of their three works Spitfire entries with Dutchman Rob Slotemaker, who ran an 'anti-skid' driving school at Zandvoort, home of the Dutch Grand Prix. Rob was so good at controlling lurid slides in race cars that he was hired to do some of the stunt driving for the crash scenes in Steve McQueen's film *Le Mans* in 1970. We did quite a bit of testing, and the Triumph people were great, with Harry Webster, their chief engineer, very involved in the project. They were tickled pink at having me drive their car after my success with the Lotus Elite in 1962 and the promise shown by the Lola Mk6 in 1963. They kept saying things like, 'Oh, this is so great, you should be driving a Ferrari', which I thought was very perceptive of them. They also paid me well, around £400, which I thought was pretty good at the time.

Mags and I drove to Le Mans in a Triumph 2000, a newly introduced 2-litre saloon. It had fully independent suspension, which was fairly avant-garde at that time. We stayed in La Chartre-sur-le-Loir at the Hôtel de France, which the great John Wyer had selected as Aston Martin's base for the works team's Le Mans exploits. It was the first of many times I stayed in that wonderful little hotel that is still there, picture perfect and a shrine to *Les Vingt-Quatre Heures du Mans*.

Everything went smoothly, apart from the fact that the little Spitfire could only just manage about 120mph downhill with a tail wind. It was a bit daunting to have big Ferraris driven by people like John Surtees and Lorenzo Bandini zipping by at almost twice our speed. Of course, the four

miles of the Mulsanne straight seemed like about 40 miles in that little car. You would soon be up to full speed after exiting Tertre Rouge and the massive camber range of the rear wheels would go to positive until you hit the brakes a couple of minutes later, when they would fold into very negative camber and make the car rather scary under braking, with a great deal of weaving. Still, we completed the race, the only one of the three Spitfires to do so, in 21st position overall and fourth in class.

Towards the end of the season a chap called David Fletcher contacted me to drive a brand-new Lola T70 sports car, which Ian Yates, an old Harrow school friend of Richard Attwood, was paying for. Fletcher was going to prepare the car at his little Esso service station, Harold Young Ltd, at Long Melford in Suffolk, but the T70 was not finished in time for the first event on the schedule, the RAC Tourist Trophy at Goodwood, so they entered their much older Lotus 23 instead. I had already driven the Lotus in a support race to the British Grand Prix at Brands Hatch, finishing seventh after quite a dice with Jackie Stewart, who was driving a Tojeiro for Ecurie Ecosse, the famous Scottish team, but at Goodwood the car overheated in the race and I retired.

So my first professional season turned out to be a bit of a mixed bag and for 1965 I kept on missing out on chances with teams like Cooper, Lotus and Tyrrell. I really wanted to drive for Ken Tyrrell, as Jackie Stewart had been so successful with him in 1964, and I think I was in the frame but it did not come about. Everyone wanted to sign for Lotus but Mike Spence beat me to a drive there, but in retrospect I think that was probably a good thing. However, I did still have the Lola T70 sports car programme.

The 1965 season

Together with John Surtees, I became very involved in early 1965 in the development of the T70 with Lola boss Eric Broadley, whom I knew, of course, from driving the company's Formula Junior and Le Mans cars. One of the first sports cars built around a full monocoque, the T70 had a very stiff chassis, good aerodynamics for the day and, with a 350 cubic inch Chevrolet in the back, it was very fast. In testing Surtees broke the Silverstone lap record at an average of 133mph, about 10mph faster than the prevailing Formula 1 record held by Innes Ireland.

I attended many test days, although I was relegated to watching for much of the time. John was Eric's development driver, and John's own operation, Team Surtees, was going to run the factory car. I spent a lot of time around them and later in the year, and in subsequent years, I did a great deal of test driving for Eric, who was very methodical in his approach to the task. Of course, in those days there was not a computer in sight, just a stopwatch, clipboard, pencil and pad of paper. All data input came from the driver except for the tell-tale red line on the rev counter and rudimentary measurements of tyre temperature. If you said, 'Oh, I only revved it to six', but that tell-tale needle was stuck at eight-two, it told its own story. As for tyre temperature, that was measured with a pyrometer that the

tyre technician stuck into the rubber at various points, so it was vital that your in-lap was a quick one so that the temperature measurements were as fresh and accurate as possible. All the same, at a place like Silverstone, which had blindingly quick corners as well as slower ones, no-one had any idea of tyre temperature at any given point on the track, so adjustments like camber, toe-in and roll stiffness involved not a small amount of guesswork.

This could lead to some funny moments. At one test I pounded round and then pitted to tell Eric how the car felt. Holding his clipboard, he had that far-away look in his eyes that engineers can have, whether they are designing race cars, space rockets or deep-sea submersibles, gazing into the sky while he listened, tapping his teeth with the end of his pencil, and then asking, 'Are you sure that's what it's doing?' And I would say, 'Yeah.' After a pause and more peering at the sky, he would say, 'Hmm… It shouldn't. Why don't you try again, and have another look?'

I think I was a reasonable development driver.

BELOW At Le Mans in 1964 Rob Slotemaker and I brought our 1,147cc Triumph Spitfire home 21st overall and fourth in class behind a Porsche 904 GTS and two Renault Alpines. It was a well-paid drive and Triumph invited us back the following year, but Rob crashed — and our team-mates won the class.
LAT Images

I liked working with Eric and I guess he and John felt the same about me as they involved me in Formula 2 tyre testing as well. Firestone contracted Team Surtees as one of their test teams and for this work we used Lola's new Formula 2 car, and I did most of the driving, at Brands Hatch every Monday. One day Firestone's technicians wheeled out a set of tyres with no tread. I took one look at them and said, 'You've got to be joking!' They said, 'Trust us, these will be fine.' And, of course, these early racing 'slicks' were superb, to the tune of several seconds a lap. So much for my abilities as an intuitive tyre engineer.

That year I was also very excited to be offered drives in Formula 2 by Tim Parnell, son of Reg, former top-level driver, Aston Martin team manager and proprietor of his own racing team. Although Tim had raced himself, after his father's sudden death the previous year he took over the running of Reg Parnell Racing. He had a Lotus 35 with a little 1-litre BRM engine, which was a rival to the Ford-based Cosworth SCA unit that most people used. It was a very impressive-looking piece of kit and on paper the project was promising, but it turned out that the team's budget was insufficient.

My first event in the car was at Snetterton in April, a two-part race. In the first part I finished ninth, a place ahead of my old Merlyn, which was now driven by rising star Chris Irwin, but in the second an oil pipe came off. Two weeks later at Pau, a classic Monaco-style street circuit near the Pyrenees, I finished eighth. But any budget the team possessed had been spent by the time of the next race, at Crystal Palace, and that was that.

As in 1964, Triumph asked me to drive a works Spitfire at Le Mans, again with Rob Slotemaker, but he crashed heavily at White House, which even in the Spitfire was a quick corner, and rolled it into a small ball. But at least the drive paid some bills.

I had a good season racing the Ian Yates/David Fletcher T70 in British events even though it was not as fast as it could have been because it was fitted with the cheaper Ford 289 cubic inch motor,

which proved to be an expensive mistake. I had a major disappointment at my third race with it, the Royal Automobile Club's Tourist Trophy, which after many years as a big Goodwood fixture in September transferred to Oulton Park in May. The RAC decided to run it as two separate one-hour races with the winner decided on aggregate, but they miscalculated how to score the event.

In the first race we had a problem with the battery and I finished second to Denny Hulme in Sid Taylor's Brabham BT8, but in the second race I beat him by such a big margin that I was close to lapping him at the end. However, in a muddle with the chequered flag Denny was given an extra lap and was declared the winner. Eric, expecting the first big win for the T70, went to the stewards, a bunch of bumble-headed old guys, and was in tears as he explained the situation to them. Finally they admitted the error but would not change the result, so we just had to accept second place. That should have been a big win for me as I had overtaken people like

ABOVE This is an early-season Snetterton test of the Lola T70 I raced in 1965 for the Harold Young team run by David Fletcher, who is holding the rear bodywork in this photo. The day was obviously a family affair as Mags is holding one-year-old Guy while three-year-old Greg poses for the camera.
David Hobbs collection

BELOW An action shot from that wet day at Snetterton. Whereas the factory T70 used a 350 cubic inch Chevrolet V8, the car I raced for sponsor Ian Yates had a cheaper and less powerful Ford V8 of 289 cubic inches.
David Hobbs collection

RIGHT In 1965 Tim Parnell offered me drives in his Formula 2 team's promising BRM-powered Lotus 35. I finished eighth here in the Pau Grand Prix, but then the money ran out.

LAT Images

BELOW My 1965 programme with the Lola T70 brought me close to winning the RAC Tourist Trophy, which that year transferred from Goodwood to Oulton Park. Here I am mixing it with real stars, hounding Jimmy Clark in his Lotus 30 with Bruce McLaren's McLaren-Elva giving chase.

Mike Hayward Collection

Jimmy Clark in the Lotus 30, which was very satisfying even though the Lotus was no match for the Lola.

I went on to win the Guards Trophy race at Mallory Park in the T70 and won again at Snetterton and Croft. Whenever the car finished a race I was in the top three.

Tim Parnell reappeared later in the summer and entered me for my first Formula 1 race, the French Grand Prix at Clermont-Ferrand, a circuit I knew quite well, in one of his BRM-powered Lotus 25s. Part of the deal was that I would tow the Lotus to the circuit behind my road car, a Ford Cortina GT, an ensemble that was not quite as basic as it sounds as relatively few people had proper transporters. With a friend called Jack Brown, who had been an apprentice at Jaguar with me, I headed down from home in Warwick to pick up the car in Slough. As we started out I put on my seat belt, which would have been an optional extra on something like a Cortina. Jack passed comment as it was quite unusual for people to use seats belts at that time, but I had

come to see that they were a good idea. So he said, 'Well, if you're putting yours on I guess I'd better put mine on too.'

About 50 miles later, not far from Aylesbury, we were humming along at about 90mph — no speed limits in those days — when a big five-ton laundry van coming the other way pulled into the middle of the road to make a turn. The driver stopped and I assumed he was waiting for us, but at the last moment he turned across our path and we slammed into the side of the van. I locked up all four wheels, blowing one of the tyres, but still hit the van hard enough to tip it over. Despite my seat belt, my head hit the steering wheel, breaking my nose, cheekbones and jaw, and I also fractured my arm. I finished up in Stoke Mandeville Hospital and needless to say I did not drive in the French Grand Prix that weekend. Jack, mercifully, was unscathed even though the dashboard ended up right next to his seat.

One of the little jobs they did in hospital was to stick a glass tube up my nose every morning to stop the wrong bits growing together. When I

RACING DRIVER INJURED IN CRASH

David Hobbs, the 26-year-old Warwick racing driver, who is detained in Stoke Mandeville Hospital following a road accident, was yesterday said to be in a "fairly satisfactory" condition.

The hospital spokesman said that he was unable to say yet when Mr. Hobbs would be allowed to leave.

David, who is married with two children, lives at 58 Blacklow Road, Warwick. He was travelling to France in a Ford car with a friend, Mr. Jack Brown, of Stonebury Avenue, Coventry.

SWERVED

It is understood that David's car swerved off the road to avoid a laundry van.

He received a broken jaw, nose and elbow. Mr. Brown was treated for minor injuries, but was not detained.

David, who is engaged in a full racing programme this year, is likely to be out of action for several weeks.

Hit a wall

A 41-year-old solo motor-cyclist was fatally injured on Sunday when his machine collided with a stone wall on Sunrising Hill, Tysoe.

The man was named as Leslie Wooding, of Ranwood Road, Kings Heath, Birmingham. He was taken to Banbury Hospital were he was certified dead.

An inquest is to be held at Banbury Police Station on July 7 at 2.30 p.m.

Driver killed

Southam motorist Mr. George Henry Wisdom (50), of 14b, Banbury Road, Southam, and his 15-year-old daughter, Jennifer, were injured in a fatal accident at Stretton, on Friday.

They were taken to the Hospital of St. Cross, Rugby. The driver, Mr. Edward Harper (22), of 121, Wiltshire Court, Nod Rise, Coventry, was taken to Rugby Hospital were he was found to be dead.

His wife, Susan (21), his sister and brother-in-law, Mr. and Mrs. John Belgrove, of 12, Chatsworth Rise, Styvechale, Coventry, passengers in his car, were injured.

DAVID HOBBS AT A FETE ON SATURDAY

ABOVE I was on my way to the 1965 French Grand Prix by road in my Ford Cortina GT, due to make my Formula 1 début in a Lotus 25 run by Tim Parnell, when I crashed and ended up in hospital.

David Hobbs collection

protested by screaming the place down, the nurse opined, 'I thought you were supposed to be a tough racing driver.' I cannot imagine what Niki Lauda went through.

Mags and our boys, Greg and Guy, were on holiday at the seaside, where I had left them to go off to do the race. So I suspect Mags, like every wife of a racing driver in those days, was waiting to hear gory news, but she certainly was not expecting to hear it just an hour or two after I had set off. My injuries put me out of action for five weeks, but I suppose if the same thing happened to me now, at my age, I would be out for about three years. This is one of the reasons why, unlike some old ex-professional racers, I do not compete in historic events.

My first race after leaving hospital was the one at Croft that I won in the Lola T70. According to my friend Brian Redman, who was there with his rich entrant, John Bridges of Red Rose Motors, he took one look at the Lola and said, 'That's what I want next year — one of those.' And in 1966 he duly appeared in one.

T70 to America

Later that season I went through one of the most dreadful periods of my career and, in fact, of my life. Ian Yates, David Fletcher and I decided to take the Lola to America and do the *Autoweek* Championship, the forerunner of the Can-Am. The six-race series took place in the autumn, starting at the Mont-Tremblant circuit at St Jovite, north-west of Montréal, in mid-September and winding up at Riverside in late October. Again we had no money, but a friend of my brother, the aforementioned John Sidwell, whom I had known since I was a very small boy, had become very successful in business and in a gesture of enormous generosity gave us £5,000, partly as a loan and partly as sponsorship. John, who was very keen on racing and fast cars, had come to Silverstone with me and I had given him some hot laps in the Lola, which impressed him no end.

It turned out that poor old David Fletcher, whom I had known for about 18 months, was a recovering alcoholic and certainly he had never had a drink in my presence. He and our one and only mechanic, Al, arrived in Canada before me, to get the car through customs and so on, and when I reached St Jovite he said to me, 'I had a drink last night. I thought it might make me sick, but I feel absolutely fine.' It seemed an odd thing to say, but I was unaware of his difficulties. That evening we went out for dinner and had enough to drink for me to feel a little off-colour the next day but David said he was fine. Perhaps I should have suspected something, but I did not even know what an alcoholic was in those days, and had never seen what the condition could be like. All of this turned out to be a very big issue as our trip unfolded.

The race itself was pretty successful as I finished third behind Jim Hall's Chaparral and Bruce McLaren in one of his own cars, beating all the locals. Our next stop was Mosport, just east of Toronto and about 300 miles away. For the life of me I do not know how we got there but when we did arrive the plan was to make the Shell garage in Bowmanville our race shop, alongside John Surtees, who had now turned up with the factory Lola. The garage was owned and run by Ronnie Mutton, whom I would see a lot of in subsequent years. It was a very eventful week.

During practice John had a big moment at turn one and his car vaulted the very dodgy guard rail and dropped into a pedestrian tunnel. He was very lucky to survive as he broke his back but thankfully he made a full recovery although he was out of action for months. In the race I was looking strong, running in the top four with some very heavy hitters, but retired with mechanical problems. Before we set off for the next race, I visited John in hospital in Toronto and later found that I was the only driver who did so.

Although we had been looking pretty competitive, our money had already run out and we did not know how we were going to get to the next races, on the West Coast. However, a little guy called Lou with a cracking girlfriend had attached himself to us over the weekend, and when he learned of our situation he said, 'Well, I'll tow you to Seattle!' Through Ronnie we got ourselves a two-wheel trailer, put the Lola T70 on that, along with four or five spare wheels, and jammed ourselves — David, Al and me — into Lou's Cadillac, along with Lou's well-endowed girlfriend and Al's toolbox, and off we set. Bad move. We should have packed up and gone home.

When I look back on it, this was a spectacular trip and I would like to do it again. I remember coming over a crest and seeing the lights of Winnipeg at night, looking as if the city was just down the road, but because the air was so clear it was much further than it appeared, 25 miles at least. We drove through Saskatchewan via Moose Jaw, into North and South Dakota, past charcoal-making teepees and finally into Seattle and onwards to Pacific Raceways at Kent, in Washington state.

Two Chaparrals were there and won both of the races, Jim Hall from Hap Sharp. I was sixth in the first race but did not finish the second. This was my first encounter with Jerry Grant, who was also driving a Lola, and he was quick. A bit like Butch Cassidy, I thought, 'Who is this guy?'

We then headed south to California for Laguna Seca and Riverside, again courtesy of Lou and his Cadillac. We did not race at Laguna, probably because we were too busy minding David and short of money, but we did run at Riverside as one of about 50 entries including big names like Jimmy Clark and Richie Ginther in factory Lotus 40s, Graham Hill and Bruce McLaren in McLarens, as well as A.J. Foyt, Peter Revson and Mario Andretti — a simply fantastic entry. I was a bit peeved because there was a new factory T70 there run by Team Surtees but John (still hospitalised), with whom I had done so much

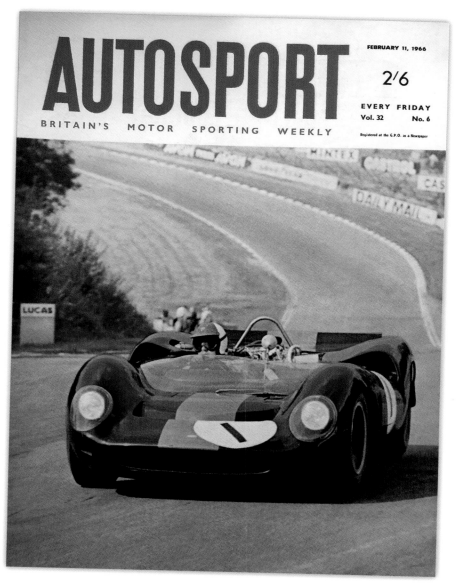

BELOW At least *Autosport* recognised my efforts with the Lola T70 in 1965, by popping me on the cover of one of their winter issues. This shot was taken at Brands Hatch during the Guards Trophy race, my last event in Britain before heading off to campaign the car in North America.

Courtesy of Autosport

testing and had a good relationship, put Jackie Stewart in it rather than me.

During practice I was standing with Jackie and Jimmy when a message came over the public address announcing, 'Mr Stewart to the clerk of the course's office.' But he was not in trouble — it was to take a phone call from Helen and find out that she had given birth to their first son. Paul Stewart went on to race himself and then, together with Jackie, set up a racing team that ultimately went on to become Red Bull Racing.

As if the trip itself was not bad enough, the race was another disaster. Al was a good guy and a good mechanic, but lack of parts and time are not great for race preparation. When I moved off, the clutch was barely working and would not fully disengage, then to make matters worse the starter held the cars on the grid for a long time, leaving my clutch dragging so badly that it burned out. So I finished up in the pits, where I was interviewed for TV by Chris Economaki. It was my first appearance on American TV and not my finest hour as all the frustration and pent-up

anger came out in a complete array of expletives. Chris, being the absolute professional that he was, took it all in his stride and we became very good friends, and in later years worked together many times. He never forgot our first meeting!

Straight after the debacle at the start of the race, I took David Fletcher to Los Angeles airport and literally put him on the plane, handing him over to the cabin crew with strict instructions from his wife not to give him any alcohol. That was the last I ever saw of him. He never recovered and died a few months after our fateful trip. He was a lovely, generous fellow with a heart of gold.

I had stayed throughout that week at the home of another ex-Jaguar apprentice, David Batt, who had moved to Los Angeles. He lived in Pacific Pallisades, a good 60 miles from the track, but with money being so tight staying with him was the affordable option. After David Fletcher's departure, he took on responsibility for the T70, which did the rounds of various teams. I was reunited with it at the 2008 Goodwood Revival by then owner Frank Sytner.

OPPOSITE My body language conveys the story. My big trip across the Atlantic for four late-1965 races — two each in Canada and the US — in the Lola T70 held so much promise and excitement, but after a fair start with third place at St Jovite it all turned to dust. *Getty Images/The Enthusiast Network*

BELOW The last of my four T70 outings in America, a 200-miler at Riverside in California, ended ignominiously, with clutch failure. *Getty Images/The Enthusiast Network*

CHAPTER 5
1966–67
SURTEES AND MORE

I suppose by 1966 I was becoming what people call a journeyman driver, getting paid to race, driving for various teams in different categories, but without a decent factory drive.

But this looked as if it would change as the season started. John Surtees, amazingly already nearly fully recovered from his huge crash in Canada only a few months earlier, was going to run a new Lola T70 in various sports car races, mainly in Britain, and asked if I wanted to drive it. This looked like a golden opportunity, a proper factory drive for a team led by one of the all-time greats, in conjunction with Lola Cars, by this time one of the country's leading manufacturers of race cars. Surely nothing could go wrong this time?

Well, lots. John never seemed to get a proper sponsor for the programme, so even though we were the works Lola team, we were always a day late and a few quid short. In the end I only took part in four or five of the bigger sports car races in Britain, but thankfully there were other opportunities interspersed between these outings.

At Mallory Park in the spring we must have had some sort of mechanical failure early in practice as John and I were watching the rest of the session together when a maroon Lola T70 came careering down the back straight and went off deep into the grass on the left, shot across the road into a ditch on the right, then hauled itself out and roared off in the direction of the hairpin

LEFT The culmination of two massively disappointing seasons driving Team Surtees Lola T70s was this race, the six-hour BOAC International 500 at Brands Hatch in July 1967. After persevering that year with a hopeless Aston Martin V8 engine, for my final race in the car 'Big John' installed a normal Chevrolet unit — and got pole. But we had various problems in the race and never figured.
LAT Images

— all without lifting off the throttle. John and I looked at each other and said, 'Who the hell is that?' On checking the entry list it turned out to be my first known sighting of Brian Herman Thomas Redman. He has remained a thorn in my side for more than 50 years and a man who can still inflict terrible damage to my body in bar situations.

I digress. I continued to do a lot of standing around at race meetings where I was supposed to be driving around. The Aston Martin Owners' Club used to sanction a big race at Silverstone and I was entered in the Lola. It rained during the race but I was in the lead group and running well when the car started to slide around in a most alarming manner, so I headed for the pits. After a brief look nothing was found amiss and so I resumed, with the same outcome. So I returned to the pits again. On closer inspection they found that part of the sump gasket had sprung a leak and was spraying a jet of oil onto the left rear tyre. But that disappointment was nothing compared with what followed.

The next disaster was down to me. Again we were back at Silverstone and the main support race for the International Trophy meeting, in front of a very large crowd. John was still with Ferrari — this was only a matter of weeks before his acrimonious departure — and chief engineer Mauro Forghieri was there with the Formula 1 team. Before the race John had been doing a great sell to Mauro about me. 'Oh, he's going to be very good, very steady, safe and fast. You wait and see how he handles Chris Amon, Bruce McLaren and Denny Hulme.'

So there I was in the middle of the front row. The starter's flag went up, already in gear, revs up, down went the flag — and my car moved slowly forward burning the clutch out. I had put the big Hewland LG600 box into third, not first. Needless to say, that was the end of any hope of a Ferrari career. I can hear Forghieri saying, 'Yes, John, I see what you mean, good boy, very quick.'

My best result with the T70 that year came on a return visit to Silverstone, for the Martini Trophy race in July. I finished third behind Denny Hulme, who had a fabulous season in Sid Taylor's similar car and cleaned up most of the races, while Bob Bondurant was second.

My last race in the T70 was at Croft, the scene of my victory the previous year after returning from the road accident. Denny and I were the class of the field for what was a two-heat race, but trouble struck again in practice when the differential broke. Our mechanic Malcolm Malone set to work with his ciggy firmly jammed between his front teeth.

It became very clear that we were not going to make the first heat. Derek Ongaro, our team manager, went off to see the clerk of the course and returned with the news that if we did only the second heat we would not be eligible for a result, but Derek decided that I would take part anyway. We had endured such a miserable season with so many mechanical problems that he thought he owed me a start. So I started from the back while Denny, who had won the first heat, was in pole position.

It rained — what a surprise in Yorkshire — and I started on wet tyres. About halfway through I thundered past Hulme to win by miles and, of course, Derek and Malcolm were delighted. To be fair, I was on Firestone wets and Denny was on Goodyear's inferior equivalent, but that is racing and it was a fabulous result.

Derek phoned John to tell him the news and he just about had a coronary. 'You mean you raced my car with no hope of a result?' John well and truly reamed us both.

That was the end of our T70 season with Team Surtees and we now prepared for another great year in 1967. Little did we know it would be very similar, if not worse.

More single-seaters

My first single-seater race of 1966 was also my Formula 1 début, which this time really did happen, at the street circuit of Syracuse on the island of Sicily. Back then there were various non-championship Formula 1 races, mainly in England, but there were a few others and the Syracuse Grand Prix was one of them. Most of the big teams turned up, including Ferrari. There were also quite a few private teams who basically

bought the previous year's cars from the factories and went racing. Some of them were able to win races too, as Rob Walker had done a few years earlier with Stirling Moss driving for him. Once again I was entered by Tim Parnell in a BRM-powered Lotus 25 for a one-off chance.

It went very well and I finished third behind the two factory Ferraris of John Surtees and Lorenzo Bandini. There were no barriers at the track, which was on public roads complete with kerbs, walls and trees, and towards the end of the race the available road got narrower and narrower as people closed in. The slowing-down lap was chaos, with just enough space to squeeze our race cars through the crowds.

Afterwards one of the best-known British journalists of the day, John Blunsden, came up

ABOVE Away with the birds. This is a stop-off at Milan cathedral on my way with John Surtees to meet Ferrari's Mauro Forghieri in Maranello. Despite John talking me up, I never did get to drive for the Scuderia. *David Hobbs collection*

to me and said, 'You're on your way now, the phone won't stop ringing.' Unfortunately he was wrong. However, my result as the first non-Ferrari finisher must have played a part in a brief visit I made to Maranello at Surtees's instigation but that never went anywhere. However, fourth in that race was Vic Wilson, a BRM privateer, and it turned out that his cousin, wealthy Yorkshire businessman Bernard White, did play a part in taking my career forward.

That year I also returned to Formula 2 and for reasons that now elude me I was back driving for Merlyn again, this time in a Mk9. The first two races were in Britain, starting at Oulton Park, the track where I had been robbed of the Tourist Trophy victory the previous year in the T70. This took place the day after Syracuse so it was all a bit of a rush and in the end it was a waste of time because it snowed and we never raced. Two weeks later at Goodwood the weather was much better but the car's Cosworth SCA engine blew up after a few laps.

The Goodwood race was where Jack Brabham and Denny Hulme showed up with a pair of Brabham BT18s fitted with a new 1-litre Honda engine, the Japanese motorcycle manufacturer's first foray into car racing. The cars, designed by Australian Ron Tauranac, were absolutely awesome and the team was accompanied by a large group of young Japanese engineers working on these new engines, which were incredibly loud. Later, after Bernie Ecclestone bought the Brabham Formula 1 team in 1972, Tauranac left and started Ralt, building highly successful Formula 3 cars, and a he also remained involved in Formula 1 designing and building cars with Honda.

There was plenty of opposition at Goodwood that weekend with Jochen Rindt and Alan Rees in a couple of similar Winkelmann Racing Brabham entries fitted with Cosworth engines, Graham Hill in John Coombs's BRM-powered Brabham, and Jackie Stewart and Jean-Pierre Beltoise in a pair of French blue Matras. One of the great things about Formula 2 in those days was that the races mostly did not clash with the Grands Prix, so lots of the big names raced and up-and-coming young drivers like me could measure themselves against

LEFT Prior to my Lola T70 races in 1966, the season started with my Formula 1 début in the non-championship Syracuse Grand Prix on 1 April, a day that happened to bring good luck. Driving Tim Parnell's BRM-powered Lotus 25, I finished third behind the works Ferraris of John Surtees and Lorenzo Bandini. That felt pretty good.
LAT Images

the stars, and, maybe, sometimes beat them.

But those two Brabham-Hondas absolutely dominated the 1966 season and usually finished first and second.

For my third Formula 2 race of the season, at Montjuïc in Barcelona, I was back with my old team Midland Racing Partnership (MRP) in their latest Lola T61, with Cosworth SCA power. The track, which was new to me, was set on the side of a hill overlooking the city and was just roadways through a park with odd bits of barrier. It was a pretty hair-raising place. I had a terrific race and came home fourth, beating a lot of fancied runners, including a World Champion, Graham Hill in his Brabham BT16. Ahead of me were just the two Brabham-Hondas split on this occasion by Jackie Stewart in the Matra. I hoped this result would lead to further decent drives.

Graham Hill was a very good and popular speaker and also enjoyed making jokes at other people's expense. At the time I had a blue and yellow crash helmet, simply because I liked the colours, and later I added a Union Jack. In the Snetterton pitlane Graham came up to me and said, 'Hobbo, it looks as if someone has been sick all over your helmet.' I was mortified, and Mags still remembers it to this day. So there was a touch of extra pleasure in beating him in Barcelona.

I seesawed in and out of single-seaters that year and did not get back into one until Reims in July, racing for my third Formula 2 team of the year. This time I was with the official Lotus operation run by Ron Harris, driving alongside Mike Spence in the latest Lotus 44. On the second lap I was part of a huge bunch accelerating out of the tight right-hander leading onto the first long slipstreaming straight when Pedro Rodríguez, immediately ahead of me in the innovative Protos, missed a gear and I went into the back of him. That was a race to forget and strangely I never drove for the team again.

There was one more Formula 2 chance when I was invited for what would be my final outing with MRP, on the Bugatti circuit at Le Mans, where motorcycle races are held nowadays. Unfortunately it was yet another unhappy ending as I got mixed up in a first-lap multi-car shunt.

My first GT40 encounter

An important opportunity came quite early in the year, in May, at what I consider the most daunting track of that era, the 8.8-mile Spa-Francorchamps circuit in Belgium. Set on the edge of the Ardennes forest, scene of some of the most gruesome battles of the Second World War, the track was on everyday public roads bordered variously by trees, telegraph poles, buildings, deep ditches and barbed-wire fencing. It was also extremely fast, with an average speed back then of around 140mph.

This was my first-ever drive in one of my all-time favourite race cars, the Ford GT40, which evolved from the Lola Mk6 that I raced at Le Mans in 1963. The Detroit-based Essex Wire Company, a supplier to Ford and one of the world's largest manufacturers of wires and cables, bought two GT40s for a racing programme. For the Spa 1,000Km I shared one with German driver Jochen Neerpasch, who went on to head BMW's racing operation, while the other was driven by Peter Revson and Skip Scott. It was a disappointing initiation for me at one of the 'grandee' circuits.

Jochen took the start of the race and when he came in to hand over he casually remarked that the car was 'running bit hot'. I got in and saw the needle of the water-temperature gauge right round against the stop, so I supposed the damage had been done by then. After a lap and a half the thing expired as I powered out of Stavelot corner, which was just about as far from the pits as you could be, a good four miles away. I freewheeled as far as I could before pulling into the yard of a farmhouse. I got out and knocked on the door, still with my helmet on. A middle-aged chap opened the door and, completely unfazed, invited me in and offered me a cup of coffee. We ended up watching the rest of the race on his television, with the GT40 parked in his driveway.

I spent most of the next day, Monday, driving back home to our new abode. Well, it was new to us. Actually it was about 350 years old, in the village of Upper Boddington, deep in the countryside north of Silverstone. I arrived late in the afternoon, just as the removal van was driving away up the lane, poor Mags having managed the

ABOVE **After twice doing the Le Mans 24 Hours in Triumph Spitfires, I had a rather more sophisticated mount for 1966. I shared this Maranello Concessionaires Ferrari Dino 206S with Michael Salmon.**

LAT Images

entire move herself while also looking after our two small children, Greg and Guy, by now aged four and two. Mags always took so much in her stride.

We set about getting organised in our new home, Hill Farm House, but I did not have a lot of time as the next races were always about to hove into view.

The Colonel

For Le Mans in 1966 I was invited to drive a pretty little Ferrari Dino 206S entered by one of Britain's leading race teams, the Ferrari importer Maranello Concessionaires, owned and run by Colonel Ronnie Hoare. It was a dream opportunity and I had high expectations.

Colonel Hoare was the absolute caricature of an English gentleman. He was so smooth, so absolutely pukka, so stereotypically English. He always used to wear the most exquisite tweed jackets with equally exquisite shirts and ties, complete with finely tailored cuffs and smart cuff links. His hair was wavy, not curly, absolutely

immaculate at all times and with just the right amount of grey to add distinction.

My co-driver was Michael Salmon, a very quick sports and GT driver, just a little eccentric, tall and gangly, and fairly well heeled as he lived in the tax haven of Jersey in the Channel Islands. Michael spoke a bit like the Colonel himself and could do the most amazing impersonation of him, with a perfect Ferrari V12 sound effect at his beck and call as well.

Our team-mates were in bigger-engined Ferraris. Richard Attwood and David Piper drove the wonderful Ferrari 365P2 Spyder, a potential race winner, while Piers Courage and Roy Pike, a talented American from Formula Junior, were in a 275GTB/C.

Our drivers' meeting with Ronnie on the Friday afternoon was like something out of a comedy film, with Ronnie speaking to us like small children. 'Nahow, when you get in, you first staahrt the engine, and then, of course, you select first geeahr to leave the pits, and first geeahr is heah, of course...' as he demonstrated the lever

position with his hand. It was daft prattling, telling us how to drive and how to do pit stops. With Michael adding his perfect imitation of a Ferrari V12 at appropriate moments, it was hysterically funny.

Unfortunately our car only lasted for 45 minutes. It suddenly quit with rear-axle failure, with me driving. Then the Attwood/Piper P2 Spyder broke three hours after that. All this was most untypical for the Colonel's cars were always beautifully prepared. The only finisher among us was the Courage/Pike 275GTB/C, which soldiered on to eighth place. I could not believe it: my chance of a lifetime in this lovely car with an absolute top team and it was over almost as soon as it had started. *Sacré Bleu!*

This was the year Ford scored its famous 1–2–3 finish with the 7-litre GT40 Mark IIs. Ford's people tried to stage a photo finish with the leading car, driven by Denny Hulme/Ken Miles, side by side with the Bruce McLaren/Chris Amon entry that had been running second. But the Automobile Club de l'Ouest, who ran Le Mans, declared Bruce

and Chris the winners because they had started further back on the grid and therefore had gone a greater distance. Poor Ken Miles never really got over the disappointment.

A new benefactor

The rest of my sports car racing in 1966 was for Bernard White, who was in the print and publishing business. His brother was Sir Gordon White, who co-founded the British conglomerate called the Hanson Group, a big name in corporate Britain at the time.

My first events with Bernard were in a Ferrari 250LM, starting with the support race to the British Grand Prix at Brands Hatch. I retired from that, but then got a second place at Croft and a sixth back at Brands Hatch. Then we went to Austria for the Zeltweg 500Km, the last round of that year's World Sports Car Championship, held on the airfield track just down the road from what is now the Red Bull Ring. Bernard entered a Ford GT40 for Innes Ireland as well as the 250LM for me. The factory

ABOVE For the second half of 1966 I drove in sports car races for wealthy privateer Bernard White, starting here at Brands Hatch with his beautiful Ferrari 250LM in a support race for the British Grand Prix. This simple paddock scene captures a bygone era, with varied vehicles from suppliers of carburettors, fuel additives, spark plugs, brake components and pistons.
Barry Charles Hitchcox/ FotoLibra

Porsches 906s went on to win on this very bumpy track while I retired with overheating and lost several fillings out of my teeth.

But the season was not over yet because I got a call from Bernard asking me to drive his GT40 in the South African Springbok series in November and December, starting with the Kyalami Nine Hours. I was to team up with Mike Hailwood, the finest motorcycle racer of all time. Mike had won nine motorcycle world championships at all engine displacements, but what really made him almost God-like to British fans were his accomplishments at the Isle of Man TT races, where he ultimately won 14 times, setting new lap records practically every year.

In fact the whole idea filled me with dread but as we needed the money I agreed to go. I had little knowledge of South Africa and its people but knew I would dislike it. Another reservation lay in the experience of the previous year's long trip to America, which had started so well but then became a nightmare in almost every respect. I also had preconceived ideas about Mike 'The

Bike' Hailwood. I did not know him but I was convinced that we would not hit it off. How wrong can you be?

We were both accommodated for almost a month by the Nucci family, who had a lovely house with a pool in the Johannesburg suburbs and it was here that I met Mike on my arrival. Immediately it became clear that all my forebodings were unfounded and right from the start we got on like a house on fire. He was a wonderful guy with many interests. He played the piano, guitar and saxophone, and was a magic mover on the dance floor. He also liked a drink or three but it was upon *les girls* that his mind was laser-focused and he had many conquests during our eight-week stay. Mike also had his preconceptions about me too, thinking I was some toffee-nosed Formula 1 person, but we had an absolutely fabulous time together. Later, after Mike married, our wives really got on too and we all remained close friends until Mike's appallingly untimely end in, of all things, a road accident caused by a lost foreign lorry driver backing across a divided highway. For Mike's poor widow, Pauline, it was a double tragedy as their young daughter Michelle was also killed.

While Mike and I were living the high life, South Africa, of course, was deep in the Apartheid era. On one occasion, our host Mrs Nucci rendered me speechless when she remarked, 'You English have such a strong class system through your schools, universities and jobs.' She said it with a completely straight face while behind her were two black girls who, with their mother, did every job in the house and garden for very low pay and lived in a shack at the bottom of the yard with virtually no facilities. Meanwhile, Mr Nucci ran a very prosperous bus service that transported black workers into Johannesburg to work and back out again to their well-guarded and totally segregated townships.

Our first race was the Kyalami Nine Hours, which had become quite a popular attraction for Europeans as it came when the nights were long and cold back home. For this event I was paired with a different Mike, Mike Spence, in the Ford GT40 while the other Mike and Bob Anderson, another motorcycle world champion turned car racer, shared the Ferrari 250LM that I had raced a few months earlier.

For the South African trip Bernard had taken on a mechanic whom we will just call 'Bob', rather than his full name, to protect the innocent. This bloke was all mouth and trousers and I had my suspicions about him from the outset because any mechanic who tells you how great he is and mentions 'tyre patch roll centres' and 'tyre slip angles' gets my antenna up. Anyway, I was to start the race, which had an old-fashioned Le Mans-style getaway. I told 'Bob' that he should park the car in its starting slot with first gear engaged, so that when I jumped in I would start the engine, let the clutch out and — pow! — gone. This pillock somehow selected reverse but amazingly I did not back the car into the wall. We retired with transmission problems while Richard Attwood and David Piper won, again, in one of David's Ferraris. Altogether they won this race eight times.

BELOW The Kyalami Nine Hours was the first race of my South African tour and for this event I shared the GT40 with a different Mike — Spence rather than Hailwood. In this shot, taken during the pre-race build-up, I am in the middle, holding my helmet and chatting to one of the circuit personnel, and Mike Spence is leaning against our steed. *www.motoprint.co.za (courtesy of Ken Stewart)*

After a few days in the sun, Mike and I set off for Cape Town, about 900 miles south-west across the Karoo, a large semi-desert area. The next race, and our first together, was near Cape Town, a beautiful city on the edge of the vast southern ocean, at a fairly short, twisty circuit close to Killarney. This was a three-hour race involving one pit stop for refuelling and a driver change. I started and by the halfway point I was leading easily. In for the pit stop and driver change. The GT40 had a huge, racy-looking fuel filler at the base of the right-hand A pillar with a big cap and hinged snap-locking clip. Well, mechanic 'Bob', having completed the refuelling, slammed the cap shut, but, unknown to us, failed to lock it on the latch.

Mike rushed off to the first corner, a sharp left-hander. As he braked hard and swung left, fuel gushed out of the filler neck and poured over the bodywork and onto the front wheel and brake assembly — whoosh! The result was that the front end of the car and Mike's face got badly singed. Now we were both pissed off with 'Bob', who had

to set to and repair the car, then tow it on a trailer the 900 miles back to Johannesburg and onwards another 500 miles to Bulawayo, in what was then Rhodesia — now Zimbabwe — for our third event at a track called Kumalo.

There were two races at Kumalo and I won one and Mike the other, so Bernard was happier, Mike and I were happier, and so, I am sure, was 'Bob'.

This was turning into quite a tour of colonial Africa as the next race was in Portuguese East Africa (now Mozambique) in Lourenço Marques (now Maputo) on a track around the port of this gorgeous, very European city on the Indian Ocean. There Mike and I spent our week at a peaceful resort alongside a salt lagoon separated from the ocean by huge sand dunes, doing lots of waterskiing and lying around in the sun.

Come race weekend, 'Bob' excelled himself. With about an hour to go before the start, he had the front of the GT40 raised on a simple quick-lift jack, the type with a fulcrum that went over-centre when the car was up and stayed put. He then lifted the rear of the car with another. Result?

The front jack flipped up and over the car, hurling itself through the windscreen. Panic! And lots of expletives from everyone. 'Bob' dashed into town to try to find a replacement, a fruitless task, while I scurried around looking for goggles and prepared for a very breezy race as we thought it best to remove all the other windows as well. The car certainly would not have passed muster in Adrian Newey's school of aerodynamics.

It was my turn to do the first stint of this three-hour race. Sod's law being what it is, rain then started to fall, making the whole effort even more unpleasant. When I came into the pits to hand over to Mike, I could not see him waiting to jump in. Then I spotted him in his regular clothes sitting at the back of the pits. He calmly waved me away, shouting, 'Oh no, dear boy, I couldn't possibly drive in the rain with no windscreen. You carry on.' Always good fun, was Mike. Anyway, somehow I managed to finish second.

Next came Christmas, which we spent in tropical heat back in the Nucci household in Johannesburg. Meanwhile, back in our freezing house in England, Mrs H was getting pretty hot under the collar, as my prolonged absence was not going well, not well at all, what with looking after our young boys, Greg and Guy, on her own and me not even being there for Christmas.

For our next race, on 27 December, we drove another 400 miles south from Johannesburg over the Drackensberg Mountains to Durban, on the Indian Ocean, for a race at the Roy Hesketh Circuit on the outskirts of Pietermaritzburg. For this event, Bernard, after our many calls to him back in England, sent out his original full-time mechanic, Roly Moat, or 'Roooorrly Moooort' as he called himself in his strong Yorkshire accent. Things did not get off to an electrifying start as Roly was violently sick over the dinner table the evening before the race. Quite a sight. I cannot remember if he had carrots for dinner, but we must have done.

The good news was that we won that race convincingly to conclude our South African schedule on a very satisfactory note. However, the promoter of the opening round of the 1967

LEFT While I was soaking up the heat in South Africa, Mags and our two boys, Greg and Guy, had a long wintry stretch without me and no doubt played many board games. I even missed Christmas and New Year with them.
David Hobbs collection

Formula 1 World Championship, due to be held at Kyalami just six days later, asked if we would take part in one of the support races as we were obviously a fast outfit. For me, that meant racing in a very competitive car in front of Grand Prix racing's finest — a real opportunity to showcase my skill. What could possibly go wrong?

There was one major dilemma. This change of plan meant a phone call to Mags to explain that I would be gone for at least another week. I had left home on 2 November and by now we were coming up to New Year. Well, as she has done all through our lives together, Mags made it very easy for me and told me it was too good an opportunity to miss. She really was a wonderful wife for a struggling driver to have and her stress level must have been very high with the real and constant danger we all faced back then. To this day she continues to be wonderfully supportive of all my endeavours.

Race day at Kyalami dawned, another beautiful hot sunny day. My race started well, down the long straight to the medium right-hander called Crowthorne, then a quick run to an uphill left-hand sweeper followed by a swoop over the brow to Sunset Bend, fast through the right-hander, a rush up to Clubhouse, brake hard, turn left — and at that moment the filler cap sprang open again. A lurid spin followed, right in front of everyone in the clubhouse. I should have gone home before that race.

Mike and I had had a lot of fun and achieved some good results, but it could have been so much better. At least I finished the season with two wins for Bernard and by now he was talking about entering Formula 1 in 1967, with me driving. And despite our terrible year with the Lola T70, John Surtees was offering more drives as well. John fell out with a few drivers over the years but he and I hit it off pretty well.

By the time I arrived back at Heathrow, wearing a light blue suit and the most amazing tan, Mags took some time to recognise me as I walked out of the customs hall. Back at home I realised how cold our old farmhouse was. At least my loyal friend Tony Barrett, who had come with me to my first race seven years earlier, had bought

Mags an electric blanket, which saved her from the worst of the cold. Mags and I spent the rest of the winter knocking down walls and scraping old oak beams to add our signature to the place. And I contacted a plumber to get central heating fitted.

Into 1967 with Lola

For the 1967 season John Surtees pulled off a seemingly incredible deal for Lola. They were going into partnership with Aston Martin and hoping to win the World Sports Car Championship with an Aston Martin-powered Lola T70 Mk3 GT, a closed-coupé version of the T70. John asked me to be his co-driver, which I regarded as a great privilege. Co-driving with a World Champion in one of the world's most important race series with a car that promised to be a potential Le Mans winner — what a great opportunity.

Sadly, as in 1966, it turned into a complete and utter disaster. The 5-litre V8 engine was very heavy and never seemed to have much power. I did a lot of the testing and we would go to Snetterton and Silverstone, me and Malcolm Malone, cigarette still stuck in his teeth, but we just could not get any speed out of it. Aston Martin would say, 'Well, it's the car.' And Eric would respond, 'It's not my car, it's your engine.'

We tried all sorts of tricks to make this T70 go quicker. One involved improving airflow to the engine. Where the cockpit roof stopped at the rear bulkhead, there was a square trough that ran down the middle of the bodywork and ended in a spoiler, wings not having come into use yet. The carburettor intakes were in the middle of this trough. So Eric tried an experiment to make sure the intakes were not being compromised. He put a huge, flat tray on the back of the car, a big sheet of aluminium with the carburettor intakes fully exposed, fastened behind the back window and extended to the rear.

This was at Snetterton, which has a very long back straight running parallel to the A12 main road, perhaps no more than 20 yards from it, with trucks passing nearby while you are doing 180mph in a race car. At the end of the straight is a hairpin, a tight, heavy-braking job. Since there

LEFT The first race for the Team Surtees Aston Martin-powered Lola T70 Mk3 GT was the Nürburgring 1,000Km. In this scene Malcolm Malone is adjusting tyre pressure at the right front and Vince Higgins, our other mechanic, is at the back of the car.
David Hobbs collection

BELOW After our promising speed in practice, the Nürburgring 1,000Km was a huge let-down as our new T70 suffered a suspension failure after only six laps with John at the wheel — so I did not get to race.
LAT Images

RIGHT Here I am with John Surtees, looking despondent as the Nürburgring 1,000Km drags on after our car's early retirement.
Jutta Fausel

BELOW Le Mans came next. This was even worse than the Nürburgring. The Aston Martin V8 engine burned a piston after only three laps and that was it. John had taken the start so again we were out before I even got behind the wheel.
LAT Images

was no data collection, the driver was incredibly important in testing and the rev counter was the only instrument you focused on. What were the revs going into a corner and, and more importantly, coming out of it? And, after chassis changes, were they different and, if so, higher or lower? So you are continually glancing at the rev counter, especially as you get nearer and nearer your ultimate braking point. You are looking up, looking down, trying to read the revs at the last split-second before you hit the brakes.

The Lola seemed no faster with this big tray on the back but it now had absolutely no rear downforce. When I hit the brakes for the hairpin the car spun like a top. It went round, and round, and round. You have never seen so much tyre smoke. Luckily, I did not hit the embankment where the road turned right. That would have been a disaster as there was no run-off, just this big dirt mound.

So we dickered around like that, with no discernible improvement, and finally we went to the Nürburgring 1,000Km. There the right

front wheel fell off, going down to *Bergwerk*. Bloody great.

Next was Le Mans. We practised and fiddled around with the car. There was some argy-bargy about spark plugs because Aston Martin wanted a different brand from the one Surtees used, and I believe Aston also tried a different cylinder-head gasket for the race engine. So we changed the plugs, and John started the race, since it was his car. He did three laps before the thing burned a piston. So I never took part in the actual race.

Next we went to the Reims 12 Hours and again the engine blew up, at which point John just about had a coronary and gave up on Aston Martin — which was ignominious for them. With a Chevrolet V8 fitted instead, our last outing was the BOAC International 500, a six-hour race at Brands Hatch, where John put the car on pole position, just ahead of the Chaparral of Phil Hill and Mike Spence — who went on to win the race. Our car? Just about everything that could go wrong did. I drove for some laps, in and out of the pits, until finally we called it a day.

ABOVE **By the time of the BOAC International 500 at Brands Hatch in July, John Surtees had ditched the Aston Martin engine and reverted to Chevrolet power, and we got pole. As ever, John took the start and here he leads into Druids on the first lap, trailed by works Ferrari 330P4 Spyders driven by Paul Hawkins (8) and Ludovico Scarfiotti (7), and the Chaparral with its high wing.** *Mike Hayward Collection*

Jaguar XJ13

At much the same time as Lola-Aston Martin testing was going on, Jaguar's 'Lofty' England asked me to become involved in the evaluation of their XJ13 racer, a rear-engined successor to the D-type. After a ten-year absence Jaguar were considering a return to Le Mans, but by this time the XJ13 was already about five years old and had languished under a dustsheet because there had been insufficient interest in pursuing the project. So the car was in a bit of a time warp but it was a beautiful, sleek machine with a wonderful 5.5-litre double-overhead-camshaft V12 engine that delivered 550bhp and masses of torque.

Norman Dewis, Jaguar's accomplished chief test driver who had evaluated all the company's new road and racing models from the XK120 onwards, was understandably a bit put out by involvement. But 'Lofty' needed unbiased assessment from a racing driver with experience of competitive cars of a similar type, like the Lola T70. The testing was done at the Motor Industry Research Association (MIRA) track near Coventry early on Sunday

mornings to keep it as 'hush-hush' as possible and away from prying eyes. 'Lofty' now lived in the next village to ours, Priors Marston, and for the first session I presented myself at his house at about 5am and we drove together to MIRA in his E-type. On arrival I found that the Jaguar chairman, Sir William Lyons, and his chief stylist, Malcolm Sayer, were on hand. The engineer in charge was Mike Kimberley, a fairly recent ex-Jaguar apprentice himself who many years later ran Lotus Cars.

We did a number of sessions like this and during one of them, in April, I lapped MIRA at over 161mph, which stood as an unofficial closed-circuit British lap record for 32 years.

Besides the MIRA running, there was one final test at Silverstone and for this I was joined by another ex-Jaguar apprentice, Richard Attwood. Afterwards we wrote up our report, pointing out some very obvious changes such as the need for wheels of 11-inch width with slick tyres instead of skinny wheels and old Dunlop R5 tyres, and recommending the use of solid bushes rather

BELOW Early in 1967 Jaguar's 'Lofty' England invited me to test the XJ13, a V12-engined sports racer that had been designed some years before but then put under wraps. The 161mph lap I did at the MIRA proving ground in Warwickshire was an unofficial British record and remained so for 32 years.
Alamy/Trinity Mirror/ Mirrorpix

than rubber ones. The car also needed some downforce. Although beautifully slippery, it probably developed lift at speed. Despite all that, I think it would have been instantly competitive as it had far more horsepower than a GT40.

But by now, sadly, Jaguar was part of British Leyland and their boss Sir Donald Stokes put the lid on the programme. However, the car still survives, although Norman Dewis crashed it at MIRA in 1971 after a mechanical failure while doing filming for launch publicity for the new V12 E-type, Jaguar's first production car with the sophisticated engine pioneered in the XJ13. Jaguar did, of course, subsequently return to Le Mans in the 1980s with Tom Walkinshaw and added another chapter of successes.

Petering out

The 1967 season was a crushing disappointment. It had started with so much promise, driving a factory-entered Lola with a factory Aston Martin engine alongside one of the greatest figures in motorsport. But it all turned to ashes.

I raced a Cobra a couple of times for The Chequered Flag and there were two more sports car races for Bernard, but none of those brought any worthwhile results. My last race of the year was the non-championship Paris 1,000Km at Montlhéry partnering Max Wilson in his Lola T70. I qualified it on the front row of a strong grid but we were out within 15 laps with an oil leak. I did about ten sports car races that year and retired almost every time.

My season had started with potential drives for yet another Formula 2 team, Birmingham-based Alexis. Only one outing materialised, at Mallory Park, and that was another disaster as the gearbox broke in practice and I was unable to start the race.

One of the few brightish spots was my World Championship Formula 1 début, at the British Grand Prix at Silverstone in Bernard White's BRM P261, which only had a 2-litre engine at a time when Formula 1 had moved to a 3-litre limit. I finished eighth, which would have got me a few points these days.

But better was to come.

ABOVE The non-championship Paris 1,000Km at Montlhéry was my last race of 1967. I put Max Wilson's Lola T70 on the front row alongside the Jacky Ickx/Paul Hawkins Gulf Mirage M1 but the engine expired after only 15 laps — a sorry end to a sorry season.
Jutta Fausel

CHAPTER 6
1968–70
THE GULF YEARS

To me it was absolute heaven. I had never driven for a big team before and my new deal for 1968 was going to give me my best chance of winning Le Mans.

I drove a Lotus Elite at Le Mans in 1962 and won my class, then in 1963 I raced the Lola Mk6 there for Eric Broadley. In 1964 and 1965, as a works Triumph driver in the little Spitfire, the people in the team all thought I was wonderful, saying I should be driving something much better than their car. Then in 1966 I drove the Ferrari Dino for Colonel Ronnie Hoare, a prospect that really excited me but in the race the car lasted only about 45 minutes. In 1967 I went to Le Mans with the Lola-Aston Martin and did not even get to race it as it blew up after three laps while John Surtees was behind the wheel.

At the end of 1967, however, I received a call from David Yorke, who had worked with Surtees over the years. John had told him that I was a good driver and David said, 'Well, if you're good enough to drive for John Surtees, you're good enough for us.' He offered me a seat, teamed with Paul Hawkins, in one of the Gulf-sponsored Ford GT40s to be run in 1968 by JW Automotive Engineering. The other car was to be driven by Jacky Ickx and Brian Redman.

They flew me to Pittsburgh to the headquarters of Gulf Oil to sign the contract. I was going to get real money: $750 a race, except at the Daytona

LEFT The 1968 Daytona 24 Hours was my first race with the fabulous Gulf Ford GT40 team run by John Wyer. Our two cars qualified first and second, but neither finished the race. Here we are side by side on Daytona's banking, my car — shared with Paul Hawkins — on the left.
Bill Warner

24 Hours, Sebring 12 Hours and Le Mans 24
Hours, for which they would pay $1,000. It was an
honour and a thrill to drive for the team.

The 1968 season

JW Automotive was a very professional and well-
organised operation. It had a proper transporter,
we drivers had the use of rental cars, and in
the paddock there was a large caravan where
we could relax and change in and out of our
race gear. John Wyer, the boss, was a terribly
overawing presence, very dark, not exactly a
laugh a minute, with little sense of humour.
Yorke was the team manager and John Horsman,
who was also very serious, was chief engineer.
There was a super team of mechanics, all good,
hard-working guys, three per car plus a tyre guy.
Wyer's wife, Tottie, handled timing and scoring,
and there were a couple of volunteers, fairly well-
off retired chaps I think, who used to come along
and do things like signalling at Le Mans. We
stayed in good hotels, no fleabags, and our team
dinners were terrific. The wine would flow, but

you were expected to be on time and ready to go
the next morning.

That team knew how to win endurance races.
Yorke would gather us together at Le Mans,
where a good lap was, say, 4:14 or 4:15, and he
would say, 'Right, we're going to run 4:21s for
the first 12 hours, and then we'll see where we
are and adjust accordingly.' They did not like
you making mistakes, missing shifts, over-using
brakes, that sort of thing. It was very controlled
driving, as even the best cars back then were
fragile, unlike now. Pit stops were always very
slick and the team had plenty of spares.

The only negative for me about the entire
experience was that Yorke's favouritism towards
Jacky Ickx was just like the way Helmut Marko
treated Sebastian Vettel in his Red Bull Formula
1 days. Yorke thought the sun rose and set with
Ickx. Of course, Jacky was the quickest driver,
although perhaps not much quicker than Brian,
but certainly quicker than Paul and me. So Ickx
always had first choice of engines and if there
was a particularly strong one he got it.

Actually, the 1968 season with Gulf did not start well, with much disappointment at Daytona and Sebring, the first two races.

Our GT40s qualified at the head of the field at Daytona but were slower than the works Porsche 907s in the race. Brian spun his car very early on in the infield kink and, going backwards at about 90mph, he let out the clutch without thinking and ruined it. Paul and I, meanwhile, were doing well when the fuel tank sprang a leak at about two-thirds distance. Someone had neglected to tape over the rivets in the side sills of the monocoque before installing the fuel bags and eventually rivet heads wore a hole in one of them.

At Sebring we went out after Paul collided with Liane Engeman, half of an all-female driving team in an AMC Javelin. Paul was very vociferous in the press box, making all sorts of politically incorrect comments about women, kitchens and bedrooms, causing quite a stir. Just recently Liane told one of my television colleagues, Will Buxton, that her team-mate Janet Guthrie was driving at the time and in any event Paul hit their car and

not the other way around. I suppose you might conclude that it was a typical racing 'he said, she said' incident.

All but one of the rest of the rounds were in Europe, starting at Brands Hatch with the BOAC International 500, a six-hour race. Jacky and Brian won, and our car finished fourth. This was a very memorable race for a very bad reason. While Paul was at the wheel, I strolled over to Clearways corner to watch the race and someone came to me and said, 'Have you heard about Jimmy?' He received a blank stare because he was referring, of course, to the tragic news that Jimmy Clark, the greatest driver of my generation, had just been killed at Hockenheim in a Formula 2 race. Jimmy had been supposed to be at Brands Hatch driving Ford's new prototype, the F3L, but Colin Chapman, his boss at Lotus, thought the Formula 2 event was more important for him. The thoughts going through my head were very jumbled, confused and questioning. If this can happen to the great Jimmy, what does it mean for the rest of us mere mortals?

BELOW Our chances in the 1968 Sebring 12 Hours were ruined when an AMC Javelin co-driven by Liane Engeman and Janet Guthrie swerved into the path of our GT40, causing suspension damage. Paul Hawkins was driving at the time and afterwards he sounded off to the media about women drivers.
David Hobbs collection

LEFT My fourth race with the Gulf GT40 team was the Monza 1,000Km and Paul Hawkins and I won it. This is one of the early laps, going onto the famous banking in fourth place behind the Jacky Ickx/Brian Redman sister car and the new works Porsche 908s of Jo Siffert/Hans Herrmann and Ludovico Scarfiotti/Gerhard Mitter.
The Revs Institute for Automotive Research/ Eric della Faille

Like all drivers of my era, however, I had brushed aside these uncomfortable thoughts by the time we rolled into the magnificent Royal Park at Monza, on the outskirts of Milan, three weeks later. The race was run on the entire 6.3-mile circuit, comprising the current track (without chicanes) plus the very rough, steeply banked oval, so it was quite a diverse challenge. There was a very wide pits straight and you actually passed the pits twice during a lap. To go onto the banked section, you came by close to the pits into a tight chicane, which had been put in a couple of years earlier to slow cars down onto the banking because it was so rough. Then you went round the whole elongated oval, including through another chicane that did the same slowing-down job before the second 180-degree banked turn, before rejoining the road course at the start of the pits straight but on its far side. With no chicane before it, the *Curva Grande* was flat out, with trees on the inside of the curve, but the base of each tree was protected by a straw bale so our safety was assured. Then there was a very fast run to

ABOVE Lots of clag! This late-race scene, with masses of rubber on the track, is at the chicane that was placed at the end of the straight to slow everyone down before they headed off round the bumpy banking.
The Revs Institute for Automotive Research/ Eric della Faille

the *Lesmo* corners, which were also much quicker than today, with a useless bit of guardrail to tip you over into the trees. It was quite an eventful lap with no run-off anywhere.

Paul and I were third on the grid behind our sister car on pole position and the Jo Siffert/Hans Herrmann factory Porsche, one of the new 908 versions making its race début. We went on to win the race, which was fantastic as it was by far the most important victory of my career so far, and it was great for Ford as well because the GT40 had not previously won the Monza 1,000Km. We had a faultless run and built up such a comfortable lead towards the end that we were able to ease off in the closing laps. The other JW car broke its exhaust and had to retire.

The fabulous Nordschleife of the Nürburgring was our next challenge. Brian Redman had never raced at the 'Ring so he convinced Mr Wyer that Ickx should drive with Paul, while Brian joined me. Together we finished sixth, the more nimble Porsches having a field day. That night the prize-giving was another epic German show of emotion, very Porsche-centric but a lot of fun. We all consumed rather large quantities of adult beverage and our jolly photograph on the facing page shows that at one glance. There is a vase on the table containing a tulip that soon after disappeared down the throat of Mr Redman, who thought it looked very tasty. Not many minutes later the aforementioned tulip reappeared. The drudgery of days away from home!

Not far geographically from the Nürburgring lies the fabulous but equally sinister Spa-Francorchamps. Race day did not so much dawn as emerge drearily into daylight, heralding a very wet and gloomy day. Jacky Ickx showed why he was the blue-eyed boy. He came around at the end of the first lap nearly a minute ahead of the next car — absolutely stunning. Paul and I persevered into fourth place. The race ended up taking over six hours but in dry weather would have been finished in under five.

During one of my stints I caught the Porsche 908 of Jochen Neerpasch, my GT40 team-mate in the Spa 1,000Km two years previously, and

LEFT At the Nürburgring 1,000Km I shared a car with Brian Redman for the first time. He asked to be switched out of the sister GT40 he usually drove with Jacky Ickx because he felt he did not know the circuit well enough and feared that he might hamper the Belgian's chances.
Gulf

LEFT Three inebriated Gulf drivers fooling around in Germany post-race. The guys seated are (from left) Paul Hawkins, Brian Redman and me. That tulip in the foreground did not remain in its vase for much longer.
David Hobbs collection

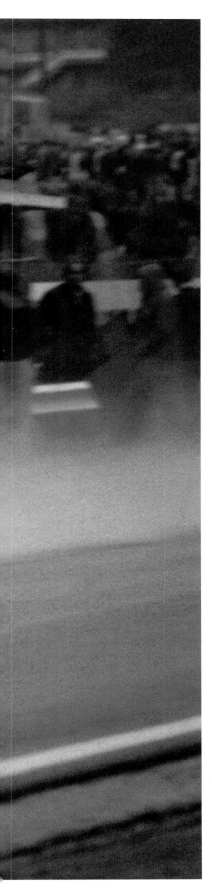

LEFT Paul Hawkins and I came home fourth in heavy rain at Spa-Francorchamps. I narrowly missed getting caught up in Jochen Neerpasch's accident when he lost control of his Porsche 908 right in front of me.
LAT Images

followed him for a complete lap, wary of pulling out into the blinding spray. Coming through Burnenville, a long downhill right-hander with houses on the edge of the track, I was able to look through the curve past Jochen and down the Masta straight. As I could not see any slow-moving cars, I decided I would pass him on the exit, but the issue resolved itself sooner than that. As we came out of the corner, Jochen suddenly spun and hit a bus shelter on his right. The impact was like an explosion, with bits of Porsche and bus shelter flying down the road. His windscreen fluttered down in front of me, but I managed to avoid the debris and get through. Actually he was lucky to hit the bus shelter because about ten feet behind it was a steep grassy slope into a meadow of cows, all with their mouths open witnessing this carnage.

Back across the Atlantic, our next race was the Six Hours at Watkins Glen, a circuit in upstate New York that was new to me. Paul and I should have had our second victory. In the race the two Gulf GT40s were running 1–2 and we were

Glen Six Hours should
have been another
victory for Paul Hawkins
and me. Towards the
end I was a lap ahead of
Jacky Ickx when team
manager David Yorke
repeatedly put out pit
signals ordering me to
slow down and let his
favoured driver past for
the win. Here I am taking
the chequered flag as
'the first of the losers'.
The Revs Institute for
Automotive Research/
David Nadig

leading, a lap ahead of our sister car, which Jacky
Ickx was sharing with Lucien Bianchi because
Brian had broken his arm in the Belgian Grand
Prix when the suspension broke on his Cooper.
This was when David Yorke's bias towards Ickx
really reared its ugly head. He insisted we slow
down to allow the Ickx/Bianchi car to pass us for
the win. From the point of view of championship
standings it made no difference to the team which
order we finished, and there were no points for
drivers back then.

The Ickx car was low on oil pressure and he
should have just stroked it home for a finish, but
Jacky was still driving like a man possessed and
it was miracle that his engine did not let go. Yorke
was getting more and more annoyed with me
for not slowing down sufficiently and every lap I
was given more 'Slow Down' and 'Easy Easy' pit
signals. Meanwhile, my co-driver Paul Hawkins
had gone out to the first corner with Richard
Attwood and they were leaning over the fence
urging me on! But remember, after eight years
of racing, this was the first really top team I had

driven for and I just did not want to jeopardise
things by sticking my neck out and disobeying
team orders. So I slowed up, and was passed.
Afterwards Jacky said to me, 'David, I like to
win.' I almost said back to him, 'You don't say.'
How his engine survived I will never know.

Most of the guys in the team felt badly about
it, as did the Gulf executives in attendance. Next
day at Elmira International Airport the Gulf boss,
Grady Davis, apologised, saying he thought it
was a rough deal, and slipped Paul and I an extra
$1,000 each in cash.

The Le Mans 24 Hours that year was in
September, months after the normal June date
because of strikes and civil unrest in France.
By then Ickx had broken his leg in a Formula
1 accident at Watkins Glen, so Bianchi was
paired with Pedro Rodríguez in the other car.
Once again Paul and I were leading when the
clutch disintegrated, losing us two hours in the
pits while a new one was fitted. Soon after we
rejoined the race the engine blew up at the end of
the Mulsanne straight.

LEFT The Gulf team added a third car to its line-up for Le Mans in 1968. As usual, Paul Hawkins and I drove together, in car 10, and we had spells in the lead during the early hours of the race.
LAT Images

BELOW Our Le Mans went wrong about five hours into the race when the clutch broke up. Replacing it took nearly two hours and dropped us totally out of contention — and then the engine blew up shortly afterwards.
Ford

All along during practice Paul and I had thought that the engine was a bit suspect, with more vibration than normal, and after the session on the Thursday evening we suggested an engine change for the race. Before embarking on this task on the Friday in the Renault garage next door to our hotel, the mechanics found that an exhaust pipe was slightly touching the chassis and thought this might be the problem. So Paul and I helmeted up, him at the wheel, drove out of the garage and blasted along the bumpy roads surrounding the village, getting up to about 150mph. We hummed and hawed but decided the engine might be all right, so they did not change it after all — and the damned thing blew up in the race. The sister car of Bianchi and Rodríguez went on to take the win, much to the joy of the team.

All the above shows not only that you do require some luck in racing but also that you need to be a complete prick at all times, even if your demands keep everyone up all night. A successful racing driver must make sure that what he thinks needs doing gets done. No pussyfooting around. Nice guys come last.

That year Le Mans finished the regular season, but Gulf and Wyer decided to go to South Africa in November for the Kyalami Nine Hours, which my best pal Jacky Ickx and I won. For this race we drove a Mirage M1, which was basically a modified GT40 that the team was evaluating for the following season. Following his Formula 1 crash at Watkins Glen, Ickx's foot was still in a short plaster cast so I did the lion's share of the race. That fuel filler problem bit me again in this race, literally in the backside. Under my race suit I was wearing a pair of Marks & Spencer string underpants, my strange choice of underwear at that time. A gallon of fuel got spilled during refuelling and some of it dripped into the car, onto my race suit and into the seat. As the race wore on the fuel on the soft skin of my backside became pretty painful but I stuck it out for the stint. As soon as I got out of the car I ripped off the suit and the go-faster underpants, washed off the fuel as best I could and applied some ointment. All the same, for the next two years you could

BELOW My 1968 Gulf season was rounded off very nicely by winning the Kyalami Nine Hours, this time driving a Mirage M1, basically a reworked GT40. For the only time in my career I was paired with Jacky Ickx.
www.motoprint.co.za
(courtesy of Ken Stewart)

play noughts and crosses on my rear end where the string had burned the skin. We were made of tough stuff in those days. But mercifully the whole thing did not go up in flames.

The Nine Hours was held on a Saturday and was followed by a fabulous day-long barbecue party on Sunday at the home of one of the main Kyalami officials, Francis Tucker, who had a wonderful house just a short distance from the track. His party, a massive affair, was the official prize-giving, so there was no question of leaping on a plane and hurtling back to Europe. Those South African racing guys really knew how to push the boat out and it all brought back memories of the trip Mike Hailwood and I had so enjoyed two years before.

Falconry

In between racing for Gulf that year, back in Britain I took part in what was then called the British Saloon Car Championship, now the British Touring Car Championship. I raced a Ford Falcon for Malcolm Gartlan and was able to compete in

eight of the championship's 11 rounds. I am not sure how I met 'Malc the Falc' but we all hit it off right away, Mags and his wife and Malcolm and me. The team was based in Pershore, a town in Worcestershire on the River Severn. Malcolm was fairly well heeled and his wife had a stable of horses and was very much into that sport. We spent many a happy hour at the Gartlan residence and had a pretty good racing year, with quite a number of podiums including two wins, one of which at Croft gave me a hat-trick. I only went to Croft on three occasions and won each time, in 1965 in the Harold Young Lola T70, in 1967 in the Team Surtees Lola T70 and in 1968 in the Falcon.

My other Falcon win, at Silverstone's big Martini Trophy meeting, was quite dramatic. On the penultimate lap, going into the very fast Woodcote corner, I was leading and Brian Muir in his Falcon tried to muscle through on the inside. His left front corner banged into my right rear and spun me around and off the track. The engine stalled and no doubt flooded a bit because it seemed to take an age to fire up

ABOVE AND BELOW When my Gulf commitments allowed, I raced a Ford Falcon for Malcolm Gartlan in the 1968 British Saloon Car Championship. I was leading Brian Muir at Silverstone when, going into the final lap, he bashed the back of my car and spun me around — but I still won the race!

LAT Images (above) and David Hobbs collection (below)

again. I wobbled off the verge and set off in what I thought would be fruitless pursuit, but the team were all hanging over the pit wall frantically egging me on, with hands, arms, pit boards, everything. I was thinking it was pointless, but I did as they urged and legged off at full pace. Halfway round that last lap, in the middle of Hangar Straight, I encountered a wounded Falcon with a bashed-in front corner, a shredded tyre and smoke pouring out of the wheel well. As I swooped past Brian I gave him a cheery wave and finished the lap to thunderous applause — well, from our team anyway. Afterwards I took a victory lap with two passengers, our two little boys Greg and Guy, who were six and four. They were very proud of their father.

I did not win the championship, but for my first season in such a big car I was very pleased, as was Malcolm. At the end of the year, things turned sour over some personal issues, involving — what else? — money, which at the time I thought very unnecessary and weird, and still do. It was such a sad way to end what had been well-rewarded fun.

The 1969 season

My second year with Gulf, when I drove both a GT40 and a Mirage (now the M2 version), proved something of a disappointment. I was looking forward to it as I now had my old mate Mike Hailwood as my team-mate, Paul Hawkins having had enough of David Yorke and gone off to set up his own team. In the other car Jacky now had another British partner, Jackie Oliver, as Brian Redman had joined the factory Porsche team.

The first two races in Florida, in a GT40, had the same outcome as the previous year — two retirements. At Daytona we were in second place when the engine started to overheat soon after the halfway point because of a crack in the cylinder block. At Sebring the weather was so hot that we knocked out the car's side windows to try to get air into the cabin, with no real effect, and dropped out about halfway through with a front suspension breakage, no doubt hastened by the very bumpy track surface. Like Ickx and Oliver, we had been running way behind the leaders and there seemed no chance of victory for either car.

Mike and I went back to our team hotel, Clayton Motel, had dinner and went to bed, only to be woken up soon after midnight by all sorts of shouting, laughter and generally joyous sounds. Somehow, due to a sudden spate of attrition for other cars, the Ickx/Oliver GT40 had achieved a miraculous win. Who said racing was fair?

After that came a fifth place in the Brands Hatch Six Hours in a GT40, then Mike and I transferred to the BRM-powered Mirage M2 for the next two 1,000Km races. We finished seventh at Spa but retired at the Nürburgring when the fuel pump packed up.

For the Le Mans 24 Hours we were back in the proven GT40. Porsches dominated qualifying with both 917s and 908s while we qualified 14th with our sister car one place ahead — but we knew we had good pace for the race. This was the year Jacky Ickx made his protest about the famous Le Mans start, because running across the road and jumping into your car did not allow you to properly do up the safety belts that we all wore by this time. So while we all did the usual

BELOW In 1969, partnered by my mate Mike Hailwood, I had two races in a Gulf Mirage, now the BRM-powered M2. Here at the Spa 1,000Km we had fuel-feed problems among various setbacks and finished an unhappy seventh.
LAT Images

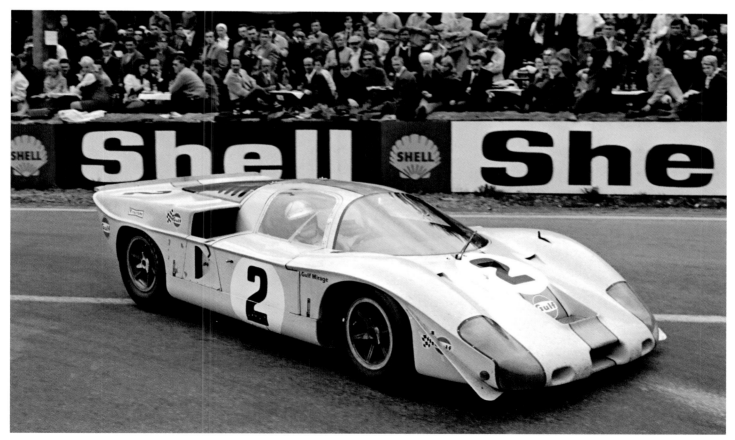

ABOVE The Nürburgring 1,000Km in 1969 was another disappointment as Mike Hailwood and I went out before half distance with fuel-pump failure.
Jim Culp

BELOW As the start at Le Mans draws near, Jacky Ickx (left) and Mike Hailwood have helmets on, while Jackie Oliver and I look thoughtful.
Gulf

OPPOSITE Trying to get a leg over, with Jackie Oliver at the centre of the action and Mike Hailwood and Jacky Ickx giving a helping hand.
Gulf

sprint and fumbled with our belts as we roared off, Jacky sauntered across the track and got away almost last.

I was in the leading group of five of six cars as we swept past the pits at the end of the first lap. Behind me, on the old high-speed White House section, poor John Wolfe crashed his private 917 and was killed. The accident also eliminated Chris Amon's factory Ferrari and another couple of cars. When Ickx arrived on the scene the road was blocked and he had to stop, so immediately he went down a lap — and it stayed like that for many hours.

In the night our race pace was pretty good. Two factory Porsche 908s, racing each other, came up behind and took a number of laps to get past, and then only pulled ahead by a fraction. For almost all the rest of my stint I had these four red lights just ahead of me until, approaching the Mulsanne kink, there was a flash of blinding light followed by an eruption of orange flame. Going into the kink hard on the brakes, I was faced with an impenetrable wall of smoke, dust and

ABOVE All-action pit stop at night as our Gulf GT40 gets refuelled and fitted with a new set of Firestones. I have just finished my stint and Mike Hailwood is clambering aboard.
Gulf

bits of flying car. I got through it unscathed and as I emerged, still doing about 100mph, I saw the back end of a 908 glued to the barrier and blazing away. A split-second later I saw the cockpit and front end going end over end down the road and suddenly the driver was thrown out. Swerving and braking hard, somehow I missed him and all the wreckage.

I found out later that the driver was Udo Schütz. Remarkably, he survived. A big man, he was perhaps somewhat protected by his girth. When I next encountered him, at a Porsche reunion at Daytona at least 35 years later, I said, 'Udo, the last time I saw you, you were bouncing down the road and I was convinced you were dead.' 'Ach, Hobbzy, vee all make mistakes,' he replied, and roared with laughter. After his motor racing escapades, he had made a fortune making shipping containers, taken up yacht racing and even won the Admiral's Cup for Germany in 1993.

This all happened on my in-lap so at the pit stop I told Mike that there would be a yellow flag for ages because a driver had been killed, as I

thought, at the kink. Hailwood did his stint and when I got back in we were still a lap up on our sister car. As you will realise, this was the cue for yet another promising prospect to turn to shit.

Near the end of my stint the brake pedal went to the floor at the Mulsanne corner and I went down the escape road heading for the city of Tours. When I eventually reached the pits I naturally reported that there was something wrong with the brakes. David Yorke stated that it was the pads but I said I was sure the problem was something else because the failure had been so sudden. He gave me one of those looks that said, 'You worry about the driving and we will take care of the car.' They changed all the brake pads, a slow procedure in those days and one of the reasons why it was wise to keep brake wear to a minimum. Resuming, I nearly ran over the pit exit marshal. Guess what? No damned brakes. *Quelle surprise!*

So after one slow lap I returned to the pits. Off with all the bodywork and wheels again, and this time they found the problem. A little pipe that

LEFT Nice outfit. Mags watches the Le Mans action in 1969.
David Hobbs collection

BELOW A hand shows us where to go after finishing third in the 1969 Le Mans 24 Hours. Also prominent in this shot are team manager David Yorke (dark jacket) and chief mechanic Ermanno Cuoghi (next to helmeted Hailwood), who later worked for Ferrari with Niki Lauda among others.
Gulf

went from one side of the caliper to the other had been nipped by a wheel balance weight. Firestone had been told to only put balance weights on the outside of the rim because the clearance between the wheel and the caliper was small, but for some reason they had not listened. So the mechanics had to change the pipe and bleed the system, by which time we had dropped behind our team-mates.

This was the year of the famous battle to the line between Ickx in our sister car and the Porsche 908 driven by Hans Herrmann. Jacky just held off the Porsche to win by 100 yards or so and we came home third, four laps down. Had the team listened to me in the first place, they would have found the damaged pipe while doing the pad change and we would have lost less time and could have won the race. Even John Horsman, the chief engineer, stated in his fine book *Racing in the Rain* that he thought Mike and I should have won.

Le Mans in 1969 turned out to be the last race for JW Automotive's GT40s as the plan for

the following year was to run factory 917s on Porsche's behalf. I had no reason to think that I would not be part of the effort.

In the winter of 1969 the team had its first test session with the Porsche 917 at Daytona, in preparation for the upcoming 24 Hours there. The team personnel had not changed much at all and various drivers assembled for the occasion. Unfortunately during one of my runs, going up onto the banking out of the infield under full acceleration, I shifted from third gear and went into second instead of fourth. This was very easy to do in the early 917s because the tubular spaceframe chassis was extremely flexible and there was a long linkage from the gear lever to the back of the gearbox. It was a trick that would be performed by a number of drivers over the next two years, but it gave the Porsche engineers, who for some reason were not fans of mine, the excuse they needed. I was immediately replaced by an almost unknown Finnish driver, Leo Kinnunen, who has remained almost unknown to this day. It was a bitter and, I felt, undeserved

BELOW In 1970 the Gulf team invited me back for Le Mans and my first and only race in the Porsche 917. This is the car I shared with Mike Hailwood, with the sister 917 of Jo Siffert and Brian Redman right behind.

LAT Images

loss. Luckily, John Surtees once again popped up at around the same time and offered me a drive in his all-new Formula 5000 car.

Once more to Le Mans

However, there was one drive left for me with John Wyer's organisation. This was the 1970 Le Mans, for which Mike Hailwood and I were recalled to drive a third team 917, alongside Jo Siffert/Brian Redman and Pedro Rodríguez/Leo Kinnunen. Like quite a few privately entered 917s, ours had the original 4.5-litre engine whereas our team-mates had the new 4.9-litre units. We qualified 10th and Richard Attwood, sharing another 4.5-litre car with Hans Herrmann, lined up 14th. In the race I drove the first stint and we soon started to move up, then Mike took over and continued our encouraging progress. At about 7pm, however, it started to rain and Mike, having decided to chance another lap on dry tyres, lost control at the Dunlop curve and hit an abandoned Alfa Romeo that had crashed there. Mike was really good in the rain so I am

not sure what happened. After he trudged back to the pits, Mike definitely got the 'Don't call us, we'll call you' treatment from John Wyer. The other two JW cars also failed to finish. The one driven by Siffert and Redman had a two-lap lead when guess what? Siffert changed down instead of up right in front of the pits. The winner was none other than Richard Attwood together with Hans Herrmann in their 917 entered by Porsche Salzburg. It was Porsche's first overall victory in the Le Mans 24 Hours.

For the rest of the season I raced the Team Surtees Formula 5000 car in Europe and America, did various Can-Am and Trans-Am races as well, and rounded off the year with Mike Hailwood again in a little 2-litre Lola T210 in the Kyalami Nine Hours. These exploits are covered in subsequent chapters.

So my days with the Gulf-backed JW Automotive team were over but I still have happy memories of racing with this top outfit. And these days everyone seems to want to paint their cars in those iconic blue and orange colours.

ABOVE Just a few hours into the 1970 Le Mans 24 Hours, Mike Hailwood crashed our 917 in the rain at the Dunlop curve, one lap from pitting to change his dry tyres for wets. In this race of attrition, with just seven finishers, my old friend and fellow Jaguar apprentice Richard Attwood went on to win with Hans Herrmann in their 917 entered by Porsche Salzburg.
LAT Images

CHAPTER 7

1969–75
FORMULA 5000

For the new Formula 5000 category, which started in America in 1968 and came to Europe the following year, John Surtees built his own car, the Surtees TS5, and invited me to drive it in the new Guards Formula 5000 Championship. Things looked promising and I thought this avenue might take me closer to my dream of driving in Formula 1. This was, after all, my tenth year in racing and Grand Prix racing waits for no man. Sadly, it all fell apart, like most of my deals involving John.

The TS5 was designed by Len Terry, who had worked for Lola and lots of other people over the years, including Lotus and Ford. Although the most successful Formula 5000 car of 1968, a Lola, had used a spaceframe, Terry specified a monocoque for the Surtees. The car was very similar to a Grand Prix machine except that the category called for a 5-litre stock-block V8 to deliver the power rather than a custom-built Formula 1 engine. John, meanwhile, had done a deal with the actor James Garner, who had found a sponsor in the form of a major manufacturer of large trailer homes based in Riverside, California.

The very first Formula 5000 race in England was at Oulton Park on 4 April 1969 and I put my TS5 on pole, with Peter Gethin next to me in the new McLaren M10A (also a monocoque) owned by Church Farm Racing, the outfit that ran Derek Bell's early cars. Rather than conventional

LEFT The Surtees TS5 was the first Formula 5000 car I drove, in 1969, and I had a very strong season with it both in Europe and the USA. This is the grid for my third race of the year, at Mallory Park in May, with Peter Gethin (7) in his McLaren M10A sharing the front row.
LAT Images

RIGHT This dramatic shot was taken during practice for my first race in the Surtees TS5, on 4 April 1969 at Oulton Park, where my efforts secured pole position.
Mike Hayward Collection

BELOW My first Formula 5000 victory for Team Surtees in 1969 came in July at Mondello Park in Ireland's County Kildare. Here I am on the victory car with Mike Hailwood (left) and Alan Rollinson, who finished second and third respectively.
LAT Images

wishbones, the Surtees had some very nice fabricated rockers in the front suspension but unfortunately they were not strong enough. In the race these rockers gradually bent, and the car kept sinking lower and lower, scraping on the ground more and more, until finally I had to pull in.

After two more rounds at Brands Hatch and Silverstone, in July we went to Mondello Park in Ireland, where I won from pole, beating my pal Mike Hailwood in a Lola. It was the first win for the Surtees marque. Mags was with me and Mike's girlfriend, Pauline, was there too. We went to the hotel after the race and, as ever with Mike, had a great time, with lots of drinking, joking and dancing. Just before midnight the manager came in and told us the party was over. 'What?' I said. 'I thought you never stopped drinking in Ireland!' 'No sir, you've got to go. Time's up.' So we shambled towards the door. Then the manager piped up again. 'Where are you going?' he asked. 'We're leaving. You told us to leave,' we reminded him. 'Ah, yes,' said he. 'But it's five minutes to twelve, five minutes until tomorrow, and then we can open up again!'

Off to America

By this time the deal with Garner had gone completely pear-shaped, so John said, 'Tell you what. I'll send you to America and you can race for me there.' He said I would get 25 per cent of the prize money, but what he omitted to mention at the time was that it was 25 per cent after he had deducted the expenses — which were considerable. But the potential rewards were still reasonable because prize money was so much more substantial in America than in Britain.

I went off to do Formula 5000 in the United States with a mechanic called Dennis Davis, a very mouthy young man who went on to work for McLaren for many years. Dennis would address John Surtees as if he was talking to some kind of servant — they had an extraordinary relationship — and when dealing with people like race officials he would say things like, 'Have you lost your bloody mind, mate?' With Dennis, I stationed myself once again at Ronnie Mutton's Shell garage in Bowmanville, Ontario, Canada as

Ronnie had said, 'You should stay at my house.' Ronnie and his wife Pat put me in their bedroom while they slept on a couch downstairs, because Ronnie thought that as a racing driver I had to have a proper night's rest. That went on for many weeks, from July until the end of September — quite a deal. Thank you, Ronnie and Pat.

First stop for me in the SCCA Continental Championship, as the Formula 5000 series was called at that time, was the Road America circuit at Elkhart Lake in Wisconsin for a 300-mile race run in three 100-mile heats. It was a long drive in a horrible little van with a trailer and we stayed at Sharp's Summer Resort, which is still there, I can attest, having been a habitué of Elkhart Lake in recent years. At this motel we had to work on the Surtees one evening and there were so many

May 16 1969 2 6

AUTOSPORT
BRITAIN'S MOTOR SPORTING WEEKLY

Spa 1000 Kms—F2 Jarama—F5000 Brands—Welsh Rally

ABOVE Although Peter Gethin beat me to the win at Mallory Park in May, *Autosport* sensibly selected me for that week's front cover.
Courtesy of Autosport

suddenly could not see anyone. Down I went through Kettle Bottom, the turn at Canada, up the hill under the bridge (which is no longer there), up to turn 14, flash up the hill to the start/finish — and there was a red flag. It turned out that there had been a massive crash behind me, down at the Kink.

On the restart, the engine went onto seven cylinders straight away. I had done one lap of a 300-mile event and I was done. Tony Adamowicz won that race — and he went on to take the championship as well.

Next came Lime Rock in Connecticut. Only a mile long and set in a natural bowl, Lime Rock is great for spectators. It was a very hairy track in those days, with a curvy downhill 'straight' bordered by steep banks on one side and a river on the other. The last turn, still going downhill, was a steep right-hander that put suspension under considerable compression before you went onto the main front straight. I finished second to Peter Gethin while Adamowicz was fifth.

It was at Lime Rock that I met a local racer by the name of Sam Posey, who was seriously into Formula 5000. Sam was to become one of my life-long best friends, competitor, media sparring partner and, finally, television colleague. At that year's first Formula 5000 race, at Riverside, Sam had a tangle with a guy called Ron Courtney and both of their cars were destroyed, Courtney's bursting into flames and burning him badly. As Sam had no car to race, his mother, Mary Moore, who was always Sam's biggest supporter, trawled the paddock with him until they found someone who would sell them a car. That someone was Lew Florence and they bought his Eagle on the spot to get Sam in the race. Mum, a scion of the family that owned AIG insurance, was very determined that her boy would do well.

We went from Lime Rock to Donnybrooke, which was later renamed Brainerd International Raceway. The owner of the track was George Montgomery, a big guy who was a pilot for Northwest Orient Airlines. He had built this track in the very north of Minnesota, near the source of the Mississippi about 120 miles north of Minneapolis, and here the mosquitoes were

mosquitos buzzing around in the humid heat, as they do in Wisconsin in the summer, that we got bitten like crazy. I thought more than once that anyone who could live in that awful place must be nuts.

I started the first heat near the front and we ran as a big group on lap one around to the famous Kink, me leading, with a guy called Jerry Hansen right with me. I had never heard of him but later learned that he was the absolute Road America ace, from nearby Minneapolis. But then, as I exited the Kink and checked my mirror, I

diabolical. I guess my gift of the gab had already started to show itself because I was booked on a breakfast radio talk show in Minneapolis before the race, probably because I was foreign and had just joined the series. I was my usual comic self and hit it off with the hosts, so every time I went to the track in later years these guys would have me on their show. As for the race, I went one better than at Lime Rock and won it, and, I might add, did so in some style as I took pole position by a huge margin, 1½ seconds, and won both heats.

At the next round, at Mosport, I qualified second but dropped out of the race with an engine problem. Then we returned to Lime Rock for another belt round the little track and this time I finished third while my new friend Sam Posey won, and I also set a lap record that stood for many years. Next came St Jovite and I won from pole, thanks in part to another big crash behind me.

Suddenly, with two rounds left, I was a contender for the Formula 5000 title even though I had missed the first five rounds. In fact I won

these last two races as well, at Thompson Raceway and Sebring, but Tony Adamowicz, who had done the entire series, beat me by just one point in the end. He was always very proud of that.

Bizarrely, the Sebring race took place a full three months after the penultimate round, on 28 December. I remember driving down to Heathrow from Upper Boddington during Christmas in my Ford Cortina and flying to Orlando, via somewhere else. When I got to this tiny airport in Orlando the baggage claim was just a rack outside the terminal in the open air. You hung around until some guy rode up on a tractor pulling a trailer, threw your case on the rack, and pottered off again. Now, with Disney and all the other attractions, it is a very different place. After picking up my case and rental car, I drove down Florida Highway 27 to Sebring, as one still does today although in much more traffic, and most of the way through built-up areas rather than orange groves. I stayed at the Clayton Motel, as I had done with the GT40

ABOVE In mid-1969 John Surtees packed me off to America to do the second half of the Formula 5000 championship series there. At my third race, at Donnybrooke, I took pole position and won. Next to me is the works McLaren M10B of fellow Englishman Peter Gethin, who also followed the money and raced on the other side of the Atlantic. *David Hobbs collection*

OPPOSITE This is the start of the final round of 1969, at Sebring, with Mario Andretti's Lotus 70 (4) leading away from my Surtees TS5 (16) and Mark Donohue's Lola T190 (10). As in Formula 1, this was a period when high wings were the norm in Formula 5000.
Bill Warner

LEFT Considering I have just achieved a cracking win, I look a little severe here at Sebring — perhaps the National Anthem is being played. The gentleman with sunglasses is Cope Robinson, Vice President of L&M, the race sponsor. Despite missing half of the races, I finished runner-up in the 1969 Formula 5000 championship standings, just one point behind Tony Adamowicz.
Don Bok

crowd. Although Mario Andretti led the race for a while in a Ford-powered Lotus, I won it. After going to the prize-giving, where I received a cup from L&M cigarettes, the sponsor of the race, I drove back to Orlando and flew home in good time for New Year.

It had been a fantastic spell for me. I had arrived on the American Formula 5000 scene against all the regulars like Sam Posey, Ron Grable, John Cannon and Eppie Wietzes and more or less blew them off straight away. Peter Gethin came over and won a race as well, but he did not stay as long as I did. The Surtees was certainly a good car and together we became quite the talking point.

Two one-offs

My 1969 season in America featured an interesting one-off drive in a USAC road race at Donnybrooke. After my win in the Formula 5000 race at that track, I received a call inviting me to drive an Indycar there the following month for Tassi Vatis, a Greek shipping magnate who

ran USAC cars for years, from dirt midgets to Indianapolis cars. Vatis's car used a Finley chassis — the creation of his chief mechanic Jack Finley — and was called the MG Liquid Suspension Special, some bright spark having thought that the Hydrolastic suspension of the Austin 1100 would be a good thing to put on a race car. I did not hit it off particularly well with Finley, who worked on the car in a motel parking lot with not much more than a hammer, a large screwdriver and a couple of spanners. In those days Indycars were designed specifically for oval tracks, very often incorporating offset suspension to suit left-hand turns, and this one did not like going around right-handers at all. It also had a turbo Offenhauser engine that I found difficult to get wound up. I did not do particularly well, qualifying tenth and dropping out after four laps. Funnily enough, they did not ask me to drive for them again.

Another guy who came on the scene at this time was a Canadian businessman called Terry Godsall, a very pleasant and rather eccentric chap from Ottawa who owned a Detroit Diesel franchise and later became Canadian distributor for Hino trucks. He knew Roger Penske and, to hear Godsall tell it, the two were like brothers. He made all sorts of upbeat comments about sponsoring me and gave me a road car for my personal use, so things looked fairly promising. He certainly took me in a new professional direction when he invited me to drive a Pontiac Firebird in a Trans-Am race at Riverside in October alongside Jerry Titus, who had won the Trans-Am title for Ford two years earlier. I cover this in more detail in Chapter 13, about my Trans-Am career, so suffice to say here that Jerry finished third while I was a retirement. As for Terry, he was to crop up quite often in the next few years.

Declining fortunes in 1970

Back at home, in 1970 I raced intermittently in the Guards Formula 5000 Championship for Team Surtees, still in a TS5, and did some testing. In contrast to my American successes of

1969, it was all very disappointing as my only result of any note was fifth place at Zandvoort — and I wrote off our two-car team at Brands Hatch. I was on the third row of the grid behind Mike Hailwood and made a great start, or perhaps even jumped it by a fraction. Either way, I climbed over the back of Mike's car, and in the ensuing start-line mêlée my car was broken and my team-mate Trevor Taylor's as well. This did not go down particularly well with his lordship.

John Surtees was married at that time to Pat, who was as hard as nails, the daughter of a builder. She was always on the pit wall, timing and scoring, and her word was law. If the officials said John had qualified fourth but Pat said he was actually second, John would be up there at the stewards' door, banging on the table. 'Pat says I'm second!' 'OK, Mr Surtees, perhaps we'll check our timing again.' Pat was a very pretty girl, always perfectly groomed, with immaculate make-up and hair, but she was also somewhat steely-eyed. I remember going to stay at their house, a huge affair at Edenbridge

BELOW The International Trophy race at Silverstone was traditionally an early-season Formula 1 event, a non-championship one, but for 1970 there were Formula 5000 cars in the field as well. Behind my Surtees TS5, on the left, is Jochen Rindt in the new Lotus 72, having only its second race and yet to show its potential. *Mike Hayward Collection*

in Kent, to the south-east of London. Meal times were a nightmare because they would spend the entire time gossiping and grousing about how John was being got at by Ferrari, or by Shell, or by Castrol — anybody. 'Well, I didn't win that race because they gave it to…'

Then we did the same as in 1969, going over to America mid-season to do Formula 5000. I arrived in July and my first race was the sixth round, at Louisville near Dallas, the Rattlesnake Capital of the World. This track, as Shakespeare might have described it, was a blasted heath, an absolute dump, and the temperature was about 2,000 degrees. I qualified third but in the race the car broke. The winner, Gus Hutchison, drove a Formula 1 Brabham BT26, a quick little car that suited the track.

I was second at Road America, seventh at St Jovite and then I won at Donnybrooke. This was quickly becoming a good track for me, to the point where they named a corner in my honour, Hobbs Hollow, now long gone. Another win came at Lime Rock and then we arrived at the

ABOVE This was my last British event in the Surtees TS5, at Brands Hatch in 1970, when high wings were no longer permitted. This is the race at which I got myself involved in a start-line tangle and wrote off not only my car but also my team-mate Mike Hailwood's — to John Surtees's considerable dismay.

LAT Images

BELOW I love this close-up 1970 shot of my Surtees TS5 at Elkhart Lake's Road America, one of my favourite circuits. As in 1969, my American Formula 5000 campaign only began mid-season, and my car, a brand-new chassis, was painted white instead of Team Surtees's traditional red.

Jim Scott

RIGHT Mags came over when the series visited Mosport in September 1970 and together we visited Castrol Canada headquarters.
Ross Jamieson

BELOW Talking technical at Sebring in 1970 with John Cannon, who was that year's Formula 5000 champion in America. Little did either of us know that I would take over his seat at Hogan Racing in 1971.
Bill Warner

daunting Mosport Park in Canada, where I had my first dust-up with Mark Donohue. Entered by the great Roger Penske, Donohue took part in a selection of that year's Formula 5000 races and thus far I had usually been able to beat him.

Penske Racing ran a Lola T192, which was not the best chassis by any means but in this formidable team's hands it was certainly superior to most. I was on pole with Donohue alongside on the front row and the race started in pouring rain. As we went through turn one — the one that had nearly killed John Surtees — we had quite a hefty touch and he disappeared from view out on my left side. So there I was again, big sigh of relief, leading comfortably after disposing of Donohue. Or so I thought. A few laps later he came steaming past on the inside going up the steep climb into the last couple of corners, and I thought, 'Where the hell did he come from?' He won the race and somehow, much to my chagrin, I also managed to get beaten by Eppie Wietzes, the local star from Toronto. It was most undignifying.

ABOVE This is 1970 at Sebring, again the last round of the championship, where I finished second to Mark Donohue. As can be seen, by now I had adopted a full-face helmet, and in America that year Formula 5000 cars were still allowed to run with high wings.

Ross Jamieson

LEFT On the Sebring podium, winner Mark Donohue basks in the attention, I look pretty cheerful, and third-placed Eppie Wietzes seems to be shattered.

Bill Warner

At Mid-Ohio I had a coming-together with John Cannon that put me out of the race. He did a little half-spin at the Carousel and shot back on the track, hitting me amidships. After the race I went to have a few words with his car owner, Carl Hogan, who seemed to take my side in the affair. As in 1969, we wrapped up the season at Sebring, where I started and finished second. This time my half-season netted me third place in the championship standings, behind John Cannon, the champion, and Gus Hutchison.

Formula 5000 champion

At those Formula 5000 races he attended, Roger Penske obviously observed my sublime talents despite the trouncing I received from his man Donohue at Mosport. I had also clocked up more wins in 1969 and 1970 than any other Formula 5000 driver. As I explain in the next chapter, Roger asked to meet me in London and offered some fantastic opportunities for the 1971 season — but there was initially a problem. Penske Racing was committed to Goodyear tyres but Team Surtees was running with rivals Firestone. So if I was going to continue to drive in Formula 5000, and the way the calendar worked it was possible, I would need to find a Goodyear team.

Roger offered to speak on my behalf to Carl Hogan, whose Goodyear-equipped Formula 5000 outfit had just won the 1970 championship with John Cannon, an expatriate Brit who had lived in the US for many years. For some reason Hogan Racing were not that happy with Cannon, so it did not take much of a nudge from Roger to persuade Carl to sign me. Hogan owned a big trucking business in St Louis, Missouri, and was a passionate character, very fond of racing.

Of course, I then had to tell John Surtees that I was leaving him. In return I received a long letter, running to several pages of foolscap, telling me what a rat I was, how I was so ungrateful, how he had put me on the map, how he had got me the GT40 drive with Gulf through David Yorke, how he had sent me to America… he could not understand how I could do this to him. Of course, he never thought to give any praise for the Formula 5000 successes and he also neglected to mention that the Formula 1 car he promised to build for me never happened. The issue was always sponsorship, which he seemed to be able to find for guys like Rolf Stommelen and Derek Bell, but never for me. So it was end of story at Team Surtees.

For 1971 the SCCA's Formula 5000 series took a major step up as Liggett & Myers, the tobacco company, became major sponsor with naming rights for what was now called the SCCA L&M Continental 5000 Championship. The series was reduced from 13 rounds to eight, but with even larger purses than in previous years. Hogan Racing ran a McLaren M10B, a terrific car to drive and with very easy chassis set-up, tended by a couple of really good mechanics. It was useful, too, to finally start a season at the first race rather than halfway through,

The first round was at Riverside in California on 25 April and I got off to a good start with pole position in the M10B, but for the two-part race I had some sort of gearbox malady. That caused me to spin on the warm-up lap of the first heat

and I was unable to start, and in the second heat I lasted only five laps before the clutch packed up. The race was won by Frank Matich, the well-known Aussie who also drove an M10B although his had a Repco Holden V8. Luckily Frank did not stick around for long that year.

The next event was a week later at Laguna Seca, also in California. I did win this one in fairly convincing fashion from the aforementioned Matich, much to the enjoyment of not only Carl and Lollie Hogan, the team owners, but also chief mechanic Bill Mayberry and his assistant Howard. They went right over the top with delight. I was pretty happy myself. After this race I had to hot-foot it back to Indy to continue practising my Penske entry for the Indy 500, which then took the entire 'merry month of May'.

My great friend Bill Pinckney, who had co-driven my Lotus Elite to our super class win at the Nürburgring in 1961, came out to join me at Indy. After showing a lot of talent as a driver, Bill had decided that he was better as a businessman and went into pig farming in Warwickshire in a

big way, and as Indiana is Hog Heaven he wanted to bone up on the latest American technologies and ideas. Between qualifying and the race at Indy I had the next Formula 5000 round, at Seattle International Raceway, and Bill came along. Formerly called Pacific Raceways, this circuit was mainly a drag-racing facility with a very hairy, fast, downhill dash through trees — charming. One morning at our hotel Bill saw his first American freight train wend its way past the dining room window and was mesmerised by a line of wagons that seemed about three miles long — a sight that still impresses me after all these years. Anyway, what else for Bill but another win, this time beating Sam Posey, my big rival at the time but long-time great friend.

Straight after the Indy 500 I headed to Mid-Ohio, not that far away, three hours or so, to test with Carl and the Formula 5000 car for the next event coming up there a few weeks later. After the test I headed back to Upper Boddington as I had had a long stretch away from home and the family. When I returned to the US, Mags and our

ABOVE This pitlane is at Seattle International Raceway, which hosted the third round of the 1971 Formula 5000 championship in the middle of my month-long sojourn at Indianapolis with Roger Penske's team. Next to the car (left) is my old friend Bill Pinckney, whom I met when I started racing Mum's Morris Oxford and who came out to the US to support me at Indy. In the background is another pal, Sam Posey, in his Surtees TS8.
Jim Culp

two boys, Greg and Guy, then nine and seven, came along and we planted ourselves at Siebkens Resort in Elkhart Lake, Wisconsin for the rest of the summer, until the boys went back to school.

There was quite a build-up for the Mid-Ohio race, the fourth round of the series, as Pepsi-Cola had commissioned a film of the event, produced by Hollywood's Bill Edgar, a highly regarded filmographer. As Sam Posey and I were the two dominant drivers, the film revolved mainly around us. L&M also used us almost exclusively for race promotions and Rod Campbell, one of the principals of General Racing, a public relations company hired by L&M, hawked Sam and I mercilessly everywhere we raced. At Mid-Ohio we went to local television and radio stations plus newspapers in Akron, Cleveland and Columbus. All the sports reporters then were stick-and-ball guys, as is still the case to some extent, and there were few gals in the sports studios. It was uphill work, I tell you. 'Nice to meet you, Mr Hobbs. Now, what is Formula 5000?' But Rod was a master and I have always thought his training of

Sam and me is what subsequently took both of us into television.

Meanwhile, for the filming at Mid-Ohio Sam and I did a lot of walking and talking on camera — more difficult than it looks — plus long, deep, searching interviews and all sorts of other camera work. Our two little boys were very impressed with the whole thing! In between I squeezed in some practice for the race, knowing all along that I was going to win it. But… pride goes before a fall. The only Formula 5000 race on film went to Sam. Although I finished second, to my mind that is the first of the losers. What a bummer! The Hobbs family had a rather subdued drive back to Elkhart Lake.

Road America was the next round, just two weeks later, and conveniently situated on the way into Elkhart Lake, where we were staying. The whole circus started drifting into town from about Tuesday and everyone stayed at Siebkens. One problem with Siebkens was that its accommodation had no air conditioning, and in July Wisconsin is hot and humid. The state bird

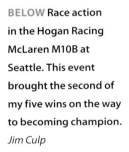

BELOW Race action in the Hogan Racing McLaren M10B at Seattle. This event brought the second of my five wins on the way to becoming champion.
Jim Culp

LEFT This grid shot is at Mid-Ohio, with Hogan Racing chief mechanic Bill Mayberry in attendance. Alongside is the Lola T192 of Brett Lunger, who became my team-mate the following year.
The Revs Institute for Automotive Research/ Suzy Dietrich

is the mosquito, some of which are about the size of a sparrow. You had to sleep with the window open, which let in not only the mosquitos but also the cacophony of noise from the bar, which saw a great deal of use, deep into the night, every night.

Most importantly, the world had spun back onto the right axis and I had another win, this time beating local hero Jerry Hansen, although there is no way of knowing what size engine he had in his Lola T192. Sam must have had a problem as he came in 13th and the popular Canadian Eppie Wietzes in his McLaren M18 was third. Needless to say, there was much celebrating at Siebkens!

Guy was a very cute and cuddly little boy, very popular with everyone. The young girls, all students, working in the restaurant loved him too, so at dinner time he would 'help' by being the water boy, topping up everyone's tumblers. One evening the top man from L&M, Cope Robinson, who came to most of the races, kindly said to Guy, 'Aren't you getting tired?' To which this cute little fellow replies, 'I'm tired of people asking me if I'm

tired!' Guy is still looking for a crack in the floor to go and hide in.

The next round was at Edmonton, Alberta, followed a week later by a one-off USAC race back at Seattle International Raceway for which Formula 5000 cars were eligible. I had decided that it would be an interesting trip for all of us, so Mags, me and the boys flew up to Edmonton from Chicago and then planned to drive the 500 miles or so from Edmonton to Seattle. I got off to a good start with another win at Edmonton, while in second place was Ron Grable, a real stalwart of American Formula 5000 racing who never had the success he was due in my opinion. Jim Dittemore, another steady runner, came third and Sam was fifth.

The day after the race we set off on our epic journey, across the Rockies through the Banff National Park and on down to Seattle. It took about three days and was absolutely worth it. I still remember some of the majestic vistas of lakes and mountains — all a marvellous and very educational experience for the boys. When we arrived in Seattle it was the time

Win number
three in 1971 came
at a favourite track,
Road America, and we
celebrated long and hard
at Siebkens, a much-
loved haunt on the shore
of Elkhart Lake.
Jim Scott

of the big unlimited hydroplane racing event
held there every year and somehow we found
time to see some of it. With all those Rolls-Royce
V12s shrieking away across the water, it was
absolutely spectacular, incredible stuff, and
extremely dangerous — they lost a lot of racers
in those boats.

As for our event, it started quite well as Sam
and I dominated qualifying, him pipping me to
pole by just 0.09 second. The USAC runners were
a long way off our pace, the best of them, Gordon
Johncock, lining up third on the grid in his Ford-
powered Vollstedt with a 'pseudo-F1' car next to
him in the form of Pete Lovely's Formula 2 Lotus
69 with a Cosworth DFV shoehorned in the back.
The race, another two-heat affair, was a disaster
and I dropped out of both heats very early on. Jim
Dittemore won the first, Sam the second.

By now both of our boys had the measles,
which they found very unpleasant. Anyway,
measles or not, we had to get back to Chicago
swiftly because the next round was the following
weekend at Donnybrooke, a circuit I really

enjoyed and where I had won on both of my
previous Formula 5000 visits. This time, however,
I had to settle for seventh place while Sam, my
nearest championship rival, retired. Brett Lunger,
who would be my team-mate the following year,
won, followed by Eppie Wietzes and Lothar
Motschenbacher, both better known for their
time in Can-Am circles.

Just one round remained and that was to be on
Sam's home ground, Lime Rock in Connecticut,
just up the road from his home in Sharon. He was
the — self proclaimed — master of the track, but
unfortunately for him I snatched this final victory
and sealed the championship title for Hogan
Racing and its driver by quite a big margin, 119
points to Sam's 70. After the race we all repaired
to the home of Sam's mother, Mary Moore, a
lovely but somewhat overwhelming woman who
hosted some super parties over the years.

The season was a fantastic start to a
relationship with Hogan Racing that lasted for
five years, a very long period in motor racing,
especially in those days. The year had also

brought a lot of fun — but then it is always easier to have fun when you are winning. It was lucrative too. The team's prize money for the year was $47,000, which aroused the interest of a number of European drivers, among them Brian Redman and even, for a while, Niki Lauda.

The 1972 Tasman Series

I have Terry Godsall to thank for my involvement in the Tasman Series during the first couple of months of 1972. This championship developed in the 1960s as a welcome winter break in Australia and New Zealand for many drivers from the Formula 1 fraternity but by this time it had evolved into a Formula 5000 contest. With financial help from Kirk White, a Ferrari parts dealer from Florida who had been part of my Penske programme, Terry did a deal with McLaren's Teddy Mayer for me to run a McLaren M18/22 in the eight-race series.

My campaign took some organising as there were massive distances to be covered not only to get out there but between the races themselves.

I took along Alex Groundsell, a very resourceful Londoner who had been my mechanic at Hogan and went on to work with me for many years, but I did not have any other engineering help so I had to have long telephone conversations with McLaren's Gordon Coppuck back in England. The bigger problem was getting shafted by Frank Matich, who not only raced but also happened to hold the Goodyear racing tyre franchise for the Antipodes. As soon as I proved I was quick, it became so difficult to get the right tyres for the car that I wound up calling Goodyear's HQ in Akron to get things sorted out. Then someone suggested we try larger rear wheels than the 15-inch ones we had been using, and the car was transformed! It made a massive difference.

When we went to Pukekohe for the New Zealand Grand Prix, the first race of the series, Frank Gardner rolled up with the first Lola T300, which was a Formula 2 car with a big engine in the back. It was small, light and nimble, and quickly became the car to have in Formula 5000. Besides Frank, the field at Pukekohe was strong

with people like Mike Hailwood, Kevin Bartlett and Graham McRae, but I had an encouraging start to the campaign with third place. In the three other New Zealand races that followed, however, my results were dismal.

Mags came over for the trip but the weather was just awful, cold and miserable, and she found it frustrating that there was no time to look around after travelling all that way. You would race on Sunday, pack up on Monday, drive or fly to the next race, and do it again. For example, at the fourth round at Invercargill, right at the bottom of South Island, we never saw New Zealand's famous fjords even though they were nearby. On top of that, she became very unwell.

While we were in Invercargill, about as far from England as it is possible to be, I spoke to the mayor at a party and told him I came from a town called Leamington Spa. He said, 'I once lived there. Our house was on Radford Road.' I said, 'Radford Road? That's one street from where I lived for ten years!' It turned out that my sister Barbara and his brother-in-law both worked at the local hospital.

Then we transferred to Australia for four races there and my results did pick up a bit. At Surfer's Paradise, which flooded the day after we raced, I finished fourth. My engine overheated at Warwick Farm, a racecourse where the grass of the equine track was temporarily protected by plywood sheets across which you lurched at racing speeds with the tail out. Sandown Park, where I finished third, was another racecourse that featured a hairpin corner bordered only by a fence, beyond which was a quarry about a hundred feet deep. It was at Sandown that Mags met Peter Windsor, the journalist, for the first time. We were renting a house near the beach and somehow we picked him up and he took over our spare bedroom. He came wandering down one morning and asked, 'Where's breakfast?', to which Mags replied, 'It's here, but you have to cook it yourself.' Peter seemed somewhat shocked that she would not cook it for him.

The last race was in Adelaide. My family come from Adelaide, as you know by now, and we stayed with Aunt Ethel, Dad's sister, whom I had

BELOW When the 1972 Tasman Series transferred to Australia for its second half, my results picked up. The last race, in Adelaide, was wonderful because all of my Australian cousins turned out to see me win.
Terry Marshall

met when Dad treated us to that round-the-world trip after selling half of his business. We had a great time at her lovely house and ate very well — no fast food with Aunt Ethel. When it came time to race, all my cousins turned up, and I won. By the time we got back to the house we were a bit tiddly from the celebrations, at which point Aunt Ethel asked me how I did. 'I won,' I said. To which she sweetly replied, 'Well, isn't that what you're supposed to do, dear?' Talk about a let-down.

On the way home we stopped for three days or so in Hong Kong, where we had a great time and promised to return. More than 45 years on, we are still waiting to fulfil that promise. And I never did return to the Tasman Series.

Fallow years

After winning the American Formula 5000 title in 1971, I drove for Carl Hogan for four more years, always with Lolas, first the T300, then the T330 and T332. I got on very well with Carl. He was a big, gregarious guy, full of fun with a drink in his hand, and his wife Lollie was great too. He

ABOVE For 1972 Hogan Racing put me in a Lola T300, complete with my reigning champion's number 1, and I also acquired a team-mate in the guise of Brett Lunger, here suited up and ready to go.
Getty Images/Alvis Upitis

BELOW At the fifth round of 1972 at Donnybrooke my engine expired in the second heat after I had won the first. Here I am leading Peter Gethin's Chevron B24, Jerry Hansen's Lola T300 and George Follmer's Lotus 70 at the start of that second heat.
Getty Images/Alvis Upitis

ABOVE Hogan Racing came briefly to Britain in 1973. This Silverstone round brought a very satisfying victory with team-mate Brett Lunger in my wheel tracks.
LAT Images

LEFT The following day at Silverstone saw Formula 1 and Formula 5000 entries combine for the International Trophy. At the start I am tucked behind the Tyrrell of Jackie Stewart, while the other prominent F1 cars are the McLaren M23s of Denny Hulme (9) and Peter Revson (10) and Clay Regazzoni's BRM P160.
LAT Images

was almost the perfect team owner, although he was a bit too obsessed with how things looked, very much like his friend Roger Penske. We never came near repeating our 1971 success, because Graham McRae came over from New Zealand in 1972 and cleaned up, then Brian Redman came on strongly with Carl Haas's Lola along with Mario Andretti in the Vel's Parnelli Viceroy car, and then Al Unser as well.

In 1973 Carl Hogan also took in the first three British rounds of the Rothmans Formula 5000 Championship. The big International Trophy meeting at Silverstone, where we raced in a Formula 5000 event on the Saturday and then joined in with the Formula 1 cars the next day, was one of the highlights of my later years in these big single-seaters. My Hogan Racing team-mate was Brett Lunger, a member of the Dupont family who had spent time as a US marine in Vietnam. Brett was a pretty tough character and not that much slower than me, although he seemed to spend too much time thinking about his racing. He and I occupied the front row of

ABOVE Back in America for the rest of 1973, I was unable to match my Silverstone glory as I did not win a Formula 5000 race in a year that saw Jody Scheckter and Brian Redman sweep up everything, the South African becoming champion. I ended up fifth in the rankings.
Jim Scott

LEFT In 1973, my second year with a Lola, now a T330, Carl Hogan gives me some advice before the action starts. This is the newly constructed Pocono Raceway in Pennsylvania.
David Hobbs collection

RIGHT I like this shot from 1974 because Brian Redman and I are in our Lola T332s and I am the one in front. That year Brian, who became champion, and Mario Andretti won three races apiece, while I won the other, at Mosport, and finished third in the championship.
David Hobbs collection

BELOW In my final year of Formula 5000, Carl Hogan added splashes of white to the T332's usual dark blue livery and produced ever bigger air boxes. This is Road Atlanta, where I finished fifth.
Bill Warner

the Formula 5000 grid, me on pole, and we absolutely blitzed the race, nose to tail throughout. As well as winning, I broke the outright lap record, which was held by a Formula 1 car — that shows how quick the Formula 5000s were. The next day, when we were running with the Grand Prix boys, my engine blew up and the lap record was recaptured by a Formula 1 car, Ronnie Peterson's Lotus 72.

I had some great races with those star drivers and others, but Hogan's operation was always a day late and a dollar short, as the saying goes. We never went testing and sometimes he tried to be too clever, re-engineering the car without any real science behind it, such as fitting a new airbox or revised wings but with no idea whether or not it made the car better. Tom Anderson, our crew chief, got a bit frustrated. Of those four years, the least disappointing was 1974, when we ran the upgraded Lola T332. I won a race, at Mosport, got some podiums, and finished third in the championship standings, behind Redman and Andretti.

CHAPTER 8

1971

MY PENSKE YEAR

At the end of the 1970 racing season I was again frustrated because there were few prospects on the horizon, even though I had finished third in the American Formula 5000 championship despite missing the first half of the season. However, my two race victories, which gave me a better 'strike rate' than anyone else in the championship, and my skirmishes with Mark Donohue, clearly piqued some interest from Roger Penske, and later that year I had a phone call from his long-time right-hand man Dan Luginbuhl.

The upshot was a meeting in London with Roger and Mark at the Grosvenor House Hotel in Park Lane where I was presented with a grand plan for 1971. I would do the Indianapolis 500, Pocono 500 and Ontario 500, and I would also drive a Ferrari 512M sports car with Mark in four rounds of the International Championship for Makes, at Daytona, Sebring, Le Mans and Watkins Glen. What a deal — I was almost giddy with excitement. I could relish a full season in the most competitive machinery available.

Early in 1971 I went over to Philadelphia to officially sign up. I stayed with Mark and his first wife in their modest home in New Jersey, along with their two little boys, one of whom, David, went on to win the 2009 Rolex 24 Hour at Daytona. Mark and I came from very different backgrounds, me a middle-class Englishman,

LEFT My 1971 deal with Penske Racing included four rounds of the International Championship of Makes. It was rarely in doubt that our immaculately prepared Ferrari 512M was the class of the field, but Mark Donohue and I were unable to win. Here at Watkins Glen we got off to a great start, with Mark leading from pole, but when everything was looking good the car suffered a suspension failure.

LAT Images

he the all-American Irish kid, crew cut and all, and cleverer than me — although that is a low bar — with an engineering degree from Brown University. He insisted on being in the workshop all hours of the day and night, even sweeping the floor if he felt it necessary, his reasoning being that, 'I can't ask a guy to sweep the floor unless I'm willing to do it myself.' I have never been sure if that is the best use of a valuable resource.

Our shiny Ferrari

After a couple of days in Philly we flew to Florida in Roger's private jet to test the Ferrari 512M at Sebring. The car was magnificent. No one had seen a Ferrari like this one, completely taken apart, painstakingly rebuilt and presented so immaculately that you could eat your dinner off the door sills and out of the engine bay. The chief engineer, Don Cox, worked very closely with Mark and between them they could work engineering miracles.

When I first drove the Ferrari I was surprised how much understeer it had in mid-to-slow

corners, at which point Mark said, 'Oh yeah, by the way we have a spool, no diff, I'm sure you'll get used to it.' I felt this was a throwback to his Trans-Am success, where the solid-axle cars really did need a spool to lock the differential. Anyway, I soon got used to it, as I was obliged to — it was Mark's car and he set it up for his driving style. The only problem was the seating position: without a quick-change seat, my legs, longer than his, were always a bit jammed up under the steering wheel, and my head bounced off the roof.

The first race with my new team was, of course, the Daytona 24 Hours. Boy, did that car cause a stir when it rolled out of the truck. No one had ever seen such a shiny Ferrari. The European pressmen were their usual snooty selves: 'It's all spit and polish. Wait until the Gulf 917s [which actually looked a bit drab] get at it… won't see 'em for dust.' Wrong! Very wrong.

One of Penske's innovations, now almost universal in racing, was aircraft-type refuelling, and this was used for the first time at Daytona. I thought John Wyer and David Yorke at the

Gulf team were going to have coronaries when they saw it. Off to the stewards: 'You can't have refuelling like that!' Stewards: 'There's nowhere in the rule book that says you can't.'

Our sparkling car got pole position by quite a margin. Better still for me, Donohue and I were very close on time, even though I did very few practice laps. When I tentatively asked Roger if I was actually going to get any practice, he replied, 'Haarbs [Hobbs], this is a 24-hour event, you're going to get plenty of practice.'

Among Penske's excellent crew was our timekeeper and scorer Judy Stropus. This was the first time I met Judy and we remain close friends to this day. Her ability to keep a lap chart of the entire race was legendary, as were her skills with the stopwatch. Many was the time race officials came to the pit where she was working and asked, 'Did so-and-so complete 59 or 60 laps, we're not sure?' Or, 'Who have you got on pole position?' Over the years she worked for a lot of the top teams.

In the race Mark and I were equally quick, and both faster than any of the Porsche 917 drivers. We led comfortably until about midnight, when Mark got caught up in someone else's crash. Vic Elford's 917 blew a tyre going into NASCAR 3 at about 215mph — no chicane then — and the car did a massive spin down the banking, raising a huge cloud of smoke and dust. Mark was first on the scene and slowed up but some hero in a Porsche 911 about 50 laps down decided this would be a good time to make up some ground and ran into our beautiful Ferrari, shunting it into the wall and causing a lot of body damage.

Back in those good old days with just two drivers for a 24-hour race, we had a small caravan as our bedsit and I was attempting to get some kip when in walked Mark. A bit groggy, I looked at him and said, 'What are you doing here? Hang on, aren't you supposed to be… Oh blimey, what *are* you doing here?' The last person you want to see in the middle of an endurance race is your co-driver. The crew, led by John 'Woody' Woodard, put about 1,000 yards of duct tape all over the car to hold it together, and we still came in third.

BELOW A pit stop early in the Daytona 24 Hours. We took pole position and led until around midnight, but then, with Mark Donohue at the wheel, an errant Porsche 911 driver smashed into our car in the aftermath of someone else's big accident on the banking.
Bill Warner

Rather amazingly, we were able to continue at Daytona after much patching up of bodywork, bringing our 'tank-tape special' home in third place. Here Roger Penske, as ever, is hands on — literally.
LAT Images (right) and Bill Warner (below)

Then as now, just a few short weeks separated the two big season-opener races held in Florida and Sebring was soon upon us. Back then the circuit was much longer than it is today, over five miles, and it ran way out to the edge of the airfield. There were a couple of very long straights using the old runways and where they intersected the turn was marked by a handful of traffic cones that soon got scattered, leading to the odd driver getting a little lost out there, trying to find the right runway in the pitch dark.

This time there was major opposition, not only from lots of 917s but also some seriously fast prototypes, including a works Ferrari 312PB driven by Jacky Ickx and Mario Andretti, and some quite handy factory Alfa Romeos. Once again we were on pole.

Mark started the race and again we led. After a couple of stints each, he was at the wheel again and was suddenly late to appear. Then he limped into pitlane with the right rear of the car all torn up. Apparently he and Pedro Rodríguez had had an altercation out in the back forty. When he got out of the car, Mark, who was usually fairly even-tempered, let loose about how Rodríguez had run into him multiple times. Mark was always a bit strange about drivers. While he considered me to be, to quote, 'a good bloke, especially for an Englishman', he had a *massive* thing about Pedro — he just could not stand him. I have no idea why as they could hardly have met more than a handful of times. Anyway, for us it was another defeat snatched from the jaws of victory, and after more generous lashings of duct tape we eventually came home in sixth place. As for the collision, no one ever seemed to be very sure who had hit whom.

Off to Indy

More excitement was on the way. As the end of April approached and after my first Formula 5000 race with Carl Hogan, at Riverside, I was back with the Penske team and headed for my first Indianapolis 500.

I was obviously a bit nervous at the prospect of this giant circuit walled in all the way around

ABOVE For the Sebring 12 Hours the Penske boys returned our Ferrari 512M to its normal pristine appearance. Again we led the race and again there was a collision, this time the fault of Pedro Rodríguez in his Gulf Porsche 917. As at Daytona, after repairs Mark and I recovered to finish sixth but the usually cool Roger Penske was left fuming.
Bill Warner

and very fast too. On my arrival, though, I could see immediately why road racers like Jimmy Clark had been successful, because the four banked turns, at just nine degrees, are not very steeply banked, nowhere as much as I expected. They also seem long, much longer than you would imagine for a 90-degree turn, and each of them is slightly different. Unlike road racing, where you take a wide approach into a corner, a late apex and then a good blast on exit, at Indy you turn in relatively early, run round the bottom of the curve, and then go up toward the wall again on the way out. Of course, we did not carry anything like the speed they do now into the turns but there was definitely a technique to handling those corners.

Poor Mike Spence lost his life at Indy in 1968 because he did not follow the accepted style. He took one look at the place and decided the other drivers had it all wrong, that you needed to run high in the corners and then come down. But cornering at Indy, with its basically flat straights transitioning into banked turns, is very different from driving through the level turns mostly found on road circuits. Once you try to turn in up high, you cannot actually get down to the apex. Driving the gas-turbine Lotus 56, Spence bounced into the wall because of this and, in a freak occurrence, the front wheel flipped up and struck him on the head.

A particularly important aspect of car set-up for Indy was tyre stagger, which was possible with the crossply tyres of the time but not with today's radial tyre construction. This was the technique of inflating the tyres to different pressures, with those on the right-hand side at higher pressure so that they became slightly larger in diameter, to encourage the car to turn left. It worked like magic.

My Lola T153, with its big Ford V8 and huge turbocharger, would reach about 230mph down the straights, so I had to lose about 60mph going into the corners. The technique was to brake with the left foot, which was foreign to me then but completely familiar now, while keeping the boost pressure up because that giant turbo also

had giant lag. This meant using just the right amount of right foot on the throttle so that you did not unleash too much horsepower while slowing down. I soon managed to pick up the technique and after my rookie test my pace was about the same as most of the other runners. I did something like 2,300 miles in practice, going round and round and round, burning massive quantities of fuel and getting through enormous numbers of tyres.

As with our Ferrari, 'Woody' Woodard was chief mechanic for the Indy campaign. Lou Spencer, who was very experienced and had worked with some top guys, Carroll Shelby and Dan Gurney among them, ran my Lola. All of Roger's crew were experienced Indy guys and they were very helpful.

Mark Donohue, meanwhile, had an all-new McLaren M16A, which was the first proper attempt at a winged car for Indianapolis, with a wedge-shaped nose and side-mounted radiators as pioneered in Formula 1 the previous year by the Lotus 72. In fact there were three of these

handsome new McLarens, all with the four-cylinder Offenhauser engine, the staple motor for Indy, and with Denny Hulme and Peter Revson driving the works entries. To give you an idea of the leap forward made by the M16A, my Lola would average about 170mph for the lap but the McLarens were soon up at the 180 mark, right out of the box. They cast a dark cloud for a lot of the top drivers.

I remember Al Unser coming over to speak to Mark and Roger about the M16A: 'You guys are going to kill this race. You're going to ruin it with these damn cars. It's hopeless.' He had a point: it had taken about ten years for lap speeds to go from 160mph to 170, and then the next 10mph increment came along in an instant, just like that. The spectacle of increased speed, however, meant there was always quite a good crowd of spectators, maybe as many as 15,000 every day, so it clearly created a story.

The whole month-long event at Indy involved so much pomp and circumstance and tradition, as it still does. There was considerable deference to former drivers and a lot of power in the hands of the track personnel, yellow jackets, some of whom were former racers. Even parking your car was a rigmarole. Gasoline Alley was made up of funny old green garages and everything had to be done according to a massive ritual. The car had to be filled up with a certain amount of fuel at the official fuel station, then more while in the garage, and then your car was pushed out to pitlane and down to your pits. Unlike all racing I had experienced, nobody did any work on the cars in pitlane. To do anything on a car, just something as simple as changing the roll bar or the springs, it had to be pushed back to the garage or towed behind a little tractor.

Understanding how the whole thing was steeped in tradition explains why someone like A.J. Foyt went apoplectic about Jimmy Clark's car being green, which was considered an unlucky colour. The place also had its hero dynasties: the Unsers, Al and Bobby, were huge names, partly because their older brother Jerry had been killed at Indy in 1959 and their father also raced; the Bettenhausens were also out in force, at least two or three of them, and the Vukoviches.

Having been there for three weeks of practice with no significant problems, everything seemed perfect for us at Penske Racing. Donohue was quickest virtually every day and each time that happened he won a free dinner, to which he usually invited me as one of his guests. Even Teddy Mayer, the boss of McLaren's factory team who went by the nickname 'The Weiner', was clicking around asking why our car was faster than his pair. Then came Pole Day, the first of four qualifying days.

The evening before qualifying began Roger Penske called the team together for a meeting at our Howard Johnson's hotel. There were about ten of us: Roger, Woody, Mark and me, two mechanics on Mark's car and two on mine, plus one or two extra guys who went around keeping things clean and neat, this being Penske Racing. Roger said, 'OK, we all need to be down in the lobby at 6am to be sure to get into the track ahead of the crowds.' I thought that seemed a trifle early. Every day we had driven down the road

at the north end of the circuit that went past the Hulman family's Coca-Cola bottling plant, the huge facility just outside turn four, and hardly seen a soul.

How wrong could I be? On qualifying day at 6am, there were cars parked on the verge outside the Howard Johnson's when we left for the Speedway, with non-stop heavy traffic as we made our way to the north gate, rather than the south gate that we had used every day of practice because it was closer to the pits. When we finally arrived I could see that already there were a lot of people there, but by the time I walked out of Gasoline Alley through the arch between the infield grandstands — wow! — the crowd was way bigger than I had ever seen before, bigger even than at Le Mans. The place was suddenly packed to the rafters. The boast of the Indianapolis Motor Speedway in those days was that the Indy 500 itself was the biggest one-day sporting event in the world, by far, and Pole Day was the second biggest, and the second day of qualifying was the third biggest. There were about 250,000 people there for qualifying. It was awesome to see.

I qualified 16th at 169.571mph, which was about the same speed Mark had done the previous year in the same car. But I do remember Mark going out in his McLaren and cranking out a superb lap — in fact it was 177.087mph — and then pulling back into the garage where all the press were waiting and getting out of his car, smiling and preening. While all this was going on, there was suddenly a massive roar from the crowd and Tom Carnegie on the public-address system announced, 'And that's a new… track… rrrrrecord!' Peter Revson in one of the factory McLarens had pipped Donohue for the pole! I have never seen anybody more pissed off than Mark was at that moment.

On race day, a Saturday, we had a similar early-morning drill, except we left the hotel an hour earlier. Now the crowd had swelled to 350,000 and we had the marching bands, cheerleaders and the ritualistic parking of the cars on the grid, all an hour before the start, and finally the famous 'Gentlemen, Start Your Engines'.

I was surprised to see no fewer than four pace cars. One of them, driven by an amateur called Eldon Palmer, went far too fast down pitlane after peeling off and ran into a temporary photographers' stand at the far end, well past the pit exit, causing some fairly serious injuries. When this occurred, of course, the race was just underway and we drivers were completely unaware of this peculiar accident.

Turn one on the opening lap is daunting. With the packed grandstand in the background filling the view, I remember feeling that the corner itself seem to loom into very sharp focus, with dust and scraps of paper flying everywhere. Once that was over, I got into the swing of the race and was able to use a version of modern drafting, although nothing like you see in NASCAR nowadays. Everything was going fine and I was up to sixth or so by the time of my fuel stop. In those days the cars carried 75 gallons of ethanol fuel that added about 550 pounds to the weight of the car, even though alcohol-based fuel is actually a little lighter than gasoline. Compared with today's

Formula 1 cars, which carry about 300 pounds of fuel and do not replenish during the race, that level of difference at Indy between full and empty was staggering, in all respects. Acceleration off the corners was badly affected, and you had to slow down all that weight on entry. Looking back, I cannot imagine how we sprung the cars for that kind of weight, adding 550 pounds to a machine that only weighed about 1,400 when empty. You would think that the thing would have dragged on the deck.

Anyway, not long after my fuel stop Rick Muther in the Sugar-Ripe Special, a Brabham knock-off, was right behind me. Coming out of turn four I heard a terrible racket and felt a sudden loss of power. Indy's old pit entry was a joke, just a slot in the wall, and by the time I had figured out what had happened, that slot was long gone. So I was now freewheeling down the front straight, thinking that I had better just park it on the grass at the entry to turn one. But I was also looking for Muther in the mirror. Where had Rick gone? Well, Rick reappeared at 'seven o'clock

ABOVE The rituals of the Indy 500 include the traditional posed shot in pitlane, with me modelling my shiny new Pyrotect fireproof race suit. Although I had witnessed huge crowds at Le Mans, it was awesome to experience Indy's 350,000-strong full house on race day. *Indianapolis Motor Speedway*

ABOVE This was my fate in the Indy 500, on lap 107 of the 200. After a sudden loss of fourth gear, my car slowed and Rick Muther, close behind, had to take violent avoiding action. He hit the inside wall near the pitlane entrance and rebounded into me. His Hawk car (left) came close to turning over while my Lola had both ends knocked off it.
David Hobbs collection

low'. When my Lola had suddenly slowed, he had only avoided me by giving his car a massive yank to the left. He hit the inside retaining wall, bounced off it like a billiard ball, and came back at me where I was unable to see him because I was focused on the other mirror. He hit me ahead of the left rear wheel and spun me around into the wall. He also spun and started sliding down the track on two wheels. The car so nearly went over on him, but luckily it toppled back on all four wheels. My Lola's oil tank split when I hit the wall and hot oil spilled all over me, including my visor, which made vision a bit difficult.

The big fear in those days was fire. I was wearing a gold Pyrotect suit but even so no driver wanted to sit in any flames. When everything came to rest, with the car in the middle of the track, I was deeply aware that I had only just stopped for fuel and had 60 to 70 gallons of it around me. So my first thought was to jump out. I stood up in the car and to look back at turn four I had to flip up my visor because it was covered in oil. It looked like the coast was clear so I set off

to run the six or seven yards across the track to the pits. About halfway across I suddenly realised that when crossing a street where the traffic is doing 150mph one's judgment can fail. So I ran faster. As I leaped up on the pit wall I had one leg in mid-air and A.J. Foyt missed me by about two inches. How I avoided being killed I do not know.

I went back to our pit, laughing nervously, and there I was interviewed by two or three people. Roger Penske was not at all amused that I was laughing, although of course that was simply due to overwhelming relief.

What had happened was that the teeth on the fourth ring of the Hewland gearbox had stripped. It turned out that for some inexplicable — and most un-Penske-like — reason the team had had a set of special lightweight gears made for the race. Nothing went wrong during all that practice mileage but come the race both Penske cars suffered this gear failure. In fact Donohue's went first, at about one-third distance, after he had led Peter Revson for much of the way. Like me, he found himself freewheeling, coming to rest up against the fence between turns three and four. His abandoned car was just left there, because that is what happened at Indy in those days, and much later in the race Mike Mosley came hurtling out of turn three, clipped the outside wall, careened across the track and nailed Mark's parked M16A firmly amidships, setting fire to both of them. So Penske had two wrecked cars instead of the glory that had looked so promising.

Mark definitely could have won the race, and I probably would have come fifth or sixth and been Rookie of the Year. Before the race everybody kept telling me I would get that prize because I was the quickest rookie by miles but it went to a guy named Denny Zimmerman, a dirt-track racer who finished eighth.

Needing replacement cars, Roger went up to Teddy Mayer and said, 'We'll have two more of those McLarens, thank you very much.' To which Mayer replied, 'I'll sell you one to replace the one you've written off, but I'm not going to sell you another one.' McLaren just did not want us to have two M16As. Roger's view then was that there was little to be gained from running me in the old Lola at Pocono and Ontario, so I did not do those races after all — and, of course, I did not get paid for them either.

The ironic thing is that in the end Al Unser won the 1971 Indianapolis 500 in an older-spec Colt, the Johnny Lightning Special, the same car in which he had won the previous year. In film of my crash, I noticed that Unser can be seen disappearing out of the bottom of the frame leaving big black tyre marks. After slowing down at the scene, he realised the yellow flags would come out and knew it was time to make a pit stop, so he gave it some serious gas and rushed around to finish his lap. His margin over Revson's

RIGHT **These three views show how the Lola came to rest in the middle of the track, very close to the Brickyard's famous row of bricks. The first driver to squeeze past was Al Unser, who went on to win the race. In the third shot I am out of the car and running to the pit wall with A.J. Foyt bearing down on me.**
David Hobbs collection

second-placed M16A was only 23 seconds at the
end, so — who knows? — perhaps that canny bit
of strategy made the difference.

Mark Donohue did win the following year,
1972, in a McLaren M16B. In the intervening 12
months, Dan Gurney looked at the wing on the
back of the McLaren and said, 'If we're going
to have a wing, let's have a real one.' So it was
that the 1972 Eagle had a wing about the size
of a Tiger Moth's and top speeds shot up even
further. From Revson's pole speed of 178mph
in 1971, Bobby Unser in an Eagle took it up to
nearly 196mph in 1972 — a staggering leap.

Le Mans with the Ferrari

My next race with Penske was the Le Mans 24
Hours, where our host was the well-known
photographer and journalist Bernard Cahier.
We stayed in a rather splendid villa and there
were various functions for sponsors and other
dignitaries. Mark Donohue was not fond of
that kind of thing, but he did join in one for
my 32nd birthday.

We were unsure of our chances at Le Mans
because the Ferrari 512M, unlike the Porsche
917s, did not have a long tail for aerodynamic
advantage at sustained high speed on the 3.7-mile
Mulsanne straight. All the same, Mark qualified
our car fourth and gave us reason for some
serious optimism.

In the race we ran really well and I had a
couple terrific stints as we moved into third spot.
Unfortunately the black cloud over our campaign
did not evaporate in the French sunshine and at
about 8pm the engine expired, with Mark at the
wheel. The really ironic thing here is that this
V12, a new one direct from the Ferrari factory,
had been installed after practice because Roger
wanted us to have a fresh engine for the race.
Our regular engines were blueprinted and
maintained by Traco, the California engine shop
that specialised in Chevrolet and had done a lot
of work over the years for Penske, but we had no
Traco spare with us. 'Woody', the chief mechanic,
and Mark were vehemently against discarding
our used Traco in favour of this factory Ferrari

LEFT The Ferrari 512M should have been a great combination at Le Mans in 1971 but its works-supplied V12 engine — replacing our usual Traco-tuned version — let go before quarter distance. Here the car is being fuelled up before the race, with Roger Penske (left) typically at the heart of things.
LAT Images

BELOW As shown in this pace-lap view taken at the Esses, our fourth spot on the grid for the 1971 Le Mans 24 Hours put us right up there with the long-tail Porsche 917s.
LAT Images

ABOVE The chaps with me in this cheery post-race group at Le Mans in 1971 are (from left) Tony Adamowicz, unknown, Phil Hill, Richard Attwood (peering over my shoulder), Elliott Forbes-Robinson, Chris Craft, Richie Ginther and David Weir.
The Cahier Archive

BELOW With my focus in 1971 very much on Penske commitments and my Formula 5000 campaign in the US, my only race in Britain that year was the Brands Hatch 1,000Km. Wealthy Spaniard José María Juncadella, seen here at the wheel, no doubt hoped that some Penske magic would rub off on his Ecurie Montjuïc Ferrari 512S. We qualified eighth and finished fifth.
David Hobbs collection

unit, but Roger — 'The Captain' as he was called then and still is today — insisted and so it was done. We loaned our used Traco to NART (North American Racing Team) for their Ferrari 512 driven by Sam Posey and Tony Adamowicz, who finished third! Had we not changed the engine, I am sure Mark and I would have won, because it was in this race that Jo Siffert, with a two-lap lead, popped his Gulf Porsche 917 into second gear instead of fourth as he accelerated past the pits while leading, the very mistake that had cost me a drive in the team.

Our final Ferrari race was the Watkins Glen Six Hours, part of a double header weekend with the sports car race on the Saturday and a round of the Can-Am series on the Sunday. Again Mark put our 512M on pole and things were looking really good. Off he went into the lead and was pulling away until, after about 40 minutes and just before I was to take over, the steering post on one of the uprights snapped off. Once again our day was over.

Even 'The Captain' was a bit perplexed that

we had had such a disappointing season with a car that was undoubtedly the class of the field. That Ferrari has become iconic, the most famous 512 in existence, and yet it never won a race. Fortunately for me, I was never behind the wheel when it broke or crashed. Many years later I did a television interview with Roger at Daytona and he said, 'Didn't you crash our Ferrari here in 1971, Hobbs?' To which I replied, 'No, Roger, I did not. It was Mark.' This was a remarkable slip in his otherwise unbelievable ability to remember everything and everybody.

Back at the beginning of the 1971 season, Mags and I stayed with Roger in his fabulous penthouse suite in Philadelphia. The whole place was a shrine to conspicuous consumption, with remote light fixtures, a television that folded down from the ceiling, and a room decked out like the interior of a 17th century galleon, all polished oak, with a giant mast, rigging, belaying pins and so on. None of this interested Roger. He had bought the place as a good deal in a foreclosure from a guy who had massively overspent putting it all together.

The day after our arrival I had a meeting with Roger in the office from which he ran the Penske empire. Back then his operation was still relatively small but nonetheless it included Hertz trucks, Goodyear tyre distribution, a car dealership and the racing team. He rattled through what he expected from me during the forthcoming season but at one point he broke off when the phone rang. Without missing a beat, he transferred from me to the person on the end of the line, a truck driver I imagined, and gave him directions to where he needed to go, plus the final-drive ratio of the truck, and told him to bear in mind the gradient on part of the route. Then he was back to me instantly. Then there was another call, this one from Karl Kainhofer at his race shop, talking about set-up and gear ratios for a test at Trenton. Again, he put the phone down and picked up our conversation right where left off, just as though we had never been interrupted.

He micro-managed the entire enterprise. Now he employs over 35,000 people and yet he is still on the pit wall at every Indycar race as chief

strategist. His memory for names, people and events is prodigious. When I was inducted into the Motorsports Hall of Fame of America in 2009, we all mingled afterwards and Roger said to me, 'Where's Margaret? Oh, there she is!' Off he went to have a chat with Mags, whom he had not seen or spoken to for nearly 40 years. Amazing.

My season with Roger Penske started with so much promise but basically turned to ashes. The year as a whole was not a total loss as I won the Formula 5000 championship with Carl Hogan, but I could so easily have won at least three of the classic endurance races, placed well at Indy and maybe at Pocono and Ontario too. *C'est la vie*, I suppose. But I look back and still find it pretty irritating that what was a good year did not become a fabulous one.

ABOVE **This was my last outing for Roger Penske. After Mark Donohue decided to miss the US Grand Prix in favour of a clashing USAC race at Trenton, I got to race the team's Formula 1 McLaren M19 at Watkins Glen and finished 10th.** *David Hobbs collection*

CHAPTER 9
1973–76
BACK HOME IN INDIANA

In the autumn of 1972, after a less than exciting season, I met Roy Woods. Roy was a half-decent driver who raced among other things a Trans-Am car in his distinctive colours, and he was also a team owner. Coming from Oklahoma, where the family had a number of oil wells discovered by his grandfather, Roy was extremely wealthy and money was not an issue. He was also an awfully nice guy, laid back and very sociable.

One of Roy's people stumbled upon Carling, the Canadian brewer, as a potential sponsor and it turned out that the boss was sold on the idea of racing as a great platform for raising awareness of its Carling Black Label beer. Unfortunately, everyone got a bit carried away and Roy Woods Racing ended up in Formula 5000, Can-Am and Indycar (for the big three 500s at Indy, Pocono and Ontario). The result of this massive onslaught, predictably enough, was that none of it proved to be very successful.

It was a lucrative year as Roy Woods paid me a retainer of $25,000, my best ever, plus a percentage of prize money, which never amounted to much. I remember doing the deal when he came over to Britain and visited us at our home in Upper Boddington with his friend Ron Tonkin, who later became one of the largest car dealers in the north-west of the US. Roy also gave me a shotgun, thinking perhaps that living in the English countryside meant I needed one.

LEFT The first attempt to run the Indy 500 in 1973, when I drove an Eagle for Roy Woods Racing, was halted after an 11-car start-line pile-up triggered by David 'Salt' Walther, whose car caught fire. Two days later the race was finally run — and three years later, oddly enough, I drove my last Indy 500 in a car run by Walther.
Getty Images/Bettmann

Indy in 1973

So in 1973 I was back at the Indy 500. The team Roy put together was led by R.W. 'Kas' Kastner, a sports car driver who became a very capable team manager with many championships under his belt — but he had no Indy experience. All of the team's mechanics were also pretty new to it as well, although my crew chief talked a good game, prattling about lots of technicalities that he did not properly understand. And as I had only raced at Indy once, in 1971, it was not as if I was an Indy expert either.

Despite that, I qualified my Offenhauser-powered Eagle comfortably, in 22nd place. In the race I passed guys like Gordon Johncock, the eventual winner, and Johnny Rutherford among others, so our chassis set-up was pretty good.

With lots of laps in the high 180s, I was heading for third or fourth place until, going down the back straight, the engine suddenly died. I freewheeled for half a lap and coasted into the pits. 'It just stopped,' I told them. 'I don't know what happened.'

It took the crew some time to discover that the reason was a broken magneto drive. They dropped in a new one, it proved to be perfectly timed, and the engine fired straight away. It was a miracle. I got back out there and I was rocketing along again, passing people left, right and centre, but I was about 25 laps down. So the fact that I eventually finished 11th tells you what might have been.

That Indy 500 was a nightmare in another respect. This was the year it rained day after day, and the race ended up being run four days late, on the Wednesday. By the time it was all over, the ground was all churned up and people camped down at turn one were covered in mud from head to foot. It was a desperate situation.

It was also the year I fell asleep on the grid. As I mentioned in the previous chapter, Indy has one of the longest pre-race traditions anywhere. You climb in, sit and wait. And wait. And wait. Marching bands, speeches, Jim Nabors singing 'Back Home Again In Indiana'. Finally comes the command to start engines. Well, in 1973 we did all that — and then it rained. So all the drivers had to shut down their engines until the sun came out again. After all that build-up, I was never keen on getting out of the car, taking off helmet and gloves, and so on, so I stayed put. Warmed by the up-to-temperature engine and returning sunshine, I just nodded off.

Then along came Roy, limping along on his walking stick, full of the excitement of watching his car compete in the Indianapolis 500 — and here was his driver dozing in the car. Roy thought that was demeaning to the whole status of the event and gave me a clip around the side of my helmet with his cane. I could not understand the fuss. After all, Denny Hulme used to fall asleep on the pit wall while his car was being worked on in practice, and later Nelson Piquet, the three-times World Champion, was another on-track power-napper. If you are not relaxed in your car, you are in the wrong job.

At the first attempt to start the race, on the Monday in very poor light and on a slightly greasy track, David 'Salt' Walther crashed hard into the wall as he crossed the start/finish line. The entire front of his McLaren was torn off, up to the bulkhead, and as the car spun around it sprayed fuel everywhere. Normally the flames from burning ethanol are not visible but because of the low light the fire from Walther's car looked like brandy alight on a Christmas pudding. In the end there were 11 cars involved in the pile-up but I was able to get through the mess and pulled up, without damage despite a clip from another car at one point. It was while speaking to a reporter afterwards that I made my infamous comment about what a joke it was that 33 of the 'best drivers in the world' could not drive down an effing straight without running into each other. Mario Andretti, in particular, was unimpressed, thinking that I was demeaning the event. I suppose he was right, but it was just an off-the-cuff remark.

When we finally did race on the Wednesday, to cap it all poor 'Swede' Savage lost control coming out of turn four and hit the catch fencing on the infield massively hard, sparking another conflagration. He inhaled flames and smoke and died a few weeks later. I was one of the first to arrive on the scene and stopped right there, as did Denny Hulme and a few others. Denny was stomping around saying 'Jesus effing Christ.' He had been burned at Indy the year before, when the bright daylight prevented him from realising that he was on fire until he saw his visor and the back of his gloves melting, leaving him with terrible burns on the backs of his hands. The race did restart but finally they called a halt to it after about 350 miles.

Later in the year at Pocono my engine broke in the race. As for Ontario, in qualifying the right rear tyre failed going into turn two, ripping off the end of the rear wing and doing quite a bit of other bodywork damage. I was unable to start the race.

Roy Woods and Carling also wanted me in

their Formula 5000 car, but I thought better of putting all my eggs in one basket and continued to drive for Carl Hogan, because we had won the championship together and we had a great personal rapport. But I did drive Woods's Can-Am car and so was kept pretty busy. More of that in the next chapter.

Indy in 1974

After the 1973 season Carling dropped all of its racing programmes with Roy Woods, having spent tons of money and got diddly-squat in terms of results — and the boss who had championed the cause had gone. However, the company remained impressed by the marketing benefits that Indy had brought. Their people had done a bang-up job with lavish entertaining of

ABOVE A picture of contemplation at Indy prior to a qualifying run.
David Hobbs collection

ABOVE Of my four attempts at the Indy 500, the 1974 race was the one where I had my best chance, with a truly competitive car.
Getty Images/The Enthusiast Network

OPPOSITE Pace lap in 1974 shows me on the outside of the third row in my 'Carling Black Label' McLaren M16C/D. The guys ahead include the biggest Indy stars, among them A.J. Foyt (pole), Gordon Johncock (fourth), Mario Andretti (fifth) and Bobby Unser (seventh).
Getty Images/The Enthusiast Network

distributors and customers, with whom I had mingled enthusiastically. So Carling decided they wanted a presence there again and turned to me. They offered me more money for a single race than I had ever previously received, $5,000, plus a percentage of prize money.

I went to General Racing in Connecticut, with whom I had been involved in Formula 5000, and they in turn contacted McLaren. Soon we had a full factory McLaren Indy 500 programme run by Teddy Mayer and Tyler Alexander, using the latest M16C/D and with a lot of interaction with the Formula 1 team. Carling were excellent at marketing, and had lots of distributors, so they put together a promotional programme that activated their sponsorship in the way it should be done. I drove one car, called the 'Carling Black Label', and Johnny Rutherford drove the other, which carried no sponsor name. Teddy and Tyler were as professional as ever, I had a great crew chief in Huey Absalom, a racing 'lifer', and engine man Gary Knudsen was a wizard. Good people, good cars.

Following the 'fire and rain' race of 1973 as well as the oil crisis of the same year, there were a lot of technical changes to the cars, to slow them down and save fuel. Above all, fuel tanks were smaller, reduced from 75 to 40 gallons, and the total fuel allocation for the 500 miles was restricted, to 280 gallons, so that you had to watch the consumption — no more pouring in unlimited amounts at stop after stop. Other significant restrictions were the introduction of pop-off valves to limit boost pressure and a reduction in maximum wing size. All of this reduced lap speeds by about 7mph.

I found the McLaren a beautiful car to drive and in practice we got it set up on Carburetion Day just the way I wanted. Although I could not match Johnny's speed — he was super-quick on ovals and this was his 16th start in the 500 — I was one of the few guys who lapped at over 190mph that year. I did some practice laps at about 193 or 194, but I could not repeat it in qualifying, hitting 184 or so. I qualified ninth, but I should have been in the top four or five.

LEFT For once my car held together and in the 1974 Indy 500 I finished fifth, which could have been third but for two errors — one mine, the other the team's.
Getty Images/The Enthusiast Network

ABOVE At Indy in 1974 I was team-mates at McLaren with Johnny Rutherford, who won the race. I found him a super guy and we got on really well. This is a pre-race photo-call for my sponsor, complete with British flag.
Edwin Ingalls

In the race the car was humming along well, but the bloody thing had picked up some oversteer that I was unhappy with, probably due to losing some tyre stagger. I tried to drive around it but eventually I decided we should attempt to fix it. I made the very bad error of coming in under green when I should have just bided my time until there was an incident. No sooner had I stopped than the track went yellow, putting me a lap down, and I never could catch up. We also got our fuel calculations slightly wrong as there were still 20 gallons left at the finish, which meant we could have turned up the boost a bit.

I finished fifth. Bill Vukovich, who was third, had practised slower than me every day of the month and I had also comfortably out-qualified him, yet he beat me in the race. There was no excuse for that: it was down to my green-flag stop and running a bit less boost. Johnny Rutherford, my team-mate, had the most unbelievable run from the back after a qualifying hitch and won the race. When he came past me, in turn one, it was like I was tied to the ground. So we finished

first and fifth. I have always felt I should have come third, behind Bobby Unser; I would not have won, but third is better than fourth, and fourth better than fifth.

To use a phrase, 'It was good, but not great.' People say, 'Wow! Fifth at Indianapolis is a great achievement!' Derek Bell has graciously said he would give up one of his five Le Mans victories to finish fifth at Indy, but I somehow doubt that. Nonetheless, my percentage of the team's $33,000 prize money for fifth place was pretty useful.

It is pleasing that I can look back and say of my career that I raced in NASCAR's Daytona 500 and the Daytona 24 Hours, finished third in the Le Mans 24 Hours, drove in Formula 1 and finished fifth at the Indianapolis 500. You have got to see things in perspective, I suppose, but race drivers want to win. I have always felt that when you finish second, as I stated earlier, you are the first of the losers.

But it was a good experience. Mags and I had a lot of fun with Johnny Rutherford and his wife Betty. We went to see the Mel Brooks film *Blazing*

Saddles and when it reached the scene where the cowboys are farting around the campfire I thought Johnny was going to die laughing. We got along so well that I convinced him to come and race in Formula 5000. Carl Hogan bought a second new Lola and, a few weeks after Indy, Johnny came to Watkins Glen for his first race in it. In the opening practice session he stuffed it in the barriers in the Esses and broke his leg. I felt pretty bad about that.

Indy in 1976

I did not race at Indy in 1975 but I returned in 1976 and it was a complete disaster. I was driving the Dayton-Walther Special, run by 'Salt' Walther — his nickname arose when he raced hydroplanes at sea — and funded by his father George, who owned Dayton Steel Foundry, a very large and successful company. When they approached me, I turned them down because I did not want to do Indy again, but they responded by offering more and more money. In the end the offer was just too good to turn down.

George was a wonderful man, but we did not see much of him because he left 'Salt' to run things. 'Salt' was unsavoury. He had a succession of women, no doubt attracted by his wealth, and we all knew not to go in the truck when he was in there shagging. His crash at Indy in 1973 had badly damaged his hands and he wore a black leather glove on the left one. In later life he served several prison sentences for drugs offences and other crimes.

The car was a McLaren, so it was basically a pretty good one, but the team's standards of preparation were shocking. Struggling on qualifying day, I went through three sets of tyres before I found one that gave me an extra 5mph, and I got into the race on the back row, 31st of 33 starters. Then, on one of the many pace laps before the race, the thing kept dropping out of gear. I thought, 'This isn't going to last long.' Going around Indy at top speed, trying to hold the car in gear, is not ideal. In fact it was a water leak that eliminated me, after only 10 laps. You could say it was a bit of a damp squib.

ABOVE I may look cheerful for the obligatory pitlane pose, but my last Indy was pretty dismal from start to finish. In the race I was out after only 10 laps.
Indianapolis Motor Speedway

BELOW Waiting for the Walther mechanics to sort out my McLaren during Indy practice. The car was potentially good enough but the team was hopeless and I could only scrape onto the back row.
David Hobbs collection

CHAPTER 10

1969–73
MY CAN-AM YEARS

Back in the early 1970s much of the racing in the United States, with the important exception of Indycars, was sanctioned by the Sports Car Club of America. The SCCA ran not only the Formula 5000 championship but also the Can-Am and the Trans-Am, and on the amateur side its affiliated regional bodies organised thousands of events, from autocross in parking lots to serious races at all the big road circuits in the country.

The Can-Am grew out of the United States Road Racing Championship (USRRC) for Group 7 cars in which I raced with the Lola T70 in late 1965. The big attraction of this series was its *laissez faire* rules… basically 'run what you brung'. Spectators and competitors alike thought this was a very cool idea. The first Can-Am series, called in full the Canadian-American Challenge Cup, took place in 1966 and John Surtees won it in the factory Lola T70. Then we had five years of McLaren domination with the 'Bruce and Denny Show' and Lola was never able to repeat its early success despite getting Formula 1 World Champion Jackie Stewart on board in 1971. Initially sponsored by Johnson Wax, the Can-Am offered awesome prize money, such that both Bruce McLaren and Denny Hulme won more money at it than they ever did in Formula 1.

The original concept of the open rule book met its match when Porsche contracted

LEFT I enjoyed my Can-Am racing most of all during 1973, driving for Roy Woods in this lovely McLaren M20, seen swooping down Laguna Seca's Corkscrew trailed by Jackie Oliver's Shadow DN2. The trouble was that by now the turbocharged Porsches, particularly Mark Donohue's awesome 917-30, were in command. *Jutta Fausel*

Penske Racing to enter the Can-Am with its turbocharged 917-10. George Follmer made mincemeat of everyone in the 1972 series and the following year, with the even more powerful 917-30, Mark Donohue was utterly dominant, winning six of the season's eight races.

My early Can-Am forays

My first Can-Am races were in 1969 at Road America and Michigan, driving a Ford-powered McLaren M6B for Bill Young, an amateur driver who had done a Can-Am season in 1968 with a Lola T70 and then decided to get various drivers involved in his efforts the following year. The car did not last the race at Road America and at Michigan I finished 10th.

In 1970 I had a one-off drive at Edmonton in the Ford G7 run by Agapiou Brothers Racing but it overheated on the first lap of the race. Then I switched to a McLaren M12 campaigned by Terry Godsall, whom we first met in Chapter 7, and did three races with that, at Road America, Laguna Seca and Riverside, and it broke every time.

ABOVE This is my first ever Can-Am race, with Bill Young's elderly McLaren M6B at Road America in 1969. I had to retire when the engine overheated.
Jim Scott

BELOW In my second Can-Am race it looks as if I am showing Denny Hulme the way round Michigan. If only — Denny is about to lap me. This race was a classic 'Bruce and Denny Show', with those two finishing first and second in their works McLaren M8Bs, while I was 10th in my M6B.
The Revs Institute for Automotive Research/Karl Ludvigsen

My Can-Am racing in 1971 started off little better. I had a couple of guest drives for a British privateer, Tony Dean, who had an ageing McLaren M8D. These races were at Road Atlanta and Watkins Glen, and again I retired both times with a blown engine. The year before, rather against the odds, Tony had actually won a Can-Am race at Road Atlanta when both of the factory McLarens broke and others had problems. That day Tony was racing a Porsche 908 and it marked the first Can-Am victory in nearly three years by a car other than a McLaren. However, Tony was best known for his transporter that seemed to go backwards and forwards across the Atlantic between every race, and on it, mixed with the spares, were Cuban cigars on which he had forgotten to pay the duty.

Then at the end of 1971 Terry Godsall came up with another plan. In 1969 British designer Peter Bryant had built his own Can-Am car designated the Ti22 but invariably known as the 'Titanium Car', 'Ti22' being the chemical symbol

LEFT On the pit barrier at Road America in 1969, contemplating Bill Young's McLaren M6B.
Jim Scott

BELOW This is a classic Can-Am car, a McLaren M8D, which I raced a couple of times for Yorkshireman Tony Dean in 1971, but with no success.
Bill Warner

ABOVE For the last two
Can-Am races of 1971
I drove Peter Bryant's
innovative 'Titanium Car'.
Here I am at Riverside,
where I managed to
knock the car's nose
on one of those white-
painted half tyres and
could not continue.
*Getty Images/The
Enthusiast Network*

and atomic weight for titanium, which was used
extensively in the construction. When Jackie
Oliver raced it in the last two rounds of 1969 it
showed good pace straight away, but early in the
1970 series, at St Jovite, the car flipped and was
destroyed. Bryant had a 'Mk2' ready towards the
end of the year and Oliver ran it at Laguna Seca
and Riverside, finishing second to Denny Hulme
on both occasions. Then Bryant and Oliver both
became involved with Don Nichols's Can-Am
Shadow operation, although the designer soon
split with Nichols and set about racing the Ti22
again. Somehow or other he and Godsall came
up with a plan to take part in the final two
California races with me at the wheel.

The first of my races in the Ti22 was at
Laguna Seca, where the car was a joy to drive
and I qualified third, right behind the two
all-conquering McLarens of Peter Revson and
Denny Hulme, and ahead of Jackie Stewart's
Lola. In the race, though, I was passing a slower
car going up to the famed Corkscrew turn and
the driver did not see me coming, resulting in a

fairly serious flank-to-flank blow that put me out
of the race.

The last Can-Am round of the season was at
Riverside, a terrific, fast, flowing, challenging
circuit out in the desert, east of Los Angeles.
Here I was unable to qualify due to some
technical problem and had to start at the back.
Right from the getaway I began to carve my
way through the field and it was all most
exhilarating. At one corner, however, I clipped
the nose of the car on one of the white-painted
half tyres used at Riverside to mark the corner
apexes, and unfortunately the damage, although
slight, meant that my race was over.

I enjoyed these races in the Ti22. It was a good
car with lots of potential and Peter Bryant was
a clever designer. He subsequently wrote the
book *Can-Am Challenger*, a very good insight into
racing and race car design.

The 1972 season

My first full Can-Am season was 1972 and I
signed to drive the new Lola T310 for the cigar-

chomping Carl Haas, the US Lola importer. Soon after the season started, however, I made a wrong decision.

When testing the new Can-Am Porsche 917-10, the turbocharged spyder version of the 917, at Road Atlanta a week before the second round took place there, Mark Donohue had a big accident when the rear bodywork flew off and he suffered a broken leg. Again I got a call from Roger Penske's man, Dan Luginbuhl, this time asking if I would substitute for Mark while he recovered. At this point I had not even raced the new Lola because it was not ready so I considered the offer very seriously, but Haas's crew chief, Jim Chapman, a truly lovely guy, talked me out of it, telling me how great the new Lola would be, that the 917-10's turbocharged engine was never going to suit road races, and so on. I also did not want to appear disloyal by asking Carl to release me from his contract for what would have been an interim arrangement.

Instead Penske took on George Follmer, who promptly won that Road Atlanta race. As it turned out, Mark missed four more races and Follmer won two of those as well. After Mark recovered, Penske expanded the team to two cars and Follmer added two more victories to take the title by a massive margin, with 130 points to runner-up Denny Hulme's 65 — and I was seventh on 39. Sticking with the Lola and turning down the Porsche opportunity must rank as one of my biggest mistakes.

I judge that Lola T310 Can-Am car one of the worst machines Eric Broadley ever designed. My first opportunity to drive it did not come until a test session at Silverstone on the Tuesday before our scheduled first race at Road Atlanta. Frank Gardner, whom Eric regarded as an excellent test driver, had done all the testing up to this point and I arrived to find him pounding round. The trouble was that he was lapping about five seconds slower than the McLaren factory cars had done a couple of months earlier, before they were shipped to the US. When I asked to have a go, Lola's people said they wanted Frank to stay in the car as he was such a good tester. Finally, he

BELOW The Lola T310 that I drove for Carl Haas in 1972 has to go down as one of Eric Broadley's least successful designs. Frank Gardner did most of the testing in Britain and certainly did not sort the car as well as I would have liked.
Bill Warner

got out of the car and said, 'It's fine, needs a few tweaks but she'll be all right; the steering is a bit heavy but it's pretty good.'

So I flew to Atlanta that evening and the car followed. After clearing customs it finally arrived at the track late on Friday evening, leaving me with just one practice session on Saturday morning and then qualifying. As I pulled out of the pits Frank's comment about the heavy steering immediately came to mind. My first thought was that someone must have forgotten to remove the lock used to keep the steering rack rigid during shipping. So at the end of the lap I came in to tell the crew, but they confirmed that the lock had been removed. Frank must have had some big arm muscles, I tell you, because I needed all my strength to turn the thing.

Road Atlanta has lots of elevation changes, especially through turns three, four and five, back up over a small brow to turn six, and then at the end of the back stretch through a huge dip, up to the bridge and back down to the start/finish straight. I did a few laps with the car scraping

the ground so came in to have that checked, but Davey Evans, our young mechanic, could not find anything amiss. OK. Back out and full on it to get ready for qualifying.

Eric's big aerodynamic trick with the T310 was to make it a flat, wide car that hardly needed a rear wing. Doing nearly 200mph, I hit the dip at the end of the back straight and the right rear suspension broke. Rather than having wishbones in the suspension, Eric had used parallel links to locate the wheel hubs at the bottom. One of these links failed, so the wheel just flopped out wide, like a wonky wheel on a supermarket trolley.

That bloody car went round and round and round. It never left the tarmac and finally stopped at the top of the hill under the bridge. For me, a total passenger, it was very unpleasant. I climbed out, did a bow, and collapsed. Back in the garage, lo and behold, they discovered that the lowest bits of the car were those pick-up points for the suspension parallel links. The scraping noise I had heard was the track surface wearing through the knuckle that secured the link.

Haas's guys managed to repair the car for the race, which I treated as a test session and finished seventh. After the first few laps it was unsettling to observe, close to the point where I had experienced that violent spin, the trackside wreckage of Denny Hulme's McLaren, which had flipped backwards when cresting a brow and landed upside-down, thankfully without too much harm to Denny.

The rest of the season was no better. I could not believe how bad that Lola was, and all the while George Follmer was cleaning up in Porsche's turbo car. Eric Broadley came to all our races, carrying with him top links, bottom links and wishbones, all as hand luggage. We changed the roll centres, the ride height, just about everything at one time or another, but nothing worked. It was dismal.

My best result was fourth place at Watkins Glen. *Autosport*'s Pete Lyons was there and later wrote in his book *Can-Am* a colourful account of my efforts that I cannot resist quoting.

'If a dull race had a bright star, it was David Hobbs. Driving the Lola hard enough to make it wobble and puff up dirt from the roadsides, he scrambled past car after previously faster car, and finally out-braked Follmer's not-so-mighty turbo Porsche in a startling inside-at-the-apex move that made him third. So fiery was Hobbo's driving that it must have overheated him. Late in the race he had to stop for the ever-popular water bucket treatment, which dropped him to fourth at the end.'

After that awful season finally came to a close, Carl Haas asked if I would drive his Formula 5000 car the following year. Even if it was only half as bad as the Can-Am car, I thought, there was no way I wanted to saddle myself with it. So Brian Redman got the drive and in four seasons he won the title three times! See what I mean about him being a thorn in my side?

Le Mans in 1972

I did take time out from racing in America when I accepted a very good opportunity at the Le Mans 24 Hours. Gérard Ducarouge, who

ABOVE I had finished my last stint at Le Mans with the Matra in third place behind two sister cars and was getting ready to mount the Le Mans podium when the gearbox broke with just an hour to go.
McKlein

headed Matra and later became Lotus Formula 1 designer, asked me to drive for the Matra team. It was a big set-up.

The French aerospace company really wanted to win their home race and entered four cars, all with the screaming V12 engine derived from the one they had been using in Formula 1. In the latest MS670s were Graham Hill with Henri Pescarolo, François Cevert with Howden Ganley and Jean-Pierre Beltoise with Chris Amon, while I joined Jean-Pierre Jabouille in an earlier MS660, which was a nice car to drive but not as quick as the later model. As you would expect from the French, the hospitality was wonderful.

The main opposition to Matra that year came from Alfa Romeo but all bar one of their cars dropped out. As for my team, poor old Amon had his usual bad luck when his car, with Beltoise driving, broke its engine after only two laps. As for my car, Jabouille had an avoidable mishap a couple of hours into the race when it ran out of fuel at the Ford chicane, but that was close enough to the pits for him to get there on the

starter motor. By the time I rejoined we had lost several laps and dropped from fourth to 12th, but then we ran very strongly and got ourselves up to third place by the halfway mark, behind the other two Matras, and we ran 1–2–3 like that through the dawn on Sunday and on past lunchtime.

This was the first year the circuit used the new Porsche Curves, a terrific addition that bypassed the old White House, a notoriously dangerous bend. On one lap, accelerating out of Arnage towards this new section with the track wet but the sun shining, I had one of the biggest moments of my entire career. The car got into a horrendous tank slapper and I really thought my last moments had come, but I twiddled the wheel and somehow it sorted itself out. A couple of laps later I came into the pits for a routine stop, expecting Jean-Pierre to get in the car, but they said, 'You're doing fine, just carry on.'

So I ended up doing a massive four-hour stint, from about 10am to about 2pm, through very changeable conditions. It kept raining and drying, raining and drying. It was petrifying and, roaring down the Mulsanne straight, I started to think it was about time Jabouille got in the car, and perhaps I was getting a bit old for all this at a mere 33. Only afterwards did I realise that they wanted Jabouille in the car for the finish, which with two hours to go was shaping up to be a Matra 1–2–3.

After that four-hour stint, with my head ringing from the noise of that V12 right behind me, Mags and I walked to the Welcome Centre, where we planned to watch this French success on French soil and enjoy the part I had played in it. As we were walking along, I said to her, 'Hang on a minute, I need to count our cars because I don't think I heard three of them go by.' We returned to the pits with only an hour or so of the race left and, sure enough, one of the Matras had stopped out at Arnage with a broken gearbox. It was Jabouille in our car.

Still, Matra took the first two places, with Graham Hill in the winning car. That gave him a 'Triple Crown' that remains unique — victory in the Monaco Grand Prix, the Indianapolis 500 and the Le Mans 24 Hours.

After the celebrations, Graham offered us a lift back to Britain in his plane. When I think about it now, this was not the brightest thing to do. We took off from the little airfield alongside the track with me in the front next to Graham, and Mags in the back. I asked how he navigated home from there and Graham said, 'I'm a zoomer.' So I asked what a zoomer was and he replied, 'I just zoom up the crease in the map.' Only three years later, of course, Graham and five members of his Embassy Hill team were killed returning from France when he crashed while attempting to land at Elstree Aerodrome near London on a foggy night.

Can-Am in 1973

The only time I drove a really good Can-Am car was in 1973. This was the Roy Woods Racing McLaren M20, the last of the Can-Am McLarens and the best. The previous year it had been Peter Revson's factory car and it was awesome to

BELOW The McLaren M20 was super to drive, but by 1973 we were up against half a dozen turbocharged Porsches. This is Road Atlanta, where I finished fourth.
Bill Warner

drive. But by this time there were half a dozen of the turbocharged Porsches on the grid and there was no way a Chevy-powered car could match them.

Porsches won all eight Can-Am races that year. Bobby Rinzler's entries took the first two, one apiece for Charlie Kemp and George Follmer, and then Penske Racing's Mark Donohue swept up the rest in the incredible 917-30, which had 1,100bhp in race trim and as much as 1,500bhp with the wick turned right up. Everyone decried Porsche for ruining Can-Am, but they just did what the rules permitted.

Watkins Glen that year was one of the best races of my career. I came second to Mark Donohue and beat all the rest of those Porsches, driven by the likes of Jody Scheckter, Hurley Haywood and George Follmer. I was also running second at Mid-Ohio when a drive shaft went, and collected a couple of fourths at Road Atlanta and Edmonton. But my team tried to be too clever and kept putting in ever-bigger engines, boring out the Chevy V8 as far as 9½

ABOVE AND BELOW Two pitlane views at Riverside, the last race of my Can-Am career. Exemplifying how I was 'best of the rest', I qualified fifth, in among the six Porsches in the race, but was soon eliminated by yet another problem with the Chevy V8 that Roy Woods's engine guy bored out to 9½ litres in an attempt to stay on terms with the turbos.
Jutta Fausel (above) and Ray Hutton (below)

OPPOSITE Sharing the Watkins Glen podium with Mark Donohue, who won not only this race but all the others that followed in his Penske-run Porsche 917-30, becoming 1973 Can-Am champion.
David Hobbs collection

litres. Our engine guy was good but the bottom end of the Chevy was not built for that sort of horsepower and we had a lot of trouble with those big pistons as well.

So that was the end of my Can-Am exploits, leaving me with a lot of 'maybes' and 'what ifs'.

Those Can-Am machines were the fastest and most powerful cars I have ever driven. It was also exceptionally dangerous racing, as the safety of these fearsome cars and the circuits they raced on was hardly considered. Their rear tyres were 20 inches across and developed tremendous grip, acceleration was incredible, top speeds exceeded 200mph at many of the tracks, and aerodynamic understanding was in its infancy. The road circuits were pretty disgraceful, with little or no Armco barrier, no run-off and things galore to hit, trees, boulders, ditches, you name it. All drivers owe a tremendous debt of gratitude to Jackie Stewart, who single-handedly made tremendous efforts to improve track safety. His perseverance, though, was not universally applauded, as safety improvements cost a great deal of money.

CHAPTER 11

1966–74
FORMULA 1

I f you look up my Grand Prix statistics, they show my rather sparse record of starting seven Formula 1 World Championship races over a period of seven years and never even scoring a point. At least I finished every race and with today's scoring system I would have received points every time, but in those days points were only given down to sixth place. A further aspect of my Formula 1 career is that I drove in quite a few of the non-championship races that took place in those days and in one of those I stood on the podium.

My first experience of a Formula 1 car came in the winter of 1963/64 when I test drove a factory BRM on a grey day at Silverstone along with Richard Attwood. I always felt it was pretty much a foregone conclusion that Richard would get the drive because his father, Harry, was a close friend of Sir Alfred Owen, the boss of Rubery Owen, the big manufacturing company that owned BRM. It was all very low key, with just a couple of mechanics tending the car and Tony Rudd, who was both team manager and chief designer, timing our laps using a stopwatch attached to his clipboard. Louis Stanley, 'Big Lou', was also there: he was married to Sir Alfred's sister, Jean, and thought he was the big-shot Formula 1 team boss, complete with such an overblown stately bearing that some Americans were convinced he was Lord Louis Stanley. Richard did indeed get

LEFT My last Formula 1 drive came in the Italian Grand Prix at Monza in 1974 in the Yardley-backed McLaren M23, the team's third car alongside its Marlboro-sponsored entries for its pair of World Champion drivers, Emerson Fittipaldi and Denny Hulme.
LAT Images/Rainer Schlegelmilch

ABOVE **My World Championship Formula 1 début came in the 1967 British Grand Prix at Silverstone in this BRM P261 entered by Bernard White's oddly named Team Chamaco Collect. I finished eighth.**
Harold Barker

a drive but not until 1968, when he competed in five races for BRM and finished second to Graham Hill at Monaco, also setting a new lap record. Richard really liked Monaco!

I have already described my first two Formula 1 races in earlier chapters, so a quick recap is all we need here. To show how times changed during my era, the Aintree 200 in 1964 (covered in Chapter 4) was one of five non-championship Formula 1 races that preceded the start of the World Championship calendar that year, and four of them were in Britain. As the Formula 1 entry at Aintree was rather thin, the organisers invited Formula 2 cars to take part as well and my Merlyn was one of those, but the occasion was not very memorable as I started near the back of the grid and lasted only a few laps before the engine broke. However, in Sicily for the Syracuse Grand Prix in 1966 (covered in Chapter 5), I had a super race to third place in a Tim Parnell-run Lotus 25 and stood on the podium alongside the two factory Ferrari drivers, John Surtees and Lorenzo Bandini.

World Championship début

My World Championship début came in 1967 at the British Grand Prix at Silverstone, which suited me very well because I could even sleep in my own bed. I was driving for Bernard White, whose Ferrari 250LM and Ford GT40 I had raced the previous year (see Chapter 5), in an ex-factory BRM P261 with a 2.1-litre V8 in Tasman specification rather than the latest 3-litre V12 version. Somewhat bizarrely, Bernard called his outfit Team Chamaco Collect, after a Spanish bullfighter friend from Marbella called Chamaco with the word Collect added because they were going to collect lots of start money. The car was also used in the film *Grand Prix* and got sprayed in different colours on numerous occasions.

As Tim Parnell was also running a P261 at Silverstone, for Chris Irwin, it was useful to be able to directly compare my performance against another up-and-coming British driver, although Chris, unlike me, had several races under his belt in his P261. So I was quite pleased when I qualified 14th, immediately behind Chris and

in the middle of the grid. Jimmy Clark won the race by a handy margin over Denny Hulme and Chris Amon while I came home eighth, one place behind Chris.

Three weeks later I took part in the German Grand Prix at the Nürburgring, a circuit I knew pretty well from sports car racing, right back to my first visit with my Lotus Elite six years earlier. Owing to the sheer length of the Nordschleife, the organisers at that time accepted Formula 2 entries to pad out the field and I was one of those, driving a Lola T100 belonging to Team Surtees. John did a lot of Formula 2 races that year but on this occasion, of course, he was in a Formula 1 seat, with Honda. The Lola had an experimental BMW engine called the Apfelbeck, with an unusual cylinder-head design featuring a radial valve arrangement, and it worked pretty well.

Jacky Ickx was the star among the Formula 2 runners in Ken Tyrrell's Matra MS5. He got pole position on our separate grid with an incredible qualifying time, quicker than all but two of the

Formula 1 drivers, Jimmy Clark and Denny Hulme, and when the race started he picked off lots of the cars ahead of him to reach sixth place overall, but then something broke in his car's front suspension. Formula 2 honours went to Jackie Oliver, whose Lotus 48 was fifth overall, between Surtees's Honda and Jo Bonnier in his Cooper-Maserati. I finished third in the Formula 2 rankings and 11th overall, once again close behind Chris Irwin in Parnell's Formula 1 BRM.

My next World Championship event was the first ever Canadian Grand Prix, at Mosport Park, another track I knew. Bernard managed to get an entry on a grid bolstered by a few locals and on a grey weekend things again went surprisingly well. I qualified the BRM 12th ahead of Richard Attwood in the works Cooper-Maserati and just behind Chris Irwin in the Parnell BRM. In the race, held in heavy rain, I had a spin and a pit stop to change my misted-up goggles but still managed to finish ninth, sandwiched between two Cooper-Maseratis, Richard's behind and Jo Bonnier's ahead. Up at the front, Jack Brabham

ABOVE **It seems likely that this spectacular photo at Silverstone was taken by one of those fearless photographers visible in the shot on the previous page.**
David Hobbs collection

and Denny Hulme scored a Brabham-Repco 1–2 after Jimmy Clark's Lotus 49 ground to a halt with ignition problems.

The following year there were three British non-championship races — the Race of Champions at Brands Hatch, the International Trophy at Silverstone and the Gold Cup at Oulton Park — and Bernard asked me to drive his BRM P261 in all of them. The car still had the 2.1-litre V8, which gave about 285bhp at its best, whereas by now the 3-litre opposition had as much as 460bhp, so it was always going to be an uphill struggle.

At Brands Hatch on a crisp March day I came home ninth in a race where Bruce McLaren gave his Cosworth-powered McLaren M7A a winning début. At Silverstone the new McLarens were dominant, Denny Hulme winning this time with Bruce second, while I was the sixth of only seven finishers. At Oulton Park I finished sixth again but this time that was also last because of the high drop-out rate, including a certain Derek Bell in a factory Ferrari alongside Chris Amon.

RIGHT With Bernard White in his BRM P261 before the non-championship International Trophy race at Silverstone in 1968. As my 2.1-litre engine was nowhere near competitive with the 3-litre Formula 1 cars, I felt that sixth place was a good result.
David Hobbs collection

BELOW Charging down Silverstone's pits straight in 1968 trailed by Silvio Moser's Brabham BT20.
Harold Barker

A call from Honda

It was a big surprise when Honda phoned. The big motorcycle manufacturer, looking to expand into car production, came into Formula 1 in 1964 but really raised their game in 1967 when they signed John Surtees, who stayed for the 1968 season as well. For the Italian Grand Prix at Monza, where Surtees had given them a famous victory the previous year, they decided they wanted to run a second car and asked me to drive it. While John stuck with his usual V12-powered RA301, Honda wanted to put me in their new alternative design, the innovative RA302 complete with an air-cooled 120-degree V8 — Soichiro Honda had a lot of faith in air-cooled engines — and a monocoque skinned in magnesium for lightness.

Surtees regarded the RA302 as a very interesting technical exercise but refused to race it because he thought it needed more development. Against his wishes, the first RA302 chassis had made its race début two months earlier in the French Grand Prix at Rouen driven by Jo Schlesser and it had ended in tragedy. In atrociously wet conditions Schlesser lost control of the car going down the hill after the pits and it turned over and caught fire with him trapped in his seat. With the magnesium burning fiercely, he never stood a chance. A second car was completed and the plan was for me to try it in practice at the Italian Grand Prix.

Before the Monza race, John and I went to Silverstone with a group of young Japanese engineers to test both the water-cooled V12 RA301 and the air-cooled V8 RA302. The chassis of the RA302 seemed a good concept, with the engine hung from that magnesium monocoque on a sort of fabricated gantry, and with attachments at the bottom of the engine to make it a fully stressed part of the chassis. However, the whole engine/gearbox/gantry arrangement flexed quite badly, and the usual procedures of stiffening springs and roll bars had little effect on the car's handling; in fact it just flexed all the more. As for the engine, to say that its power band was narrow would be an understatement.

ABOVE Over the years I crossed paths a lot with John Surtees, not least at Honda. Seen with John at the wheel, this is the novel Honda RA302 that we both tested at Silverstone and I drove in practice for the Italian Grand Prix at Monza. Its engine was air-cooled and it had a lightweight monocoque skinned in magnesium.
Private collection

RIGHT This close-up taken in the Monza paddock shows how the Honda RA302's air-cooled V8 engine was suspended from a gantry-like structure running between the intake trumpets. Honda used air cooling for its motorcycle engines and was convinced that the technology could transfer to road cars after development in Formula 1.
The Revs Institute for Automotive Research/ Eric della Faille

BELOW My ever-loyal home-town newspaper kept local residents informed when I got the Honda drive.
David Hobbs collection

David Hobbs picked to drive for Honda

DAVID HOBBS, the former Coventry engineering apprentice, is to partner John Surtees in the Honda works team in the Italian Grand Prix next month.

He will also drive for the Japanese company in world championship events in America and Mexico.

Mr. Hobbs, who is 28, formerly lived at Warwick. He now has his home at Upper Boddington, near Banbury.

He said he was thrilled to be picked for the factory team. "It is every racing driver's dream," he said.

It gave no power below 7,800rpm and blew up at 8,600rpm. Drivability was not its strong point.

Testing the alternative cars back to back, I found the more conventional RA301 far superior in every way. In that car I broke Silverstone's prevailing Formula 1 lap record, held by Chris Amon in a Ferrari, so it was obviously a pretty good weapon.

When we got to Monza, Honda wanted me to try both cars again, so quite a lot of time was wasted on Friday and Saturday while I jumped from the V8 to the V12 and back again. Both, of course, had very different characteristics in every department. Finally, late on Saturday, Honda's Mr Nakajima asked me which one I wanted to race. This was a no-brainer, so I did some more laps in the V12 but only ended up 14th on the grid as very little time was left. Apart from anything else, I was mindful that the V12 was also a safer prospect.

This was the famous race where Mario Andretti, driving a third Lotus 49, and Bobby Unser, who had replaced Attwood at BRM, commuted between Italy and America. They practised at Monza, got on a plane and went to Indianapolis to take part in the Hoosier 100 on Saturday afternoon, then jumped out of the cars and flew back on the Sunday morning for the Grand Prix at Monza. Imagine that happening today. At one point in all this I took a taxi with Bobby and his mother, a mainstay of the Indy paddock, and as we drove through Milan, passing some of the most gorgeous historic buildings in the world, Bobby said, 'Ma, look at those terrible old buildings, they need to knock 'em down and shape this dump up a bit.' Mrs Unser was not amused.

When the race started Surtees initially took the lead, from pole, and a furious contest developed, this being Monza before the chicanes with everyone slipstreaming like mad and the lead changing all the time. Then, at the first Lesmo on the eighth lap, Chris Amon's Ferrari crashed, jumped the pathetic guardrail and disappeared into the trees — but to my relief I later saw him watching the race from behind the

ABOVE In the pits at Monza with the Honda RA301, the car with a conventional water-cooled V12 engine. I chose to race it in the Italian Grand Prix in preference to the air-cooled RA302.
David Hobbs collection

LEFT In the race at Monza I moved up the field nicely and kept going until my Honda's engine let go at half distance. My team-mate John Surtees went out early in the race after becoming involved in an incident while trying to avoid Chris Amon's Ferrari.
LAT Images

ABOVE A typical
Monza slipstreaming
bunch, with me
holding off Jack
Brabham and
Jochen Rindt in their
Brabhams and Piers
Courage and Pedro
Rodríguez in the BRMs.
David Hobbs collection

barrier. Surtees was right with him and crashed as well. I was running a good race and moving up the field but at half distance the engine expired so that was the end of what could have been a useful result.

Honda had spoken encouragingly about John and I doing a full season with them in 1969, but at the end of 1968 they withdrew from Formula 1 to concentrate their energies on developing a new production engine to conform with upcoming US legislation on emissions. I could have had a very full season in 1969, as I continued to race for Gulf in the Ford GT40s and Mirages and for Surtees in Formula 5000.

I did not take part in any Formula 1 races in 1969. The following year, as illustrated in Chapter 7, I took part in Silverstone's International Trophy race, which was another of those non-championship Formula 1 events with other cars added to boost numbers, in this case from Formula 5000. It was a disaster because the Surtees TS5 broke early in the first race of this two-part contest.

Racing with Penske

The next time I got the chance to race in Formula 1 was at the end of the 1971 season in the US Grand Prix at Watkins Glen. This was an entry from Roger Penske with backing from Kirk White, who was a partner in our Ferrari 512M effort that year (see Chapter 8). It was a bit of a botch.

Two weeks earlier Penske Racing had fielded a McLaren M19A for Mark Donohue's Grand Prix début in the Canadian Grand Prix at Mosport and he had finished a brilliant third. The next weekend the Penske team was scheduled to run a USAC race at Trenton and then switch back to the McLaren for the Glen another week later. However, the USAC race was rained off and rescheduled for the same date as the US Grand Prix. The team deliberated about what to do and asked me to step in should they decide that Mark would do Trenton. In the end Mark tried to do both, the two circuits being about 300 miles apart, and really messed me about. I practised in the M19A for about five laps, then Mark drove about 50, mucking around with it, putting in his beloved locked diff and so on. Finally, he decided he was going to do the Trenton race after all and leave me to drive in the Grand Prix.

I had done no set-up for a track that I knew pretty well by that point and because I had done so few laps I was only 22nd on the grid. In the end I finished 10th but we could have done so much better had I had the use of the car in the lead-up to the race.

Swansong in 1974

Three years passed before I raced again in a Grand Prix and this was a somewhat bittersweet arrangement because it came after Mike Hailwood's big crash at the Nürburgring driving a third factory McLaren M23.

This was the year McLaren had managed to snatch Marlboro tobacco sponsorship from BRM, but the team still had a contract with the cosmetics company Yardley, its previous main sponsor. So Teddy Mayer and Phil Kerr, the

ABOVE Despite deciding to race at Trenton rather than Watkins Glen, Mark Donohue spent most of Formula 1 practice in the McLaren M19A that I was going to race. It was very frustrating and in this shot it shows.
David Hobbs collection

BELOW At Watkins Glen I finished 10th in the Penske-run McLaren, but with a decent amount of practice I could have been in the points.
LAT Images

ABOVE The 1974 McLaren line-up at a pre-season photo shoot. Johnny Rutherford (foreground) and I represent the team's Indy campaign while Denny Hulme (centre) and Mike Hailwood are the face of Formula 1 — but somehow new signing Emerson Fittipaldi missed this official gathering.
LAT Images

commercial guy, put together a deal to run a third McLaren in Yardley colours for Mike. Meanwhile, Emerson Fittipaldi had jumped ship from Lotus to drive alongside Denny Hulme in the Marlboro-liveried cars. It turned out to be a good move for Emerson because he went on to win the World Championship that year.

Driving the third car in a team is never going to be great but Mike started the season well with a podium finish in the South African Grand Prix and was having a reasonable year when he crashed in the German Grand Prix at the Nürburgring and finished up in the Adenau *Krankenhaus* with a broken leg in the next bed to Howden Ganley, who had also crashed, driving the horrible Japanese Maki.

As I had done a good job for McLaren at Indy a few months earlier, I got the call to act as 'super sub' for the upcoming Austrian and Italian Grands Prix. Formula 1 was in a healthy situation back then with more entries than places on the grid and I was determined that I was not going to be one of the six who failed to make the cut.

The then-fabulous Österreichring — now the much shorter Red Bull Ring — was new to me. I qualified 17th while Emerson was third and Denny sixth. Back then, before separate qualifying sessions were introduced, all practice laps counted and the grid was simply decided by everyone's best from all the laps. I was not helped by the fact that it was my first time at this daunting track and I had Henri Pescarolo hanging around the McLaren pit and mumbling, '*I can go much faster than 'e ees going, they should put me in ze car.*' Additionally I had Phil Kerr 'engineering' my M23 and he did not want to make any of the changes I suggested. It once again confirmed that my nice-guy approach did not work. To be successful, you have to be an asshole, plain and simple, and I should have insisted on any changes I wanted. It was not as if there was any data being collected to prove me wrong — in those days the driver was the data. But I did not want to rock the boat. In the end I had a pretty clean race, overtook a lot of cars and finished seventh, just out of the points again.

Monza was more familiar territory but I had various problems in practice and started down in 23rd place. Again my race pace was good as I pulled my M23 up through the field to finish ninth, just behind Graham Hill. Emerson was second, just a few feet behind Ronnie Peterson, while Denny came home sixth.

McLaren decided to put Jochen Mass in the car for the last two races in North America. This was a big personal disappointment because Mosport Park and Watkins Glen were two very familiar tracks. I do not know why McLaren chose Mass instead of me as he had raced most of the season for Surtees without much luck and with lots of retirements. In 'my' Yardley McLaren he finished 16th at Mosport and seventh at Watkins Glen, and I like to think I would have done better than that. Anyway they signed him as their number two for the following year.

My little sojourn with McLaren ended up being my last two Grands Prix and left some unanswered questions.

LEFT After Mike Hailwood was injured at the Nürburgring in 1974, I was drafted in for two races in the Yardley-sponsored McLaren M23. Here I am at the first, the Austrian Grand Prix, with Phil Kerr, who served as my race engineer — but he was better in his normal role of looking after sponsors. *LAT Images*

BELOW My two McLaren outings in 1974 both yielded finishes, in seventh place at the Österreichring and, as seen in this shot of heavy braking in the M23, ninth at Monza. *LAT Images*

CHAPTER 12

1976–81
ROOF OVER MY HEAD

Apart from my very early years and with the important exception of the fabulous Gulf Ford GT40s, most of my racing had been done with the wind buffeting my crash helmet — but all that was about to change. For the rest of my career, right through to my final professional race, I had a roof over my head and a windscreen in front of me.

In 1976 I not only got the chance to race in the US for BMW and take part in the Daytona 500 in a Chevrolet but I also became a Jaguar factory driver. That seemed appropriate for a former Jaguar apprentice but it turned out to be a great disappointment.

Big cats

Jaguar decided to run two factory cars in the 1976 European Touring Car Championship (ETCC), using the skill and experience of Broadspeed, a very successful team run by Ralph Broad, someone I had known for a long time and a fine engineer, an engine man, very prickly and funny. Ralph had a good track record in this championship and others, having won with Minis, Anglias and Cortinas.

For a brief period Jaguar made a two-door coupé version of the XJ12 saloon. Called the XJ-C, it was a pretty, swoopy-looking car with a very powerful 5.3-litre V12 engine. Jaguar thought it would be an ideal racer but the

LEFT The three years when I raced a BMW 320i Turbo, from 1977 to 1979, were good times. Here, at Road Atlanta in April 1978, Porsche 935s had just been admitted to the IMSA series and I am surrounded by a gaggle of them, headed by Peter Gregg (59) with Hurley Haywood tucked in behind.
Bill Warner

ABOVE As a former
Jaguar apprentice who
had early success in my
father's XK140, it was a
dream to drive for the
Coventry marque in 1976.
Wearing a pinstripe suit,
I attended the March
1976 London launch at
which great success was
foolishly promised.

Getty Images/Popperfoto

programme was typical of Jaguar — a screw-up.
As I explained in Chapter 5, the company had
earlier eschewed a return to racing when it had
a golden opportunity to do so, with the XJ13 that
had proved so fast at MIRA. Now, more than
10 years since the XJ13's gestation, there was
not really any model in Jaguar's range that was
remotely racy except for this coupé. Jaguar at
the time was owned by British Leyland, a huge
conglomerate run by the high-profile chairman
Lord Stokes (formerly Sir Donald Stokes), who
surrounded himself with myriad flunkeys, none
of whom knew anything about racing.

Jaguar's racing return with a two-car team was
announced with a massive fanfare at the Hilton
Hotel on London's Park Lane in March 1976. It
turned out to be a massive failure.

Even the magic of Ralph Broad, who extracted
incredible horsepower from the engine, was not
sufficient. The rules of the championship did not
allow a special spaceframe chassis to be built,
as Chevrolet or Ford would do for the Trans-
Am, so the starting point was the XJ-C's regular
monocoque structure. Because it was such a big,
heavy car, everything was stressed and things
kept breaking. It needed massive brakes, but this
caused problems with suspension points ripping
out of the chassis. Those were beefed up but that
just made the thing even heavier. Then engine
cooling proved to be a huge issue.

Testing and development went so badly that
the first ETCC race came and went without us.
In desperation Ralph decided to enter Derek Bell
and me in the second round, the Salzburgring
Four Hours in April, in one of Broadspeed's
Triumph Dolomite Sprints, with which the
team had swept the board the previous year.
The Austrian track was a challenging, very
picturesque one with lots of elevation change
and some good corners running up and back
down a narrow valley. Even this outing went
belly-up as the engine failed early in the race.

In the end the Broadspeed Jaguar team only
did one race that year, with one XJ-C. That was
the eighth round in September, the Tourist
Trophy at Silverstone, where I was teamed

with Derek again. We proved that the car was fast by taking pole position, but in the race we floundered around until the right rear wheel came off when the half shaft broke.

That was it for me and Jaguar. All the no-shows put a big dent in my plans for the season, which ended up being a bit of a sparse one. The Jaguar effort limped into 1977, which saw a string of retirements interspersed with just two finishes, the better of which was a second place for Derek Bell and Andy Rouse at the Nürburgring.

Beginnings with BMW

My first race of 1976 was the Daytona 24 Hours, where I had last competed with Roger Penske's Ferrari 512M five years earlier. This time I was in a very promising BMW thanks to a deal put together by Mike Bailey, a good friend.

I first met Mike when I was at Riverside, California in 1970 for one of my early Trans-Am races. Afterwards we had a chat in the failing light and I remember having to pause every few minutes while a huge Boeing B-52 bomber took off from nearby March Air Force Base and

ABOVE The V12-engined Jaguar XJ-C coupé built by Broadspeed to take on BMW was too heavy and unreliable. After various false starts, Derek Bell and I gave the car its début in the Tourist Trophy at Silverstone. We took pole and led the race but I had a driveshaft break.
McKlein

LEFT At a time when unrest was rife within British Leyland, Barry Foley has this take on Jaguar's troubled racing programme in his weekly 'Catchpole' cartoon strip in *Autosport* magazine.
Courtesy of Autosport

RIGHT Coca-Cola sponsorship provided a Daytona double in 1976: NASCAR driver Benny Parsons joined me in this works BMW CSL for the 24 Hours and a fortnight later I made my NASCAR début with Benny's team in the famous '500'.
David Hobbs collection

BELOW Chatting with BMW Motorsport Director Jochen Neerpasch in the Florida sunshine in 1976 —two races in the CSL led directly to three rewarding seasons with the 320i Turbo.
David Hobbs collection

flew low over our heads. That was an awesome sight, watching those B-52s that could fly non-stop around the world armed to the teeth with hydrogen bombs. Once I walked down to the base and looked through the fence to see them sitting there full of fuel and ready to take off, their massive wings drooping down to the ground like great birds of prey.

Mike, thanks to his close ties with Coca-Cola, put together sponsorship for me to share a works-supported BMW CSL with NASCAR star Benny Parsons in the Daytona 24 Hours. The car was run on BMW's behalf by long-time Porsche racer Peter Gregg thanks to an arrangement made with Jochen Neerpasch, the young and dynamic BMW Motorsports boss against whom I had once raced. As well as Peter himself, the team finished up with two other top drivers in the shape of Brian Redman and John Fitzpatrick. I drove with Benny because the Coca-Cola deal included a NASCAR outing for me in his back-up car in the Daytona 500, which followed the endurance classic just as it does today.

The 24 Hours turned out to be a pretty mixed-up race. Somehow water had got into the circuit's central fuel supply and every car suffered, some worse than others. Benny and I finished 10th after being stranded out on the track with fuel-related problems, but Redman and Fitzpatrick won the race driving Gregg's car, as he was taken ill during the event.

Going straight from one debacle to another, I became one of the few Brits ever to race in the Daytona 500, the great NASCAR classic. It was pretty disastrous because the second-string car run by Benny's team, the L.G. DeWitt outfit, was awful. Whereas Benny was driving the latest Chevrolet Impala, my car was an older and well-used Chevelle. The crew chief was a guy called Tex Wood, who was about as redneck as you can get. He wore snakeskin boots, a scruffy old oily T-shirt and a big hat. His tool kit consisted of a hammer and not much else.

While Benny and the other regulars were going around at about 184mph, I was doing 178mph. So Benny said to me, 'You must be doing something wrong', and got in the car. He did 178mph too. 'Well, that seems to be about what it'll do,' he said as he walked back to his Impala. But I drove it anyway.

I did quite well in the frenetic 125-mile qualifying race on the Thursday. As we came off Turn Four for the first time, with me right in the middle of the pack, everyone ahead scraped either down the wall or against each other and there was debris and rubber flying everywhere. After thinking that NASCAR might not be such a good idea after all, I managed to hang on and finished eighth. I was still only doing 178mph and the top guys were in a race of their own. Commentator Chris Economaki was one of those who once said Formula 1 is unfair because you can only win if you are in a top car, but the same is true of NASCAR.

My position in the 125 put me on the eighth row for the 500. In the big race the rear roll-bar link broke, stiffening up the front too much. That made the nose of the car start to push severely and eventually, after 68 of the 200 laps,

ABOVE Benny and I had a troubled race at Daytona but we did finish, in 10th place. Clearly one of us got a whack from another car at some point.
Bill Warner

the right front tyre popped, pushing me into the wall at Turn One.

I had been to all the drivers' meetings where we were warned not to let a wrecked car roll down the banking, and certainly I was not about to let that happen because I could see that these guys were all madmen. I kept the thing glued to the wall, looking in the mirror until the exit of Turn Two, where I let the Chevelle slide down to the apron to get out of the way. Tex fiddled around with it for about half an hour before we parked it behind the wall. This was the year Richard Petty and David Pearson had their coming-together on the last lap, with Pearson winning by wobbling across the line. Benny, meanwhile, finished third.

I did another NASCAR race at Michigan in August, this time in a Ford for a team in Richmond, Virginia owned by Junie Donlavey, who devoted his life to NASCAR. I qualified about midfield, but when the race started the car seemed to come alive and I was passing people left, right and centre until only Cale Yarborough

ABOVE Riding the banking in the 1976 Daytona 500 in the DeWitt Chevrolet Chevelle. I went pretty well in this disappointing car in the 125-mile qualifying race, finishing eighth, but ended up against the wall in the 500 itself. *David Hobbs collection*

LEFT A rear roll-bar link broke during the Daytona 500, putting the front right tyre under extra duress. Eventually it blew, sending me into the wall. *David Hobbs collection*

and Darrell Waltrip were in front of me. This was more like it! Then I spun coming out of Turn Four, round and round, the full 360, back facing in the correct direction and straight into pitlane. Old Junie looked through the window net, eyes as wide as saucers, and said, 'That's the finest bit of driving I ever seen.' I just batted my eyes and said, 'It was nothing.' Meanwhile, my heart was about to explode! The race went rapidly downhill from there as the wheel nuts on the right rear were not tightened and the wheel fell off on my out lap.

The Coca-Cola deal also included a second race with the BMW 'Batmobile'. This was the Sebring 12 Hours, where Benny Parsons and I teamed up again while Peter Gregg and Hurley Haywood shared the other car. Much to Peter's chagrin, I shot off into the lead and held it for some time until the vibration damper on the front of the crankshaft gave up. The only comment from the BMW crew was, 'Oh yeah, they're always doing that.' I thought that was weird — why not fix it?

A boost with BMW

At the end of 1976 Teddy Mayer called to ask if I would be interested in driving a factory BMW 320i Turbo that McLaren was going to run on behalf of BMW in North America in the IMSA GT category. I think part of Teddy's *raison d'être* was that I was starting to become known for my television commentary work and this could parlay into publicity. It all sounded most promising and I agreed to join.

My first obligation, early that winter, was to go to Paul Ricard in the south of France to try a 320i, at that stage still without the turbo engine. After a few laps I came in and reported that I thought we needed to stiffen the rear roll bar, to which they said, 'We don't have a rear roll bar! The way the car is designed and sprung it doesn't need a roll bar. We can adjust it in other ways.' That was surprising but I accepted it.

The second assignment, in January 1977, was to attend a week-long pre-season driver training and fitness programme, something that supremo Neerpasch considered very important. Virtually every BMW driver at national and international level came along and it all started in a car park at BMW's headquarters in Munich. There, lined up in echelon, were 20 examples of the new BMW 323i, the latest addition to the 3-series range with a six-cylinder engine. We were paired up and allocated our cars for the drive to our training base in St Moritz, about two hours away in Switzerland. Jochen then proceeded to give us all a severe pep talk dressed in his ankle-length leather coat, hands behind back, striding up and down the line of drivers, looking just a bit like… well, you know. His theme was that we were all driving BMWs for the company and had to conduct ourselves safely and with the utmost courtesy to all other road users. *'To make sure,'* he said, *'I vill lead ze way, so follow me.'*

We all climbed aboard and waited for Jochen, who stuck his 323i in first gear, dropped the clutch and, with wheels spinning, roared out of the factory gate. It was unbelievable! So we all followed, hurtling through Munich, then into open country at a steady 110mph, up the mountain into Hans Stuck's home town of Garmisch-Partenkirchen, through there in about 30 seconds, and on towards the Swiss border. I was following Ronnie Peterson's car and his passenger, Gunnar Nilsson, kept looking over his shoulder at me with a mad smile and lots of thumbs-ups. When we reached the Swiss border, all the German drivers sailed straight through, but not me. *'Ah, Herr Hobbs, vehr are you going, anyzing to declare?'*

By then I was panicking because I had no idea where I had to go if I lost the group. Anyway, I got over that delay and on we went, still at relentless speed. Then it started to snow. First Harald Grohs spun off, much to Gunnar's amusement, then a couple more cars got right out of shape. Eventually we drove into this pretty-as-a-picture village — narrow streets, bottle-glass windows in the shops, mothers shopping, pushing strollers and holding *das kinder* by the hand. There was slush on the road and as we roared along the streets it splashed over the pedestrians, one car after another. So much for decorum.

BELOW My first race in the BMW 320i was the 1977 Daytona 24 Hours, sharing this non-turbo version with Ronnie Peterson and Sam Posey. We were out by quarter distance with an engine problem.
Bill Warner

After the village we broke out onto a high, sunny, snow-free area of meadows and Ronnie and I realised that we were on our own. We stopped to confer and he said, in his lilting English, that we had better turn round. Not far back down the road we found the rest of our group standing around looking sombre. Jochen had his hands behind his back again and a very sheepish Marc Surer was staring at a rather bent Fiat. The driver of the Fiat was bleeding profusely. Then a large lorry pulled up behind our cars and an enormous, surly-looking driver got out, jack handle in hand. At this point Jochen suggested that we might leg it to the hotel and meet later.

This was going to be a serious training week — up early to swim, green tea and muesli, then gym and cross-country skiing, gruel and a nap, more swimming and more gruel, then bed. However, on our first evening in the hotel lobby I encountered Ronnie, in an amazing full-length fur coat, with Hans Stuck, saying, 'Are you ready, Hobby? We're off out for a night on the town!' I am no shrinking violet but even I had to decline

BELOW For my second BMW outing of 1977, the turbo installation was deemed ready to race. After starting only 28th on the grid at Road Atlanta, it felt a great result to work myself up to fourth place in this 100-mile race — one position gained every couple of laps!
Bill Warner

this invitation, so off they went, as they did every night of our stay.

When we finally got around to the racing season, the 320i Turbo was to be run and operated from McLaren Engines North America, based in Livonia, Michigan. They had some really great people there. Tyler Alexander, who had been with Bruce McLaren from the outset, ran the factory, Gary Knudsen was the top engine boffin ably assisted by Wiley McCoy, and the team manager was Roger Bailey. I had known Roger since we first met at Snetterton when I was racing Mum's Morris Oxford. Roger was about 20 then, the same as me, and a mechanic on some bloke's car, but soon he moved into Formula 1, first with Cooper, working alongside a certain Ron Dennis, then Tyrrell, then Ferrari with Chris Amon.

Our first race was the Daytona 24 Hours, where I was teamed with Ronnie Peterson and Sam Posey. Like so many racing programmes, the whole affair was running late, so for this race the car was a non-turbo version. Even without the turbo, the 320i did not last any time at all and

we soon retired with an engine problem.

Our first race in turbo form was in April at Road Atlanta. Like many of the IMSA rounds, this was a short race, only 100 miles, so I drove alone. The car was pretty quick, with good performance, but it had terrible turbo lag because it had a great big single turbocharger on its little 2.0-litre four-cylinder engine. When the turbo was off it had absolutely no power at all, because it had low compression, but once the turbo boost came up it had all the compression you could ever need. I started 28th on the grid and finished fourth, just off the podium.

As the car had a distinctly wobbly feel at Road Atlanta, it obviously needed some suspension help. So Roger had the team put a rear roll bar on it! When the folks in Germany found out, they gave Roger tremendous grief for doing that and told him to remove it because 'the car wasn't designed to have it', but he stuck to his guns.

The next event was at Laguna Seca and the handling was transformed thanks to that rear bar. I took pole, breaking the old GT record by about five seconds. Come the race, I shot off into the lead, but the engine eventually broke. It had very small spark plugs that could not stand the pressure and heat, and one blew out. But clearly the potential was there.

That year I won four 100-milers, at Mid-Ohio and Sears Point, and then at Road Atlanta and Laguna Seca on return visits to those two tracks. Other than the Mosport Six Hours, a World Championship for Makes event where I finished eighth with Ronnie, I won whenever the car held together, and it was particularly good on shorter tracks. BMW were pretty happy with it all. We were up against the Porsche 934, which was a Group 4 car, but we could easily handle that. The bigger challenge was Al Holbert's Chevrolet Monza, which was far more reliable and went on to take the championship.

Spectators loved the BMW because on the over-run huge bursts of flame would come out of the exhaust beneath the driver's door as soon as you touched the throttle again. The turbo itself was right by the footwell on the driver's side and

your feet became incredibly hot because the thing reached at least 1,000 degrees, so we had to fiddle around with that until it was tolerable. We had a bit of a problem with the aero as well. There was a big wing on the back but the car had quite a lot of understeer so eventually we came out with a huge cow-catcher for the front. This was very effective but it was all guesswork. 'What do you think? Is that long enough? Should we make it three inches or five inches? Let's make it five inches, so if it's too long we can cut a bit off.'

Meanwhile in Germany BMW were running a similar programme for Stuck and Peterson. Their car kept blowing up and BMW eventually put it down to the idea that the quality of fuel was better in America than in Europe. Even the German car eventually got a rear roll bar as well, and around the Nordschleife at the Nürburgring Ronnie was 19 seconds a lap quicker with the bar than he had been without it. So we were vindicated on that little issue.

I remember having dinner at the end of 1977 with IMSA founder John Bishop and some of our BMW people. We were talking about the new Porsche 935, which that year had appeared in numbers in Europe and started to clean up. We knew that if the 935 was admitted to the IMSA series we would be chopped liver, because it had a much bigger engine — a 3-litre initially but with potential to be enlarged — and its flat-six format was perfect for twin turbos. John promised us that he would not let the 935 into the series but Jo Hoppen, competition director for the Porsche/Audi/Volkswagen combine in North America, got all over John and he buckled.

Despite being up against Porsche 935s in 1978, BMW carried on and I won twice. The race I remember best that year, partly because it was one of the wins, was at a circuit that was new to me, Hallett in Oklahoma. After flying to Tulsa, we drove 35 miles west to this track in the middle of nowhere. If you have seen the movie *Oklahoma!* you will, like me, imagine attractive vistas of cornfields, but all I saw was ugly scrub, with stubby little trees and tumbleweed blowing about — and masses of small oil pipelines just a few

inches across but visible wherever you looked. We arrived at our motel very late, after midnight, and the door was answered by an Indian with a perfect English accent. It turned out that he had moved to the US from Northampton, just a few miles from my home in England, and was building up a chain of motels, with five or six of them already. It was very strange. As for the race, Hallett, a short track, just 1.8 miles, suited the BMW perfectly and I won easily.

My other win was at Sears Point in California, just north of San Francisco. This was another début visit — and I won most times I went there subsequently. Something about Sears Point and I just seemed to hit it off. In 1978 I had a great race with Don Whittington in a Porsche 935 and beat him to the flag by two seconds with everyone else a lap behind.

The little BMW suited me extremely well and I really enjoyed driving it. Once we had the bigger spoiler on the front, the car would rotate very nicely, and when we increased the size of the rear wheels, to 18-inch diameter, it was even

better. The engine gave about 675–700bhp, which is a lot for a small four-cylinder turbo, and it had a beautiful little five-speed ZF gearbox. As it was not possible to change the gear ratios, all we could do was alter the final drive; for a fast place like Brainerd (formerly Donnybrooke) you used a tall ratio and for somewhere like Laguna Seca you had a much lower one.

As in 1977, we also took in the Watkins Glen Six Hours, a World Championship for Makes round, and again my co-driver was Ronnie Peterson. This 1978 season was the one in which he and Mario Andretti were pretty much cleaning up in Formula 1 with the ground-effect Lotus 79. On his way to the Glen, Ronnie had stayed at Mario's place in Nazareth, Pennsylvania and was very impressed, telling me that he had never seen so many motor-driven toys.

Driving with Ronnie was a joy but it always felt a bit awkward that I was the one who set up the car. I would say, 'Look you're the Formula 1 star, you should do it.' Ronnie would reply, 'Hobby, it's your car, you set it up how you like and I'll

just drive it.' Considering his legendary speed, I was always pleased that our lap times were very similar, although it seemed a bit suspicious to me at the time.

Race day dawned and of course the team wanted our star to do the first stint, so off Ronnie went. Unfortunately he did go off, and just tagged some catch-fencing. One of the safety fads of the time, this type of chicken-wire fencing was put up in several rows, secured by wooden posts, with the posts for the first row partially sawn through so that they snapped easily in order to slowly arrest an errant car. Anyway, some chicken wire hooked itself around the BMW's rear axle and then wound up around the propshaft. Ronnie appeared in pitlane dragging about 50 feet of catch-fencing with him, complete with wooden posts bouncing along.

So that was another race prematurely terminated and we all went home. It was the last time I saw Ronnie. Two months later he died from injuries sustained in a pile-up on the opening lap of the Italian Grand Prix at Monza.

We had a third season with the BMW 320i Turbo in 1979. It started well with a nice four-race sequence of results: second place at Laguna Seca, another Hallett win, then seconds again at Lime Rock and Brainerd. After all of our short races, the big question towards the end of the season was whether we should compete in the Pabst 500 at Road America. We all wondered, 'Should we even bother to go? A 500-mile race? It will never last.' Luckily we decided to give it a go and the team hired Derek Bell, endurance expert without peer. We won, much to the surprise of us all. Just finishing the race had been our target.

Winning that race was extraordinary. We beat some good teams too. The black Interscope Porsche 935, winner of that year's Daytona 24 Hours, was a bit faster than us, thanks to the long straights at Road America, but kept dropping back for various reasons. Finally one of the drivers, Ted Field or Milt Minter, bounced off some scenery and had to come in to straighten out bodywork. Barring problems, we were then home and dry because they could not catch us again.

BELOW Here at Sears Point in 1979 I am pretty close to the wall as I chase Bill Whittington's yellow Porsche 935, just visible beyond the turquoise back-marker 911 Carrera RSR of Luis Mendez.
David Hobbs collection

LEFT The BMW 320i Turbo was too fragile for us to embark on long-distance races with any optimism, so it was astonishing that it went the distance to win the 500-mile race at Road America in 1979. Derek Bell holds aloft our Pabst Trophy, presented by former racer and beer magnate Augie Pabst. *David Hobbs collection*

LEFT In my second and third IMSA seasons with BMW, 1978 and 1979, the Porsche 935 became the car of choice and Peter Gregg used his to great effect to become champion both years. Here Gregg (left) has a post-victory pow-wow at Road Atlanta in 1979 with Ed Conway, the track's long-time commentator. The man who finished third looks like he would prefer to be elsewhere. *David Hobbs collection*

Gary Knudsen always felt that he could have got a lot more horsepower out of the engine but told me that BMW would not allow him to. In due course this motor became the basis of BMW's 1.5-litre turbo Formula 1 engine that Nelson Piquet used to such good effect in his Brabham to win the World Championship in 1983. Our programme was a convenient test and development deal for that Grand Prix campaign — and what followed showed that we could have had a lot more horsepower.

Our McLaren team also felt they could have made other significant changes to improve the car considerably. They looked at the rule book and thought they could lower the 320i by raising the floor and dropping the sills — which is what Zakspeed did in the end with their Ford Capri. They cut and chopped it so that the whole thing was much lower and smaller, like a sort of 90 per cent replica of the real thing. BMW should have done the same. Instead they terminated the programme at the end of the 1979 season.

BELOW There was an odd postscript to my racing with baby BMWs. Back in Britain in 1979, I was asked by Bob Driver, an old acquaintance who lived in the next village, to do a round of the County Championship, a one-make series for mildly modified 323i models. Bob owned a BMW dealership in Suffolk — hence the county allegiance.
David Hobbs collection

French interlude

Seven years after my previous run in the Le Mans 24 Hours, with Matra, for the 1979 race I was invited to drive one of a pair of Mirage entries for Harley Cluxton's team, sharing with Derek Bell. The car, the M10, was basically the same design as the one in which Derek and Jacky Ickx had won Le Mans four years earlier, but with smoother, lower, open bodywork designed by John Horsman. It was hoped to run these seasoned machines with Renault turbo engines, as in the previous couple of years, but in the end they reverted to the Cosworth DFV with which they had started life.

It was my 40th birthday on the Saturday of the race and the previous evening Harley and his main sponsor, Ford France, put on a terrific party in the Moët et Chandon hospitality suite. It was a bright spot of an otherwise difficult weekend.

The Mirage was certainly fast and we qualified fifth, the best non-Porsche. For a couple of hours during early evening our car led the race, but then an exhaust manifold cracked and put us back to

about sixth place. By now it was proving to be a tough race for me personally as I was having real difficulty with extreme wind buffeting around my head, because I am taller than Derek and the car was tailored around him. It showed in our respective lap times, so after the sister Mirage retired Horsman decided to transfer one of its drivers, Vern Schuppan, to our car. During the night, when the weather was terrible, Vern lost control in the Porsche curves and hit the barrier after the headlights suddenly switched off, probably because of water interfering with the electrics. He got back to the pits for bodywork repairs but by the time our car resumed it was way down the field. After a fuel stop with less than an hour to go, Derek was ready to set off for his last stint but the engine refused to fire. *Fin.*

I was as disappointed by my performance at Le Mans as Horsman was, but it had a silver lining. The following year I had a one-off drive for Roy Woods, my old Can-Am entrant, in the Lumbermens 500 at Mid-Ohio with one Brian Herman Thomas Redman, who had re-emerged from enforced retirement after breaking his neck three years earlier. Our car was a Lola T333, a Formula 5000 single-seater that had been converted to Can-Am spec. One of the main rivals was Brad Friselle's Frisbee run by John Horsman and driven by Hurley Haywood and John Morton. Horsman made the strategic error of thinking that, after Le Mans, my best days were behind me, and told his drivers not to worry about our car as I was driving. To his chagrin, Brian and I won handily.

M1 mediocrity

In 1980 BMW went into a bit of a hiatus and it was a very thin year for me. Jim Patterson, BMW's competition chief in North America, was very keen to continue racing and wanted to keep me with BMW. As the BMW/McLaren partnership had ceased, we were now dealing with a group up in Connecticut, basically a club racing outfit who were friends of Jim's. Now the plan was to run a BMW M1 in Group 5 form as opposed to the more standard Group 4 version that BMW

ABOVE After seven years away from Le Mans, I had a good opportunity for the 1979 race, sharing this Mirage M10 with Derek Bell. We led for a couple of hours on the Saturday evening but then a succession of problems ruined things.
LAT Images

ABOVE Sharing with Brian Redman, so often a rival but on two occasions a driving partner, I had a very satisfying win in the Lumbermens 500 at Mid-Ohio in 1980, driving a Lola T333 for my one-time Can-Am entrant Roy Woods.
David Hobbs collection

RIGHT Post-race with Brian, happy with our day's work in the Lumbermens 500 at Mid-Ohio.
Michael Botsko

raced in front of Formula 1 crowds in the Procar Championship of 1979 and 1980.

Nothing much happened with the M1 until 1981, when we ran it in three of the big endurance races in North America. At the Daytona 24 Hours, sharing with Marc Surer and Dieter Quester, we got the car to the finish, albeit only in 16th place. At the Watkins Glen Six Hours, this time with just Surer and me driving, we had to park it with an engine problem. Finally I drove the M1 with Hans Stuck in the Mosport Six Hours, where we qualified a good seventh in the thick of a load of 935s, but when we got to the track on the morning of the race the throttle slides were jammed shut and we could not start the engine — and could not take up our grid position. Eventually the mechanics freed up the slides and we started the race many laps down, both driving like maniacs. We finished 14th, but we were way behind people we had out-qualified. I really enjoyed driving with Hans, one of the best endurance racers and extremely quick in anything.

I also raced a BMW M1 twice in Europe that year. The car was owned by Steve O'Rourke, the astute manager of the band *Pink Floyd*, through his EMKA Productions company. After Derek Bell, Steve and I finished second in the Silverstone Six Hours, I had high hopes for the Le Mans 24 Hours. Then Derek got the call from Porsche to partner Jacky Ickx in a 936, which was terrific for him but unfortunate for me. They duly went on and won the race. Meanwhile, Steve instead hired Eddie Jordan, who at the time was a driver but became better known for running his own Formula 1 team and then becoming a pundit for British TV.

I had the flu and felt like rubbish the whole Le Mans weekend, and my mood was not helped by the car going most of the distance before the engine expired with a couple of hours left. As far as I was concerned that went against a major rule of endurance racing: if your car is going to break, you want it to do so early in a race, not after you have dragged around all day and all night. Steve only drove on the Sunday morning as he had been busy with a *Pink Floyd* concert in London

the previous evening, so I did long spells at the wheel before his arrival. There was an annoyance during the second hour when a spin at the Esses — my only one in 20 Le Mans visits — resulted in a long stop for repairs to the nose and radiator, dropping us right back through the field.

Another BMW adventure that year was to take part in the most famous race in Australia, the renowned Bathurst 1000, which has always attracted a huge crowd. There I drove a BMW 635CSi in black-and-gold John Player Special colours with one of the big Aussie stars, Allan Grice. In fact I went back again the following year with the same team, this time sharing with another famous Aussie racer, Jim Richards.

The start of IMSA GTP

As well as racing the M1 in 1981, we had another BMW programme. Two years earlier IMSA's John Bishop had got all the team owners together at Hallett for a meeting and announced a new idea. Instead of having the series dominated by highly modified GT cars such as Porsche 935s, which

ABOVE In 1981 I twice drove *Pink Floyd* manager Steve O'Rourke's BMW M1 in Europe. Here, at Silverstone for the Six Hours, Derek Bell (right) joined Steve and me in the car and we finished second. My BMW chum Hans Stuck (left) drove another M1.
David Hobbs collection

BELOW Le Mans in 1981 was a big disappointment. After Derek Bell was poached by Porsche — and won the race — his place in Steve O'Rourke's M1 was taken by Eddie Jordan. We were a long way down the field throughout and the engine blew with two hours to go.
LAT Images

would remain as a class in the series, he would introduce a 'GT Prototype' class, for proper sports cars with closed bodywork. For the 1981 season the GTP era came to life.

Jim Patterson did a deal with March to run a BMW-powered GTP car derived from the M1. The March M1C was rather undeveloped and I think BMW in Germany never really wanted to do it. The 3.5-litre straight-six engine was totally inadequate compared with the 350 cubic inch Chevy V8s we were up against. It was probably 200bhp short — not even close. Our first test was in Britain, at Donington Park, and some young kid was hurtling around in a Formula 3 car with everyone watching, saying, 'He's the next big thing.' That was Stefan Johansson when he was about 19. Now he is in his 50s and still racing Le Mans prototypes after a long career in Formula 1 and Indycars.

My first race in the March was the Six Hours at Riverside, partnered by Marc Surer. The bodywork fell off and all sorts of other things happened but we still finished sixth behind five Porsche 935 variants. The next race, at Laguna Seca, was a short one where I drove solo and again finished sixth. Lola had also developed an IMSA prototype, the T600, and at Laguna it was wheeled out for the first time. It was a beautiful GTP car, definitely superior to the March. The man seated within, Brian Redman, won this début race, and lots more, to take that year's championship.

Jim and the team then decided that what the March really needed was the BMW four-cylinder turbo unit rather than the straight-six. However, the installation in the back of our prototype needed a team with the skills of a McLaren to make it work. The turbo engine required considerable intercooling because we ran high boost with a single turbo. It had a lot of throttle lag and generated a huge amount of heat, which gave all sorts of cooling issues, not helped at all by the long pipework from the turbo to the radiator and back to the manifold. The concept never worked and the lag was hopeless. My best result was fourth at Portland in a short one-hour race. So ended my first spell with BMW.

ABOVE The 1981 March M1C was designed for IMSA's new Prototype category but it never worked, either with its original straight-six engine or the four-cylinder turbo installed later. Here I am at Lime Rock cresting the brow in The Uphill.
The Revs Institute for Automotive Research/ Geoffrey Hewitt

CHAPTER 13
1969–85
TRANS-AM AND A TITLE

My Trans-Am career began in 1969 with an invitation to take part in that season's final race. It was a competitive year involving a lot of star drivers, with Mark Donohue in Penske Racing's Sunoco-backed Camaro, Peter Revson, George Follmer and Parnelli Jones in Mustangs, and Dan Gurney, 'Swede' Savage and Sam Posey in Chryslers.

Terry Godsall, the Canadian businessman from Ottawa whom we first met in Chapter 7, was running a Pontiac Firebird in partnership with Jerry Titus, who had been Trans-Am champion two years earlier. Godsall had seen me doing well in Formula 5000 and wanted to involve me in his Trans-Am efforts, so he entered a second Firebird at the season finale at Riverside. Jerry finished third behind the two Penske Camaros of Donohue and Ronnie Bucknum while I retired right near the end of the race. The Pontiac was not that bad a car and Jerry got a few top-three placings over the season.

Given my success in Formula 5000, Terry expected that I would instantly win Trans-Am races, despite the fact that I had no experience of the car, the team or the series. He was the sort of guy who could have been a real fairy godmother in my career if only he had organised his effort properly. Such men are good at business and tend to think they can be successful at running a race team as well — but usually they know nothing

LEFT My first Trans-Am season with DeAtley Motorsports in a Chevy Camaro in 1983 came rather out of the blue but certainly worked out well. I had a terrific run of results and became champion. This photo was taken at Brainerd, Minnesota, a track I always enjoyed.
The Revs Institute for Automotive Research/ Geoffrey Hewitt

ABOVE My first Trans-Am race was at Riverside in October 1969, joining former champion Jerry Titus in Terry Godsall's team with a second Pontiac Firebird. Here I am leading Jerry but only he reached the finish, in third place.
Getty Images/The Enthusiast Network

BELOW In 1970, after Jerry Titus was killed at Road America, I did two more Trans-Am races for Terry Godsall but was unable to make enough of a mark in his new-model Pontiac Firebird. This damp scene is at Seattle, Washington, where the engine let go after only a few laps.
David Hobbs collection

about running race cars. Racing can be a strange environment and things do not always work out the way they might in everyday life. In the end, however, Terry Godsall was good for me.

Sadly Jerry Titus was killed in 1970 from injuries sustained after hitting a bridge at Road America, one that it is no longer there. The team regrouped, built up another Firebird and asked me to drive it in the end-of-season Trans-Am rounds at Kent and Riverside, directly after giving me a race in their McLaren M12 Can-Am car at Road America. I retired at Kent but finished ninth at Riverside.

Fast-forward to 1983

My real Trans-Am career did not start until over a decade later. In 1982 I drove for John Fitzpatrick in the various Porsches in his stable and we had a good year. After the season was over Mags and I were at home in Upper Boddington one evening when the phone rang.

'John Dick here.'

'Hello, John. And who are you?'

ABOVE Posing for pre-season photography in 1983 with Trans-Am team-mate Willy T. Ribbs and our DeAtley Motorsports crew, which included John Dick (second from right). *David Hobbs collection*

'I'm calling from Portland, Oregon, where I work for Neil DeAtley. We are going to run a Trans-Am team next year with Chevrolet Camaros. We will have Budweiser money and intend to win the championship. It's going to be a fully funded team and we would like you to drive one of the cars.'

So I replied, 'OK, sure.'

And he went on, 'The Dickey brothers are going to be the mechanics.'

'Uh-huh. And your name is?'

'John Dick.'

'Sounds to me like there's an awful lot of dick in this team.'

He shrugged off that comment and continued.

'You've always been a hero of mine. You've got lots of experience, and I know you've done long-distance driving. I know you're used to having a roof over your head. I've watched you for years, and I think you'd be a great fit in the team, plus I really like working with mature drivers.'

Mature? I responded, 'It sounds very interesting and I'd love to do it, but it seems about as likely as me flying out of the window with Wendy hot on my heels.'

'No, no, this is real. It really is real.'

Two weeks later the postman delivered an airline ticket to Portland. Off I went early in the New Year and there was John Dick to pick me up at the airport. He was a little guy who looked like Brains from the TV show *Thunderbirds*, with glasses, nicely combed hair, very neat, very fastidious. We went to the race shop and, sure enough, there was a pair of Camaros, painted up in Budweiser colours. It turned out that the other driver was going to be Willy T. Ribbs. Now we had Dick, Dickey and Willy. The shop was right next to a huge sales site for heavy construction machinery belonging to the team's owner, the aforementioned Neil DeAtley, a contractor who built roads and railways, and an interesting guy who had done some racing himself.

So I went to the Portland track to test. Americans often go on about how bad the weather is in Portland, but while I was there, in the middle of winter, it was beautiful and spring-like. Despite not having driven a big sedan like this in over ten years, I broke the track record after a handful of laps. So we signed a deal and they paid me $5,000 a race plus a percentage of prize money. It turned out to be a very good year and the start of an excellent chapter in my racing career.

I got on very well with John Dick and his wife Joan. They lived in a lovely apartment overlooking the Willamette River, with beautiful views. John is still around and recently rejoined Rahal Letterman Lanigan Racing as Head of Research & Development for their Indycar team.

The first race of the 1983 Trans-Am season was at Moroso, Florida, which now goes by the name of Palm Beach International. Practice went well with Willy and I next to each other on the second row of the grid. Tom Gloy in his factory Mercury Capri led the first few laps but was then passed by my team-mate until he spun and lost places, leaving me in front. I had a bit of a tussle when it came to lapping Paul Newman and that allowed Gene Felton to get past in his Oftedahl Racing

Pontiac and win by less than a second, with me in second place and Willy fifth. Paul, of course, was a huge film star but he was also a very strong competitor.

It was at Moroso, before the weekend started, that Budweiser's man asked for a private chat with me. It went like this.

'I suppose I ought to tell you before the season starts that this Budweiser money is not coming from their sports budget. It's from their minority budget, and it's really for Willy to win the championship. We'd very much like Willy to win the championship if possible.'

This was the first I had heard that Willy's ethnicity — he is an African-American — had anything to do with Budweiser's involvement. In due course I also learned that the DeAtley Motorsports team received Budweiser payments only for results, which is never a good arrangement because the entire venture becomes predicated on doing well. I never discovered whether or not Budweiser's funding was any different for a result achieved by Willy rather

than me, like, 'If David wins the team gets 10 grand, but if Willy wins you get 30', but you can imagine how this hidden agenda bothered me.

At the next race, in West Virginia at Summit Point, a circuit I had never been to before, I started second and won by half a minute. Tom Gloy in the Lane Sports Mercury Capri, our biggest rival throughout the series, came second with Paul Newman third in Bob Sharp's Nissan 280Z Turbo, while Willy crashed out. As Felton retired, that put me at the top of the points standings — and there I remained for the rest of the year.

In fact I increased my points lead at the third race because I won that too. This was at Sears Point in California, where I had become a bit of an ace because I had won there twice with BMW. The way the track flowed just suited me, although the first time I went there, in 1977, I remember driving through the gates and thinking, 'Is this the track, this funny little bit of road?' The place was very basic in those days. Anyway, Sears Point was just as good for me in the Trans-Am car as I qualified third, took the lead on lap five and

ABOVE Popping a giant beer after winning at Summit Point — no champagne in this Budweiser-sponsored series.
David Hobbs collection

BELOW My next Trans-Am win came at Sears Point, California. This time Mags was there to celebrate with me, loyally dressed up in the right gear.
David Hobbs collection

ABOVE This is Brainerd, where I finished second to team-mate Willy T. Ribbs. Generally I had the edge over Willy in 1983, but he was a tough competitor.
The Revs Institute for Automotive Research/ Geoffrey Hewitt

BELOW My Camaro, seen again at Brainerd, was a terrific race car, with excellent handling, a powerful, reliable engine, and a great team running it.
The Revs Institute for Automotive Research/ Geoffrey Hewitt

led the rest of the way, with Felton second, Gloy third and Willy seventh.

The fourth round was at Portland, the team's home track, and I qualified second. During the race the car gave a massive lurch so I pitted, thinking something had broken, but as there was nothing wrong I can only think the reason was a patch of oil. I finished fourth and this time Willy won. That put us 1–2 in the championship, well ahead of everyone else.

By now Willy's nose had become a little out of joint because I was proving to be quicker than him, although he was certainly a tough competitor and a very good driver. I felt that he could be his own worst enemy at times, occasionally seeing things in racial terms or, when I beat him, wanting to blame anyone but himself. He was genuinely very quick but, luckily for me, not quite quick enough.

The team had a blip at Seattle International Raceway as both cars dropped out and Elliott Forbes-Robinson, the defending series champion, won in his Huffaker Racing Pontiac.

We returned to winning ways at Mid-Ohio, where I finished second to Willy. Then I swept the board at Road America, winning from pole, leading every lap, and setting fastest lap. Afterwards we went to my favourite haunt, Siebkens, to celebrate and had one or two drinks too many.

The team took another 1–2 at Brainerd, Willy ahead of me. I missed the next round, at Trois Rivières in Canada, because of a clashing commitment with John Fitzpatrick in the Spa 1,000Km driving a Porsche 956, so DeAtley put John Paul Jr in my car and he won. Then we made a return visit to Sears Point, where I took pole position but dropped out with fuel-pump failure, leaving Willy to win. Next came Riverside and I won there, beating Willy by 12 seconds, and with that I had the championship more or less locked up with one round left. As it turned out, Riverside was the last significant race I ever won.

The season finale was in Las Vegas, in the parking lot at Caesar's Palace as a support race

to the Formula 1 US Grand Prix. To become champion, I only had to finish the race and I did just that, with fourth place. It was one of very few races in my career where I just cruised around, protecting my position, something I did not like doing — but I really wanted that championship and I won it at the age of 44.

I never did learn whether Budweiser paid Neil DeAtley anything like the bonus his team would have received if Willy had become champion. As it was, Willy was second in the standings, with

ABOVE One more view of me on the way to my 1983 Trans-Am title. That year I had four wins and three second places.
David Hobbs collection

LEFT A mere 24 years after I started racing, I became Trans-Am champion. With me is Nicholas Craw, a former racer who was President of the Sports Car Club of America (SCCA) at the time, and now is a top man within the FIA.
David Hobbs collection

148 points to my 158, and he was named Rookie of the Year.

DeAtley certainly ran a very good team. He was the perfect owner, just assertive enough to keep everyone on his or her toes, but not micro-managing the way a lot of owners do. John Dick was a good engineer, the Dickey brothers were terrific mechanics, and our Camaros were well prepared, with really good, reliable engines.

More Trans-Am in 1984

As far as I was concerned, Chevrolet were always cagey about whether or not the DeAtley programme was a works one but our link man at the company, Herb Fishel, used to tease me about being Chevrolet's 'journeyman driver'. Chevrolet certainly meddled in 1984, deciding that DeAtley Motorsports, as the championship-winning team, should move up from Camaros to Corvettes. This was not a good thing and the season was a huge disappointment.

At the first race, Road Atlanta, the brown stuff really hit the fan. During the morning warm-up

Willy T. Ribbs had a run-in on the back straight with Bob Lobenberg. Back in the pits he went down to Huffaker Racing and tried to pull Lobenberg out of his car. There was a fight, with punches thrown. John Dick went over to try to calm things down and Willy spat in John's face. That was it. Neil DeAtley fired Willy on the spot. After scrambling around to find a substitute driver, DeAtley put Darin Brassfield in Willy's car for the race and he won it, with me third. So Darin and I became Budweiser team-mates for rest of the year.

Goodness knows why Willy lost his rag so badly but I have always thought that resentment may have lingered about not winning the championship the previous year. Straight away Ford snapped him up, seeing that here was a very quick, telegenic, black driver, and put him in Jack Roush's team. Willy spent years with Ford and won a lot more Trans-Am races, including four in 1984 alone, although he never became champion.

At the next round, Summit Point, I finished second to the aforementioned Lobenberg and headed the points standings, but it went downhill from there, mainly because the Corvette was not as quick or as reliable as the Camaro. The Corvette was more complex, its independent rear suspension was difficult to tune, aerodynamically it was lacking, and things broke quite often. By contrast, the Camaro with its live rear axle, and decent stay rods to help with location, handled really well.

One highlight, however, was the Detroit Formula 1 weekend. That street circuit around the downtown Renaissance Center was another that I took to like a duck to water and I led the opening laps. For this race we added water-cooled brakes but the system ran out of water early on and I ended up pushing the tyres and brakes too hard, causing me to slip back to seventh place at the end. There was no way you could nurse the brakes around that circuit and keep up any kind of speed.

Towards the end of the season we raced at a rinky-dink joint outside Dallas called Green Valley. Virtually none of our Trans-Am crowd, me included, had been there before, but I was always pretty good at picking up new circuits quickly. I qualified third there, only to drop out of the race with a stub-axle failure.

The season ended on a mildly upbeat note with third place at the Formula 1 weekend in Las Vegas. All in all it had been a very mediocre campaign, with no wins, a solitary second place, three thirds and one fourth. Tom Gloy was champion and I was eighth in the standings.

I made one more Trans-Am appearance after that, at Detroit in 1985, driving a Camaro for the Peerless team, qualifying ninth and finishing tenth. Pre-race testing of that car was interesting. It was towards the end of June, one of the longest days of the year in terms of daylight, and I flew in from England on the day of the test. I arrived in Detroit at about 2pm, rented a car, drove the 80 miles to Michigan Speedway and started testing at around 5pm. Because it got dark so late, I was out on that damned track until 10pm, so for me, with body clock on UK time, it was 3am by the time we called it a day!

BELOW **My best performance of 1984 came at the Formula 1 Detroit Grand Prix weekend, where I led until the big Corvette ran out of brakes.** *The Revs Institute for Automotive Research/ Geoffrey Hewitt*

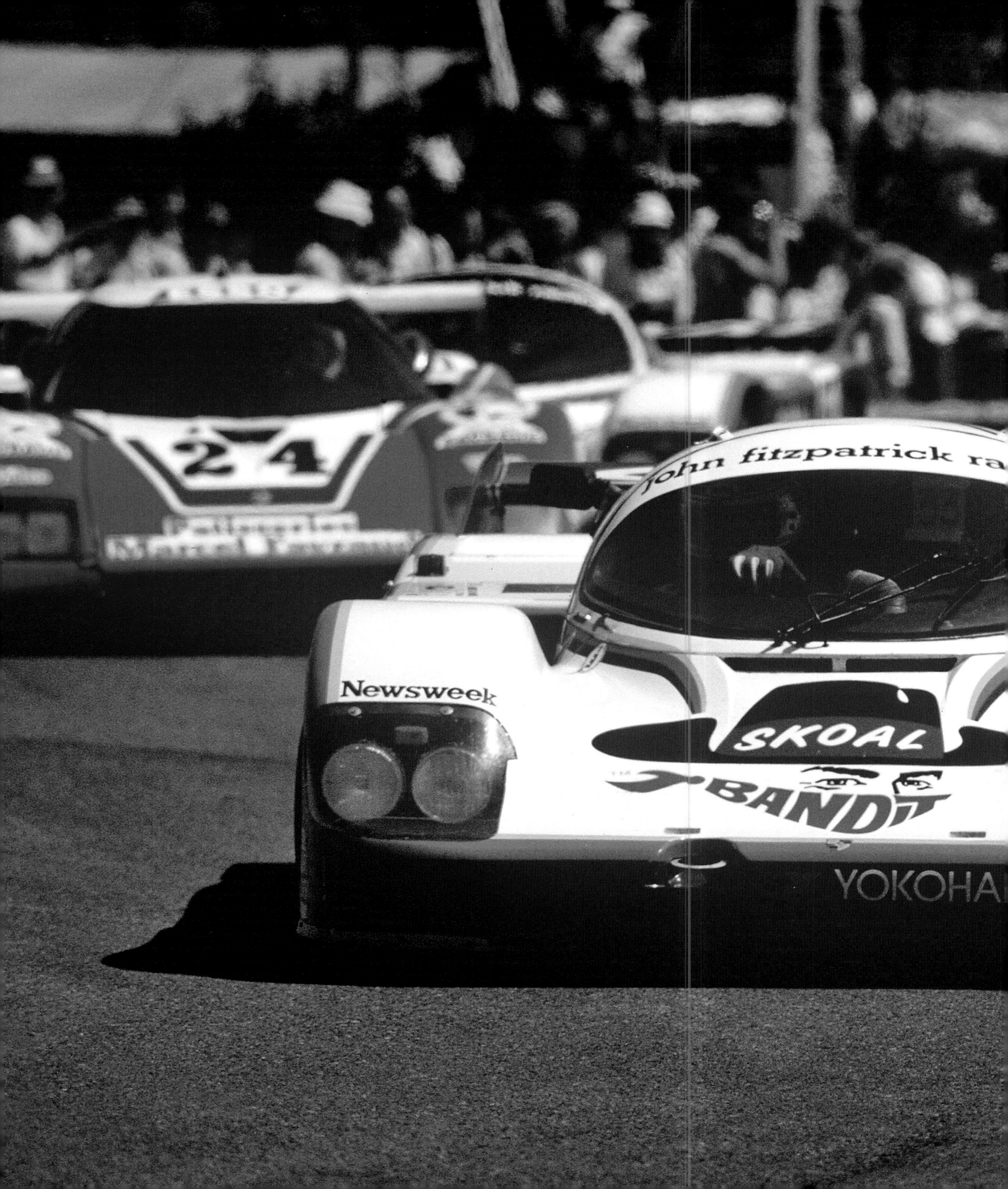

24
john fitzpatrick ra
Newsweek
SKOAL
BANDIT
YOKOHA

CHAPTER 14

1982–93
FITZ AND THE FINAL YEARS

John Fitzpatrick and I had crossed paths on various occasions. We both come from the same part of England, the Midlands, and while I concentrated mainly on single-seater racing Fitz had always competed with a roof over his head and had a lot of success. He had also followed in my footsteps to race in North America and won the 1980 IMSA championship driving a Porsche 935 for Dick Barbour.

For the 1982 season Fitz was looking to put together his own team. It was great timing for me. I had enjoyed my stint with BMW, but the last two years had rather fizzled out as BMW North America lost interest in racing and concentrated on other ways of building the brand. I was wondering what to do next when Derek Bell said, 'Give old Fitzy a call, he may be looking for a driver.' So I did. John was quite excited about the prospect and signed me up to drive his Porsche 935 K3. Perfect!

For sponsorship, Fitz did a deal whereby Wayne Baker, another IMSA regular, would bring his existing sponsor to Fitz's team. This was Jerry Dominelli, who had an investment company in San Diego that promised impressive returns for its clients. Dominelli's full name was Jerry David Dominelli and his company's identity was always displayed on the car as 'JDavid'. A few years later it emerged that Dominelli was a swindler whose money-making promises were a gigantic Ponzi

LEFT My best result at the Le Mans 24 Hours came in 1984, driving this John Fitzpatrick Racing Porsche 956B with Sarel van der Merwe and Philippe Streiff. We finished third.
Bill Warner

scheme. Lots of clients got fleeced to the tune of $82 million in total and Dominelli was sentenced to 20 years in prison. I invested some money with him just before it all blew up but I was one of the lucky ones and got it back.

Fitz, of course, had no knowledge of this and put together a well-drilled team that he called John Fitzpatrick Racing. Fellow Midlander Dave Prewitt was the team manager and the mechanics were led by New Zealander Max Crawford, who now runs Crawford Composites in North Carolina and does a lot of work for NASCAR.

Racing in 1982

For the 1982 Daytona 24 Hours, my first race with Fitz, we were strong favourites and qualified second, the best of the 935s, but after just 59 laps the car had a mechanical failure while John was driving and I never got a go. Six weeks later we went off to Sebring for the 12 Hours and again we qualified second fastest, and again we were the favourites, but Fitz flipped the car going down to the hairpin after just seven laps. He was

humming along through the long, fast right-hander and suddenly it was bouncing along on its roof after a very un-935-like suspension breakage. So, two races down and I had not even got in the thing during a race.

I was just packing up at Sebring when one of the mechanics from Ralph Kent-Cooke's team came rushing over and said that Ralph was having trouble in the heat. Could I come over and drive instead of him? So I jumped in that car, a Lola T600 co-driven by Jim Adams and Eppie Wietzes. It was fantastic. I had raced the March-BMW M1C against Brian Redman in a T600 the previous year and the difference was chalk and cheese. I only did one stint, which allowed Ralph to recover, but the car's excellence has very much stuck in my memory. The T600 retired later with engine problems.

Thereafter Fitz and I had a pretty good year in the IMSA series, winning a couple of races. The big one was the annual 500-miler at Road America. By now the Lola T600 was really coming on, particularly the Interscope Racing entry

BELOW Backed by fraudster Jerry Dominelli's 'JDavid' investment company, the John Fitzpatrick Racing Porsche 935 K3 was a fine race car but here in the Daytona 24 Hours, my first event of 1982, it broke before I even had a chance to drive it in the race.
Bill Warner

ABOVE After the early demise of John Fitzpatrick's Porsche 935 at Sebring, I was invited by Ralph Kent-Cooke's team to do a race stint in his Lola T600. The car was a joy to drive.
Bill Warner

LEFT In 1982 I put my name on the Pabst 500 Trophy at Road America for a second time, driving with John Fitzpatrick (left) in the 935.
David Hobbs collection

ABOVE This is the fabulous Reinhold Joest-built Porsche 935 'Moby Dick' at Le Mans in 1982. Fitz and I finished fourth and 'best of the rest', behind the three brand-new works Porsche 956s.
LAT Images

RIGHT This wild-looking device is the Group 5 Nissan Skyline that I drove in the 1982 Kyalami Nine Hours with Masahiro Hasemi and British rally driver Tony Pond. I crashed it in the race.
www.motoprint.co.za (courtesy of Malcolm Sampson)

driven by Danny Ongais, while the 935 was beginning to see the end of its days as newer GTP cars were developing fast. I have always loved Road America and told Fitz we should have that race in the bag because Danny was almost bound to screw it up. He did, and we won. We also won the next race at Mid-Ohio, which was very satisfying.

With a decent budget John Fitzpatrick Racing was able to afford a second 935, a replica 'Moby Dick' built by Reinhold Joest, and he and I drove this in the Le Mans 24 Hours. This was the year Porsche brought out the new 956 for Le Mans. The factory had three of these Rothmans-sponsored cars and a great line-up of drivers — Derek Bell, Jacky Ickx, Jochen Mass, Vern Schuppan, Hurley Haywood, Al Holbert and Jürgen Barth. We found ourselves running fourth in our 'Moby Dick' and thought we were looking in very good shape because the 935 was robust and the chances of those unproven 956s finishing seemed remote. But all three of them did finish — first, second and third! So we were an irritated and frustrated fourth, but we won the IMSA GTX category.

At the end of the season I returned to an old stamping ground, South Africa, and did the Kyalami Nine Hours in a Group 5 Nissan Skyline with the rally driver Tony Pond and Masahiro Hasemi. We qualified 10th in this spectacular turbocharged beast, behind various Porsches and Saubers, but in the race I crashed it at the sharp right-hander going up to Leeukop.

All in all my switch from BMW worked out pretty well and racing with John was always a very light-hearted affair without corporate pressure. This was also the year I met two excellent guys who added to the sponsorship of John's cars and went on to become the original partners in my Honda dealership in Milwaukee, Wisconsin. One was Ron McIntyre, who owned a company cleaning ships' bottoms and a restoration business. The other was Gary Wassell, who owned a large janitorial firm in San Diego. Ron is a great enthusiast and with his son-in-law Stan still attends lots of races, including Le Mans.

The 1983 season

In 1983 Fitz acquired his first Porsche 956 and ran it in the FIA World Endurance Championship. However, we first tested the car at Willow Springs, California, one of my least favourite tracks, a place that I find both horrible and dangerous, before it was shipped across the Atlantic for its races in Europe.

Meanwhile, we still had our original 935 in the US and we gave that its farewell run in the Riverside Six Hours. For this event Fitz also entered his 'Moby Dick' and recruited Derek Bell and Rolf Stommelen to drive it. About halfway into the race Rolf had a slower car move over on him and clipped the rear bodywork at Turn Six. Unbeknown to him, the knock caused one of the rear wing struts to break. Going down the

ABOVE This very poignant photo of me with John Fitzpatrick (centre) and Rolf Stommelen (right) was taken just before the start at Riverside in April 1983. Fitz ran two 935s that day and during the race Rolf was killed in the 'Moby Dick' version he was sharing with Derek Bell. It was the team's darkest hour.

David Hobbs collection

Nürburgring. In between each of those I took
in a Trans-Am race in the US, so I logged up a
few air miles on my way to becoming Trans-Am
champion that year.

At Le Mans, Fitz put Dieter Quester and
me together in one of two Porsche 956s he was
running. We were doing all right, circulating for
several hours in third place, until the car died
on me at around midnight between Arnage and
the Porsche curves. I did the heroic job required
at such moments, removing the massive rear
bodywork by myself to examine the engine, but,
like most drivers, I did not have the foggiest
notion of what I was looking at. It turned out that
the drive to the fuel-injection pump had broken.
In response, Porsche chief engineer Norbert
Singer came out with the classic line, '*I haf never
zeen one of zees sings break before. It ees incredible. I
haf never zeen zis before.*' Yeah, well, you've seen it
now, pal.

More 1,000Km races followed, starting at Spa-
Francorchamps where Fitz and I finished third,
beaten only by two Rothmans Porsches. I had to
miss the next World Endurance Championship
race, at Brands Hatch, because of a clashing
Trans-Am commitment, so Derek Warwick took
my place and, blow me down, he and Fitz won
in pouring rain.

Next came the only championship round
outside Europe, the Fuji 1,000Km in Japan, and
just getting there was a story in itself. When
practice day dawned, Fitz and I both turned a
few exploratory laps before he got back in for
some serious stuff. After only two or three laps,
the left front tyre exploded and John had a huge
crash. Thankfully unhurt, he wasted no time in
issuing curt orders about packing up and getting
the wrecked 956 back to the US, then returned
to our hotel to check out and arrange the earliest
possible flight to San Diego.

I was with John at the hotel front desk when he
tried to get the manager to call the local PanAm
office. A very blank face stared back at John
standing there, flapping his arms and saying,
'PanAm… airplane… flying.' Waiting her turn
was a Japanese lady looking just as such ladies
are supposed to, like Madame Butterfly, with a

long backstretch at 200mph the wing came off
and the car plunged into the wall at Turn Nine. At
first the word was that Rolf had a broken leg but
would be all right. Later we were told that he had
died of a heart attack in the ambulance.

It was a truly ghastly experience for the
whole team, especially for John, who had to
deal with the aftermath. I still remember the
cheery breakfast we had all enjoyed together
that morning at the HoJo's on University Avenue.
Who would have thought that the day could have
turned so ugly. We won that race but it was a
truly sorrowful occasion.

In Europe for the World Endurance
Championship we did three 1,000Km rounds
before the big one — Le Mans. We finished fifth
at Monza, eighth at Silverstone and sixth at the

ABOVE Another Le Mans, another retirement. I shared the JDavid-sponsored Porsche 956 with Dieter Quester in 1983 and ran well until the car stopped out on the circuit during the night while I was driving.
Bill Warner

LEFT I did a full World Endurance Championship programme in 1983, missing only one race because of a Trans-Am commitment. My best result in the JDavid Porsche 956 came here at Spa, where Fitz and I finished third.
LAT Images

long, shimmering dress down to to her ankles and dark hair bundled up high in the style you see in movies. She turned to John and, with a full-on London accent, said, 'You looking for a flight, mate?' John's jaw dropped, as did mine, and we peered incredulously as this apparition speaking like someone from Notting Hill. She said, 'My father was the cultural attaché in London for five years and I went to Chelsea College.' It was another unforgettable moment in life.

With a replacement 956, we took in a couple of lesser 1,000Km races in Italy. At Imola John and I finished second to a Lancia, and then at Mugello, where Thierry Boutsen joined the team, we were fourth. With that, Fitz decided to retire from driving, his Fuji shunt having persuaded him that it was time to stop.

We did one more race that year. In December. Thierry and I went to Kyalami for the annual endurance event there, this time reduced from its usual nine hours to 1,000 kilometres. We were joined by Desiré Wilson, who was the best female driver of her era, and a South African. In the race

I was going through the long right-hand corner before Sunset Bend when the clouds erupted in a classic South African downpour. The car in front of me, the Reinhold Joest 956 of Bob Wollek, Stefan Johansson and Chico Serra, spun and that caused me to lose control of my 956 as well, crashing into the Joest car and climbing up on its roof. Later when I drove for Reinhold we shared many bawdy jokes, especially after a few drinks, about how my car had fornicated with his.

Into 1984

My 1984 season looked like being entirely in the US as I was going to defend my Trans-Am title with DeAtley Motorsports as well as do an IMSA GTP season with Bob Tullius and his Group 44 team's Jaguar XJR-5. The Jaguar plan, however, turned into just one race, the Daytona 24 Hours. I drove with Tullius himself and Doc Bundy.

The car, designed by Lee Dykstra, had a big problem that manifested itself at Daytona. The 5.3-litre Jaguar V12 kept throwing its auxiliary drive belts, which were located at the front of the

BELOW The mating game. At Kyalami at the end of 1983 one of Reinhold Joest's Porsches spun in front of mine and we ended up in this indecent coupling, memories of which gave Reinhold and me much mirth when I raced for him in later years.
www.motoprint.co.za (courtesy of Stuart Falconer)

engine, against the bulkhead. Changing a belt meant that the engine and transmission had to be separated from the chassis to get access — a massive palaver. We were leading when our car threw a belt and it took at least half an hour to change the damned thing. We still finished third, my best result in the Daytona 24 Hours.

I thought Tullius himself was an impossible individual. At the drivers' meeting he ran through a list of tedious instructions. 'Don't do this, don't do that, keep your uniform clean, don't get stains on it, blah, blah, blah... And don't even *think* of going faster than me.' He actually said that, and he was not kidding. Strange duck — although his achievements in sports car racing are undeniably impressive.

As for Fitz, by this time the JDavid scandal had detonated and suddenly he had to rethink his racing operation, all the while with federal investigators looking deeply into the whole thing before concluding that John's relationship with the fraudster had been entirely innocent. Fitz moved his team to England, based at Silverstone,

and was able to replace some of the JDavid backing when Guy Edwards brokered a sponsorship deal with Skoal Bandit, makers of chewing tobacco, to do the World Endurance Championship again. We had an improved version of the 956, the 956B, which was basically a customer version of the previous works specification with more progressive power delivery and better fuel consumption, thanks mainly to Bosch Motronic engine management.

Again Le Mans was the key race. I shared the 956B with Sarel van der Merwe and Philippe Streiff, who was on the verge of a Formula 1 career. Whenever I had a Grand Prix driver partnering me I used to worry about being outshone, but Streiff was nowhere near my pace and I found him a bit of moaner; sadly a testing accident in Brazil five years later left him paralysed.

After qualifying sixth fastest, right among the quickest Porsche 956s, we looked in good shape for the race — until the first lap of morning warm-up on the Saturday. The throttle immediately stuck open on our brand-new factory engine and I had

ABOVE The Group 44 team's Jaguar XJR-5 was a potential winner in the Daytona 24 Hours of 1984 but for its V12 engine's tendency to throw auxiliary drive belts. I was leading, partnered by Doc Bundy, when exactly that happened, but we were able to salvage third place.
Bill Warner

to do a whole lap using the ignition key to slow down. When the plenum chamber was removed, the mechanics found the cause — a rag had jammed the butterfly wide open.

In the race an intense battle developed during the night between us and the Joest 956 driven by Klaus Ludwig and Henri Pescarolo, but at 6am we took what looked to be a pretty solid lead. About 20 minutes later the car went down to five cylinders. After going in and out of the pits for a fix, we disconnected the fuel from the malfunctioning cylinder and removed its spark plug, and then ran flat out on five cylinders for the next nine and a half hours. How the engine survived I cannot imagine, but it did, and we finished third. It felt like a pretty heroic result — but it was a potential win that got away.

The problem with the failed cylinder was a burned valve, which we put down to that incident in the morning warm-up. With the butterfly stuck wide open, the engine ran very lean for that one lap and the affected cylinder was the one that gave up.

ABOVE At the Le Mans 24 Hours in 1984 these guys achieved third place with the Skoal Bandit Porsche 956B (from left): team boss John Fitzpatrick with his three drivers — me, Philippe Streiff and Sarel van der Merwe.
Courtesy of John Fitzpatrick

BELOW This is the pre-race parade at Le Mans in 1984 with me and driving partners Sarel van der Merwe and Philippe Streiff. After the JDavid scandal blew up, Fitz's new sponsor was Skoal Bandit, a brand of chewing tobacco.
Bill Warner

Le Mans apart, Thierry Boutsen was usually my co-driver for 1984, although occasionally I raced with Guy Edwards, Rupert Keegan and Franz Konrad. After Le Mans, I was on the podium twice more in 1984, with second places in the 1,000Km races at the Nürburgring and at Mosport in Canada.

Thierry and I really should have won at the 'Ring, one of the very first races on the shorter, modern circuit. The 956B came from the factory with a spool, a solid rear differential rather than the more usual limited-slip type, and it had its shortcomings, particularly in the wet. Anyway we decided to put in a limited-slip and guess what? It rained at the 'Ring, as it so often does. So while the factory cars were skating about, we roared off into the lead. When I came in for a fuel stop we were nearly a lap in front. As at Le Mans, at the 'Ring all the fuel came from a central source and each pit had its own brand-new pump. Our pump stopped working, so Thierry had to go back out while they fixed it and do a slow lap. That lost us the race and we had to settle for

ABOVE Celebrating at Le Mans in 1984. To my left is Klaus Ludwig, who shared the winning Porsche 956 with Henri Pescarolo, and next to him are John Paul Jr (red suit) and Jean Rondeau, who co-drove the second-placed 956.
Tony Henton

BELOW Mags and I post-race at the Club des Pilotes at Le Mans in 1984. With us is my old racing friend Bill Pinckney, whom I had got to know in my first season, way back in 1959. Soon after this poor Bill was killed when he crashed his light aircraft.
David Hobbs collection

second place — another one that got away.

As in 1983, I did a lot of criss-crossing the Atlantic. Twice there were gaps in my schedule that allowed me to take up invitations to drive a Porsche 962 owned by Bruce Leven, a wealthy and very pleasant fellow who owned Bayside Disposal, a waste and scrap business, and named his race team after it. The 962 was a modified 956 created by Porsche specifically to meet IMSA GTP rules. IMSA's John Bishop was very safety conscious and one of his requirements was that a driver's feet must be behind the centre line of the front wheels. The 956 as a consequence was never eligible for IMSA racing but Porsche cared enough about the North American market to rectify this with the 962, which had its front wheels placed five inches further forward. Bruce bought the first customer 962 in the US and campaigned it all year. When I drove with him we got a good second place in August in the Road America 500, with celebrations afterwards in Siebkens of course, and we finished fourth at the three-hour Daytona Finale in November.

The 1985 season

I did a lot of juggling with race suits in 1985. DeAtley's Trans-Am team moved on to IMSA with a Chevy-powered March 85G prototype and I did one race with them before they decided to shut up shop, followed by three more IMSA races for Bruce Leven in his Porsche 962. My European programme in Porsche 956s comprised two races for Fitz, including the Le Mans 24 Hours, followed by one with Richard Lloyd Racing. Later in the year there were also three outings with Hendrick Motorsports in their Corvette GTP car.

I should have won the three-hour Miami Grand Prix, my first race of the year. Our DeAtley March was in the lead and I had set a lap record that still stands to this day as the Miami layout of that time was never used again. Somehow my co-driver, Darin Brassfield, let Derek Bell in Al Holbert's Porsche 962 pass him for victory on the very last lap even though there was little room to do that round the Miami street circuit. I was furious because Brassfield was a pillock to make that error. So we finished second, well ahead of

LEFT My two Trans-Am years with DeAtley Motorsports segwayed into a brief but promising IMSA dalliance at the beginning of 1985 with this March 85G. But for an unforced last-lap error by my co-driver, Darin Brassfield, we would have won the Miami Grand Prix.
Bill Warner

BELOW This wheel-waving shot of Bruce Leven's Bayside Disposal Racing Porsche 962 was taken in 1985 at Mid-Ohio, where Bob Wollek and I finished second.
The Revs Institute for Automotive Research/ Geoffrey Hewitt

a similar March with double World Champion Emerson Fittipaldi at the wheel.

Before Le Mans I had another couple of podiums in Leven's 962 at Road Atlanta and Mid-Ohio. At the latter, where we finished second, my co-driver was Bob Wollek, who sadly died far too young when he was hit on the back of the head by a truck's large side mirror while cycling for fitness near Sebring in 2001.

As a warm-up for Le Mans with John Fitzpatrick Racing, I partnered Austrian driver Jo Gartner in the Silverstone 1,000Km, where we dropped out around the halfway point with an engine failure on Fitz's 956B. For the 24 Hours we were joined by Guy Edwards, a genius at finding sponsorship who became very wealthy. We had a pretty good run, qualifying 12th but coming through to finish fourth in a race won by Joest's 956 driven Klaus Ludwig, Paolo Barilla (a pasta magnate) and 'John Winter' (a German businessman called Louis Krages who did not want his mother to know about his racing).

In second spot at Le Mans was the Richard Lloyd Porsche 962 that I then drove in a World Endurance Championship round with Jonathan Palmer at Hockenheim, where we finished fifth.

I ended the season with three IMSA races in the Lola T710 Corvette GTP car run by Rick Hendrick's team. This was a GM-funded project using a lovely Chevrolet-branded Buick turbo V6 engine, smooth as silk and seriously powerful. I did a lot of testing at Road Atlanta, usually with both Rick and Lola's Eric Broadley in attendance.

Unfortunately the car proved to be unreliable and there were failures in all three of my races. The first was with the South African Sarel van der Merwe, who was always great fun and got his place in Rick's team after a recommendation from me. He and I did the 500-miler at Road America but a fault in the turbo waste gate halted us around the halfway mark. Then I teamed up with Vern Schuppan at Watkins Glen, where I remember that the car, despite not being particularly quick though the Esses, hit 211mph by the end of the back straight. We

ABOVE Together with
Jo Gartner and Guy
Edwards, I finished fourth
at Le Mans in 1985 in this
Porsche 956B run by
John Fitzpatrick Racing.
Porsche-Werkfoto

LEFT At the end of 1985
I did three races for Rick
Hendrick in this Corvette
GTP car before returning
to BMW the following
year. This is the last of
them, at the street circuit
in Columbus, Ohio.
*The Revs Institute for
Automotive Research/
Geoffrey Hewitt*

qualified quite well, seventh fastest, but this time it was the gearbox that could not take the strain. Finally I did a street race in Columbus, Ohio but dropped out after only 13 laps.

Back to BMW

Just as I was getting going with Hendrick Motorsports, BMW re-emerged out of the blue saying that they intended to return to IMSA in the GTP category and wanted me to join them. This put me in something of a dilemma and at Road America, my first race with Hendrick, I found myself dashing between motorhomes for discussions. Herb Fishel, the Chevrolet boss, really twisted my arm to stay with Hendrick and Rick backed him up, saying things like, 'You love driving for us… you and Sarel get on so well… you understand the car...' But like an idiot I went back to BMW.

BMW had had a change of management at the top and were promising big things. It was certainly positive that they chose to hire McLaren North America for engine development and race

preparation. The car was based on a March chassis and the engine was a reworked 2-litre version of BMW's four-cylinder Formula 1 unit that in 1.5-litre form had powered Nelson Piquet's Brabham to the World Championship title in 1983. It was decided that a singleton car would début at the Daytona Finale in November prior to a full season with two cars in 1986. Joining me as co-drivers for this first race were Davy Jones and John Andretti, Mario's nephew.

The BMW was immediately quick and in practice I had a huge battle for pole with Sarel, who was really motoring in the Corvette GTP car that I had walked away from. He snatched the top spot on the grid with me alongside but we both retired from the race, my car with gearbox problems and his with a handling issue. It was clear that our car and its very powerful BMW engine had potential.

Over the winter BMW decided to stretch the engine to 2.2 litres by lengthening the stroke. This introduced some intense vibration and it was so bad in early testing that fuel lines

BELOW On my return to BMW, my first race was the Daytona Finale in December 1985, partnering with Davy Jones and John Andretti. The car was quick and I qualified it second but its gearbox broke in the race.
Bill Warner

ruptured and we had several fires in the engine bay. Nevertheless, we were entered for the Daytona 24 Hours with two cars, one for the 'senior' pairing of John Watson and me, Wattie having now finished in Formula 1, the other for the youngsters Jones and Andretti.

By now BMW's North American competitions boss, my old friend Jim Patterson, was very ill with cancer but he was determined we should race at Daytona despite the vibration problems. Even the pre-event media tour had a setback. I went to Orlando with a smart BMW PR lady with several TV interviews scheduled but sadly it was the day the space shuttle *Challenger* blew up and no one wanted to know about our plans. In the end, however, the team pulled out of the Daytona 24 Hours.

Our first race of 1986, therefore, was the Miami Grand Prix four weeks later. John and I could only qualify 11th and we finished ninth, a few laps down.

Three weeks on from Miami it was the Sebring 12 Hours and there was still a vibration

ABOVE In 1986 BMW's handsome new turbo cars were plagued with engine vibrations and we only started two of the IMSA season's first six races. At least John Watson and I finished this one, at Miami, but in the other, at Road Atlanta, the car caught fire on the first lap.
Bill Warner

BELOW My co-driver with BMW in 1986 was John Watson, who had reached the end of his Formula 1 career and turned to sports cars.
LAT Images

ABOVE Once the engine vibration was resolved at mid-season, the hugely powerful BMW prototype really started to show its potential. We always qualified well but often the car broke in races, as here at Columbus.
David Hobbs collection

problem going into that race. I spent an hour in a public phone box at Sebring trying to persuade the upper management that it had to be fixed before we could race the cars. Again we did not start.

Much against my advice, we did run in the spring race at Road Atlanta, where BMW had a big hospitality area on the inside of Turn One and about 150 dealers, wives and employees showed up. At the end of lap one Wattie came into view with the car on fire and pulled up in pitlane right in front of the dealers while the car burned merrily away. Sarel van der Merwe won in the Corvette seat formerly occupied by me.

BMW called a halt and finally, using a lot of rubber bushes to absorb the engine vibrations, they fixed the problem. Our first race back was at Watkins Glen in July and there the car was magic. During practice I held pole for some time until Davy Jones pipped me, but we filled out the front row. At the start Davy shot off like a scalded cat and I ran second, then an overheating issue struck our car and we limped home sixth. Davy and

John Andretti hung on and won, despite some problems near the end. Things were looking up and the car was obviously quick.

We were very competitive at Portland but somehow Wattie got hooked up in the safety harness at a driver change, losing a lot of time and leaving us in fourth place.

At Road America our pair of cars occupied the second row. Davy had a massive crash at the famous kink on the opening lap — surprisingly he was unharmed — and this left Wattie well and truly in the lead. My decision to leave Hendrick and go back to BMW suddenly did not look so stupid after all. After I took over I came up to lap Derek Bell in the second-placed Porsche, which was about four miles behind as the Road America track is quite long. That pass would have given me considerable satisfaction. However, as I went down to Turn Five the poxy engine just stopped. I managed to limp the car slowly to the pits but the crew could not fix it. Early the following morning they tried again to fire up the engine and immediately it burst into life. A wire had dropped off the ECU and put the fuel setting onto full rich, so in the chill of that hour the engine was able to run. This proved to be my last race at Road America, close to Elkhart Lake where Mags and I now reside for part of the year.

Neither car finished the street race at Columbus so our final chance of winning that year was at Daytona's three-hour race in October. I put the car on the front row and led the race until fuel-feed problems developed at one-third distance, leaving us ninth at the finish. Maybe there was dirt in the line or perhaps the team screwed up.

Immediately after that race BMW decided to drop the programme. I had a contract for three years so it was very disappointing. With the backing of a big manufacturer I had rather hoped to finish my career on a high, perhaps with another couple of championship titles to my credit. It was particularly painful, too, that by now the BMW had become the odds-on favourite to win the title the following year as it had proved itself to be by far the quickest car in the series.

The 1987 season

I started the 1987 season with the two Florida enduros — the Daytona 24 Hours and Sebring 12 Hours. At Daytona I drove an Ian Dawson-run Zakspeed Ford Probe with Whitney Ganz and Gianpiero Moretti, the founder of the Momo steering wheel company, but its engine broke. Then at Sebring I had the joy of driving with my son Greg and Chip Robinson in the BMW-powered Gebhardt JC853 in the IMSA Lights category. The car was pretty good but unfortunately we retired.

I reconnected with Bruce Leven, who was still running a Porsche 962, and we did the Riverside 500 together, finishing a lowly ninth. Then I received a surprise phone call from 'Kas' Kastner, one of my old Indycar engineers, who was now running the highly successful IMSA Nissan GTP programme. Elliott Forbes-Robinson had been injured at the Riverside race when a tyre let go and he slammed into a concrete wall, so I was called in as a substitute. As I mentioned earlier (Chapter 9), Kastner and I never really hit

BELOW This neat-looking car is the Zakspeed Ford Probe that I drove with Whitney Ganz and Gianpiero Moretti in the 1987 Daytona 24 Hours. We qualified it 11th but in the race its engine broke.
Getty Images/ Bob Harmeyer

ABOVE A proud moment — father and son racing together in the Sebring 12 Hours. The car is a BMW-powered Gebhardt that went quite nicely, but Greg and I, joined by Chip Robinson, were soon out of the race.
The Revs Institute for Automotive Research/ Ken Breslauer

RIGHT I had a surprise summons to drive Nissan's GTP ZX Turbo at Laguna Seca in 1987. I have to admit that I really did not do this handy machine justice and fifth at the finish was disappointing.
Kenneth Barton

it off and our racing philosophies were different. The event was at Laguna Seca and I did not really do the ZX Turbo justice, qualifying sixth and driving a poor race to finish fifth, although that IMSA season was pretty competitive with the Group 44 Jaguar, several quick Porsches and some nimble Pontiac-powered Spice cars.

I did not race at Le Mans in 1986 because of the BMW programme, but for 1987 I returned with that 24-hour maestro Reinhold Joest and had high hopes that I could finally win the thing. We had a new Porsche 962C, a strong driver line-up with Sarel van der Merwe and Chip Robinson, and the professionalism of the Joest Racing team that had won this race in 1984 and 1985. In my mind, and seemingly everyone else's, we were the favourites.

Forgive me if you feel you have read this already, but the engine burned up after about 20 minutes, with Sarel driving. There had been an issue with the fuel supply at the track, low-grade fuel having been provided to all the teams from the central supply, much like the Daytona fiasco

of 1976. When this problem was discovered, everybody adjusted their engines except, for some extraordinary reason, the Joest team. It was so un-Joest-like. This was my last race of the season although, of course, by now I was working hard at broadcasting.

Into 1988

I started the year at Miami driving with Elliott Forbes-Robinson in the Hendrick Motorsport Corvette GTP car but that came to nothing.

For 1988 Reinhold Joest again signed me for Le Mans and we also did a warm-up outing at Silverstone, where I finished fourth with Bob Wollek and Philippe Streiff. This was a big year at Le Mans with a very strong entry led by three factory Porsche 962s, five works-supported Silk Cut Jaguar XJR-9s and two Sauber-Mercedes C9s, plus lots of very capable privateer teams mainly with Porsche 962Cs, including the Joest car that I shared with Didier Theys and Franz Konrad. The factory 962Cs qualified in the top three places, the one in third spot driven by three Andrettis

ABOVE At Le Mans in 1987 I drove for the renowned Reinhold Joest, sharing one of his two Porsche 962C entries with my chum Sarel van der Merwe and Chip Robinson. We had very high hopes but our race was over after less than half an hour when a piston burned out.
LAT Images

ABOVE My second Joest Racing experience at Le Mans, in 1988, was much better. Against one of the strongest fields in years, including five of the new Jaguar XJR-9s, I finished fifth with Didier Theys and Franz Konrad.
LAT Images

RIGHT I am proud that I drove for the great Reinhold Joest. Here we are at Silverstone in 1988.
LAT Images

— the great Mario, son Michael and nephew John. Like me, Mario was desperate to try to get a Le Mans victory on his resumé, but neither of us managed that. We finished fifth, one place ahead of the Andretti car, while one of the Tom Walkinshaw Racing-run Jaguars took victory, with Jan Lammers, Johnny Dumfries and Andy Wallace driving.

I then did the Nürburgring 1,000Km for Richard Lloyd in his modified Porsche 962 with yet another co-driver who was new to me. This was Martin Donnelly, whose career ended two years later with a huge Formula 1 crash in a Lotus at Jerez. It was a two-part race and we were classified seventh.

The rest of my racing that year was in the US driving for the Budweiser-backed Peerless team, with whom I had done a deal to return to the Corvette GTP alongside the two similar Hendrick cars. The car now had a V8 engine rather than the turbo V6 and my co-driver was Jack Baldwin. Unlike Hendrick, Peerless was not supported by GM, but the team had some good

ideas, trying different aero packages as well as ABS brakes, which were a novelty in racing at that time. We made a strong début with fourth place at the Columbus street race but retired at Del Mar and Tampa.

The 1989 season

Peerless pulled the plug for 1989 and sold the car, so my only drive that year was at Le Mans, for Richard Lloyd's GTi Engineering outfit. My co-drivers were an experienced Swede named Stefan Andskar and one Damon Hill, the future Formula 1 World Champion and son of Graham, against whom I had raced a quarter of a century earlier — that made me feel my age over the weekend of my 50th birthday.

Rather than having the usual spaceframe chassis, Lloyd's Porsche 962 had an aluminium monocoque designed by ex-Lotus/Hesketh Formula 1 man Nigel Stroud, plus radical bodywork that was supposed to give us massive downforce and much-reduced drag. The venture was sponsored by Porsche Great Britain, with

ABOVE For three races at the end of 1988 I became reacquainted with the Corvette GTP racer, now run by Peerless Racing. My best result was fourth place here at Columbus. *The Revs Institute for Automotive Research/ Geoffrey Hewitt*

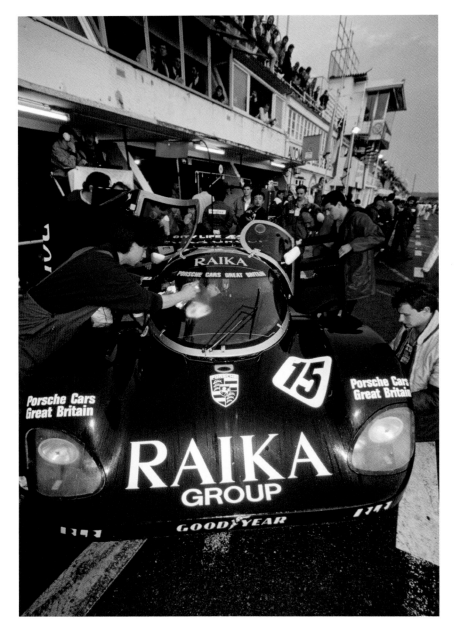

Swansong year

By now my driving career was petering out. After doing only Le Mans in 1989, my race tally in 1990 was two, both rounds of the World Sports-Prototype Championship.

At Suzuka I drove a Spice SE90C for Dave Prewitt, my old team manager from the Fitz years. My co-driver was Philippe de Henning, a French guy who was into L. Ron Hubbard and his Church of Scientology. Sponsorship from this source manifested itself with our car having the title of Hubbard's book *Dianetics* emblazoned across it but whatever money was involved was insufficient because this was a real shoestring affair. My strongest memory of the trip remains a vivid one. When the team's interpreter took us out for a sushi dinner, the fish presented for us to eat had been delicately sliced up but was still alive with its tail flapping. That was truly gruesome.

My other race of 1990 was with Jonathan Palmer at Dijon in a Joest Racing Porsche 962, a car that was now thoroughly outclassed by the big Sauber-Mercedes C9. As I was now racing so infrequently, I was no longer fit enough. Dijon is all big swooping right-handers and after three laps of practice I could not hold my head up. I went to a pet shop and bought a dog lead and hooked it up to my helmet to support my neck. Come race day, we finished eighth. That was really the end of my professional driving career — but not quite.

A postscript

Three years later, in 1993, I got a call from an old television mate, Terry Lingner, who had signed me to work for ESPN. Terry had come up with the idea of a made-for-TV series for well-known drivers over 50 years old — and I fell into that category. He called it Fast Masters and we were all to drive identically prepared $750,000 Jaguar XJ220s running on Goodyear tyres and sponsored by Havoline. Tom Walkinshaw Racing's Tony Dowe was in charge of all the machinery.

The six-race series was run entirely at Indianapolis Raceway Park between June and

lots of fanfare, car clubs on hand, PR ladies rushing around watching our every word to the press, all the bells and whistles. But the car was so slow. On the Mulsanne straight we were 25mph down on the Jaguars and no quicker than anyone else through the Porsche curves. And the engine blew up.

That turned out to be my final run at Le Mans. I took part 20 times and never won. I did return as a television pundit, ready to share my years of secrets on how to win the race that meant the most to me, and broke my heart so many times.

August. Five of the events were qualifiers for the Championship Finals in August and different drivers, mostly from NASCAR and Indycar backgrounds, took part in each qualifier. The cars were capable of 220mph but in the tight confines of IRP, part oval and part road circuit, 120mph was about the maximum.

After the opening round, which saw two of the expensive Jaguars totalled, I was in the thick of the action for round two. I won my heat from Benny Parsons and then finished second to Brian Redman in the feature event, which meant that I qualified for the Championship Finals.

There were ten of us in the Championship Finals, split into two groups of five. Three from each eight-lap heat would go through to the 12-lap final with a $100,000 first prize. In the first heat George Follmer won from Parnelli Jones, David Pearson, Bob Akin and Ed McCulloch, a drag racer who had surprisingly won the first round. In my heat Bobby Unser won from Brian while I finished third after fighting off

Johnny Rutherford, who spun out trying to catch me, leaving him last with fourth place going to Eddie Hill, another famous drag racer.

In the final the early battle for the lead was between Follmer, Jones and Unser. With three laps to go a yellow was thrown for debris on the track. I got a brilliant restart and went from sixth place to fourth, with George, Parnelli and me three-abreast going into Turn Four. That resulted in a scuffle and Parnelli finished up in the wall and broke a rib while George limped out of the race. After another yellow, I battled with Brian for third place but he just pipped me at the flag, while Unser pocketed the hundred grand and Pearson finished second.

That was it — I never pulled my crash helmet on again in anger. I had raced and won in each of five decades of motorsport, a feat that few people can match, and I never hurt myself. According to my great friend Brian Redman, that was because I was never going fast enough. What a pal. Again! See what I mean about a pestilence for life?

ABOVE **Although I officially retired as a driver in 1990, three years later I reported to Indianapolis for the Fast Masters contest, which ran over the course of six weekends, culminating in a finals day. Here are the 10 finalists (from left, back row then front row): Eddie Hill, Bob Akin, me, David Pearson, Brian Redman, Johnny Rutherford, Ed McCulloch, George Follmer, Parnelli Jones and Bobby Unser.** *David Hobbs collection*

CHAPTER 15

1976–2017
FORTY YEARS IN TELEVISION

I can trace the origins of my television career to my earliest racing days, with Mum's Morris Oxford, Dad's Jaguar XK140 and my own Lotus Elite. The main circuit commentator at Silverstone at that time was Keith Douglas, who in 'real life' was a senior figure in the motor industry, first with Smith's Industries and later with the industrial giant GKN. Keith was incredibly enthusiastic about motorsport and did everything he could to promote it, particularly at grassroots level.

One of Keith's initiatives to foster interest was to set up a series of pub seminars and rope in a few drivers, including me, to be on the panel. He would sit us down just as if we were on a television show and ask us about forthcoming races and invite questions from the audience as well. I proved to be quite good at this, pulling the legs of the other drivers and making funny comments. The audience always seemed to enjoy my contributions.

Over the years I became regarded as someone who gave interesting media interviews and provided good publicity value wherever we were in the world. When I started driving in Formula 5000 in North America in 1969 I was immediately able to establish myself in this way and one key ally was Rod Campbell. Working with Jim Kaser and Dick van der Feen, Rod's company, General Racing in Connecticut, got the contract to handle

LEFT The NBC Formula 1 team of Leigh Diffey (left), me and Steve Matchett broadcasting live from the Monaco Grand Prix in 2017. *NBC*

RIGHT My first steps at public speaking came in the early 1960s at events run by commentator Keith Douglas in pubs around the English Midlands. Here in 'The Green Man' near Silverstone I am listening while Keith holds the script, Chris Summers describes a lurid moment and Robin Sturgess observes.
Russell Douglas collection

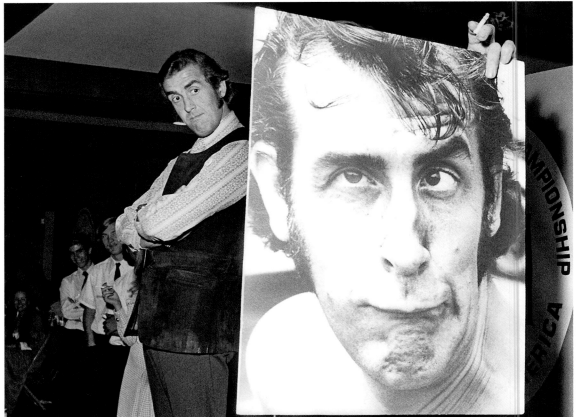

LEFT Where did they find that silly snapshot? This public humiliation occurred at a speaking function during my championship-winning Formula 5000 season in 1971. Cope Robinson of sponsor L&M manages to hold both the blown-up photo and one of his employer's products.
David Hobbs collection

public relations for L&M when the tobacco
company came into the series as title sponsor.
Rod soon sussed out that the best blokes to have
speaking to the press were Sam Posey and me.
We were the most willing to talk — and still are.

Wherever we pitched up for a race, Rod would
drag Sam and me around the local TV and radio
stations. These would be in, say, San Francisco if
the race was at Laguna Seca, or Sacramento when
we went to Sears Point. We had a good line in
verbal sparring and enjoyed putting ourselves
across as real enemies. These wars of words
became quite a big thing and soon Rod would
have us on the public-address system at a track
doing the same sort of thing.

'Well, David, what do you think of Sam as
a driver?'

'I think he's a crock of shit.'

All the while we were really close friends and
remain so to this day. I was delighted when Sam
agreed to write the foreword for the book.

These verbal punch-ups continued wherever
we competed together, including later in Can-

Am and then endurance racing, and each of us
became known as very quotable individuals.
Reporters knew they would get some good lines.
So my reputation grew.

Breaking in with CBS

In 1975 I met Ken Squier of CBS. The network
had decided to cover more racing and Graham
Hill, always a very amusing man, was going to
be their new expert analyst. That November, as I
related in Chapter 10, Graham was killed when
he crashed his light aircraft with five members of
his team on board. So Ken said to me, 'Why don't
you try for the job? I'll set up an interview with
Clarence Cross.'

Clarence Cross was a Vice President of Sports
at CBS and the interview took place at his
office on 57th Street in New York only a week
or two after Graham's death. It was the most
embarrassing experience of my entire life. All my
interview skills developed over the years went
right down the tubes. He knew nothing about
racing except for the Indy 500, which I had done

three times with a best result of fifth place. This obviously did not sound that great to him. The conversation went like this.

'Well, I was also the Formula 5000 champion.'

'What's Formula 5000?'

'It's a series for cars that look like Indycars, except that it's road racing.'

'Oh yeah? What's road racing?'

I needed something familiar. Try nearby.

'Well, for example, a track like Lime Rock.'

'What's Lime Rock?'

The interview got worse… and worse… and worse. Sweat was pouring down my spine, soaking my shirt. When it was finally over, Clarence gave me a look that I knew meant only one thing. 'Don't call us, we'll call you.'

When I told Ken what had happened he was disappointed because he wanted to work with me but he just had to shrug his shoulders.

Just a few weeks later, in January 1976, I was in Daytona for the Coca-Cola deal that provided me with drives in a BMW CSL in the 24 Hours and Benny Parsons's second-string NASCAR Chevy in the 500. So I was installed for a while in Daytona, staying at my regular hotel, the Hilton down on the beach. This was quite close to where Ken hosted his popular *Ken Squier Show*, a one-hour radio broadcast live before an audience in the Hawaiian Inn, one of those dreadful hotels along the strip. It would start with girls dancing the hula with candles and flames flashing everywhere (somehow their grass skirts never caught fire) and then after all this fun Ken would host his show.

Ken had been pushing CBS for years to cover NASCAR live on television and that year he finally persuaded Clarence Cross to come down to watch the Daytona 500 and get a feel for what NASCAR was all about. Clarence brought his wife and they arrived a few days before the 500 to take a break from the New York winter. As I was competing in the 500, Ken asked me to come on his show one evening. Many of the top drivers were there and specifically I remember Richard Petty, Cale Yarborough and David Pearson. They all wanted to be on the *Ken Squier Show*.

Clarence and his wife happened to drop in

that night I found myself sitting at a table with them. Timing is everything! My turn to appear came round and I went on with Ken for my five minutes or so of repartee. I had had a couple of gin and tonics, so I was right at the top of the cam but had not yet started to fall off the far side. Whatever I said, the audience absolutely fell about. I picked on Richard Petty, I took the piss out of Cale Yarborough, and so on. When I returned to the table, Mrs Cross leaned over and spoke to me.

'You shouldn't be driving race cars,' she said. 'You should be on the stage.'

I responded, 'Don't tell me, tell him!', pointing at her husband.

To which Clarence said, 'Well, I guess I see what you mean. I see hope now.'

Thereafter I stayed in regular contact with Clarence Cross. With my IMSA commitments for BMW that year, I spent a lot of time in Atlanta, where my HQ was the spare bedroom at the condo of Mike Bailey and his wife Judy in The Vinings. In those days you could not fly direct from Atlanta to London, so for my trips to and from home I usually went via New York. One time I had some hours to kill in New York so I rang Clarence to ask if he could do a quick meeting and he agreed.

He and I had talked earlier about the possibility of me being on the CBS team with Ken for the Pocono 500 Indycar race, although he really wanted Roger McCluskey, the big-name Indycar driver. By the time of our meeting McCluskey had decided to drive in the race, which was just a few days away, and the commentary seat was vacant. I wanted it. As Clarence and I chatted, it was getting quite late in the day, with the setting sun shining through the west-facing windows of his office. Finally, he yielded. 'OK, we'll try you out for the Pocono 500.'

I met Clarence's boss, who said he had heard that I could be amusing and instructed me to be funny, to be succinct and to get my facts right — and to have a good race. We agreed on a fee of $800, a first-class return ticket to and from London, and an expenses allowance of $75 per day. That was a bigger daily allowance than I

have ever received since from a network!

At Pocono I remember doing my very first stand-up with Ken, an on-camera appearance on the grandstand roof to open the broadcast. The cameraman squinted through his eyepiece and kept saying, 'Step back a bit… a little more… just a bit more.' Meanwhile a five-storey drop got ever nearer. Thereafter, I thought that I did a pretty good job, and it helped that I knew the drivers quite well by now, especially as a few weeks earlier I had just driven in the Indy 500 for the fourth time. Big Al Unser, driving for Vel Miletich and Parnelli Jones, won the race and it happened to be the first Indycar win for a Cosworth engine.

Afterwards I called Clarence and asked what he thought.

'Yeah, it was OK.'

'Anything else?'

'No.'

'Well, was I any good?'

'Oh yes, you were fine.'

About a week later I received a call asking if I would like to do the Trenton 200 with Ken. That was where I first met a young CBS assistant, Diane Keogh, who has become a great friend with whom I have worked for one network or another right up to recent years. Soon after the Trenton race I introduced her to Jim Patterson, the competitions manager for BMW in North America, and love blossomed. Soon they were married but their years together were sadly cut short when Jim died of cancer in 1986, just as he got BMW back into IMSA with the turbo GTP car that I drove that year.

After Trenton it all took off with CBS and I worked on every subsequent race broadcast for 20 years.

Many of the races were recorded on tape and we added the commentary later. It was a fairly arduous business and we always seemed to be put in a studio in the middle of the night, because we were a fair way down the food chain. Mainly we did this in a studio on the west side of Manhattan, just a miserable sound booth with a tiny monitor, grainy and hard to see. If you

ABOVE Early days with Ken Squier, who was so pivotal at the start of my television career and who became a long-time and much-valued colleague at CBS.
Getty Images/CBS

made a mistake in your commentary you had to go all the way back to the beginning of a segment and record it again as there was none of today's technology that allows instant audio edits.

Some of those early CBS shows were produced by IMG, the huge marketing company founded by Mark McCormack. The boss of TWI, their TV operation, was the father of network announcer Al Michaels. Susan Friendly, daughter of network pioneer Fred Friendly, worked there as well and she was a fun-loving girl, true to her name. I also worked alongside legendary announcer Vin Scully on one of the early *Superstars* TV competitions in America.

Between 1977 and 1980 I travelled to selected Formula 1 World Championship races for CBS. I remember going to the French Grand Prix at Dijon in 1979 where René Arnoux's Renault and Gilles Villeneuve's Ferrari had that famous last-lap wheel-banging match for second place. Poor Ken kept mangling names, calling Arnoux '*Re-NEE*' and his car a '*RAY-no*'. I would suggest to him that the proper pronunciation was '*RER-nay*' and '*REN-oh*', to which he would nod and say, 'I know that', and then go straight back to his versions. The evening before the race Diane Patterson (*née* Keogh) decided to ask our lap charter/race reader, Andrew Marriott, another long-time friend and my co-writer of this book, to sit down with Ken and go through all the pronunciations. The next day the music rolled and Ken welcomed everyone to '*DIE-jon*'. The one word Andrew had forgotten to rehearse was the circuit itself!

For me that weekend was memorable for more than just that fantastic Arnoux/Villeneuve climax to Sunday's race. It was the July 4th weekend, which of course meant nothing to the French, and on the Monday I was due in Daytona to drive in the Paul Revere IMSA race, which in those days was run on the road course the day after the NASCAR race on the oval. Between them CBS and BMW agreed to pay for me to fly by Concorde as it was the only way I could get there in time.

So, straight after the French Grand Prix, Ken and I got in a rental car and drove from the track to a field where we boarded a helicopter that took us to Dijon's airport, a backwoods place. Here we were joined by Mario Andretti, at that time the reigning Formula 1 World Champion with Team Lotus, and we got in a small plane for the hop to the old Le Bourget airport, in the outskirts of Paris, where Charles Lindbergh landed after his famous solo flight across the Atlantic in 1927. We took a cab from there to the main Charles de Gaulle airport, where I remember calling my niece Sheena on her 21st birthday from the VIP lounge. We caught the 9pm Concorde to Dulles airport in Washington, arriving two and a half hours before my departure time thanks to supersonic flight. We took another cab to what was then Washington National airport for the last leg to Daytona.

While I was waiting in the lounge at Washington National, a young racer walked in who was also heading for Daytona. When he spotted me he nearly dropped his bag! He had waited at home specifically to watch the French Grand Prix, which had been tape delayed and aired on CBS at about 2pm, finishing at 4pm. He headed for the airport at 6pm, and there I was standing there. He was dumbstruck. Despite the epic journey, my BMW failed to finish in the Daytona race.

That year Ken and I also did the United States Grand Prix at Watkins Glen in which one Derek Daly was driving. At this stage, with my racing career continuing alongside my embryonic television work, I found myself asking, 'Why is Derek Daly driving that Tyrrell and not me? Who the hell is Derek Daly anyway?' Derek went on to race Indycars and then begin a television career of his own in America, eventually replacing me at ESPN in 1992.

The 1979 Daytona 500

In 1979, after years of trying, CBS finally did a deal to broadcast the first live, flag-to-flag coverage of a NASCAR race, the Daytona 500. Bill France was scared stiff that no one would come to watch the race in person, preferring to see it on television, but even Big Bill could not see the big picture, that people all over the country would watch it. NASCAR had a problem in that elsewhere in the US it was regarded as

very redneck and regional, not a candidate for national coverage. Of course these television guys were all from New York, which is like a different country compared with the rest of the US, cities like Milwaukee and Cleveland, Kansas City and St Louis. Those guys up on Madison Avenue did not have much clue about how the wider world really works.

So CBS covered the Daytona 500 and it was a big deal. Ken and I did the race commentary, Brock Yates and Ned Jarrett reported from the pits, and Marianne Bunch-Phelps did some other angles such as interviews with Bill France and race grand marshal Ben Gazzara. CBS had a top production team, everyone keen as mustard and hard-working, with Mike Pearl and Mike Fishman producing and directing respectively. The music they used was great, the soundtrack from the film *The Electric Horseman*, and the production values were impressive in every way. But in the end it was the race itself that made the broadcast so momentous. The script could not have been better.

The first 15 laps ran under yellow flags because the track was still wet from rain the night before. Once the field was released, Donnie Allison, Cale Yarborough and Bobby Allison battled at the front until, on lap 32, Donnie lost control and forced the other two to take evasive action. All three cars spun forever through the backstretch infield, which was very slippery after the rain, Donnie losing a whole lap and the other two dropping back by a couple of laps. After the consequent yellow, a massive bunch, as many as 18 cars, made up the leading pack but gradually cars were eliminated — and all the while the original leaders made up ground.

With 22 laps to go, Donnie Allison retook the lead and Yarborough was right with him, having used caution periods to unwind his two-lap deficit. These two guys were just flying, round and round and round, pulling away from everyone else, with Richard Petty soon half a lap down in third place. Coming down to Turn Three on the last lap Donnie threw a block on Cale, they weaved around for bit, then Cale busted through and they crashed into each other and slid along the wall. When their cars came to rest, they immediately got out and started fighting. Meanwhile Richard Petty came round and won his umpteenth Daytona 500. Then Bobby Allison hove into view on his slowing-down lap, jumped out of his car to help his brother, and ended up in the brawl as well. It was great television, with Ken and I becoming ever more hysterical.

Up in New York and all over the north-east, meanwhile, there was heavy snow and as a consequence the television audience was much bigger than predicted, about six million or so, and suddenly vast numbers of people knew exactly what NASCAR was. That race put NASCAR on the map.

After they discovered NASCAR, CBS dropped most other forms of racing and I ended up doing rather less for them. In NASCAR I generally only did the top three races of the day — Daytona 500, Michigan 400 and Talladega 500 — and there were occasional Indycar, Formula 1 and Le Mans roles.

Branching out with ESPN

As the 1980s progressed I started to give more thought to the fact that my driving career was not going to continue forever and I needed to build up my television work. Opportunities with CBS were not frequent enough, so I started to wonder about approaching the ESPN cable channel. In those days the networks were pretty dismissive of cable television and my CBS contract was about three feet thick with all the things I could not do for other stations, but I had covered a few races with TBS, including the SCCA Runoffs at Road Atlanta with Mike Joy. He absolutely flabbergasted me: at Road Atlanta I could not believe how Mike seemed to know every single driver and their chief mechanics — thousands of them! Eventually I phoned ESPN and spoke to their motorsports producer, Terry Lingner, about a job.

'You're a network guy. Why would you want to work for us?'

'Yes, but you guys do a lot of racing, all that IMSA and so on.'

BELOW I have sat in hundreds of commentary booths with this great man — Bob Varsha has been a wonderful friend and colleague and was the instigator of this book.
David Hobbs collection

'Well, we'd certainly be glad to have you work for us, but are you really sure you want to do this?'

'Why not? The more the merrier, and I'm sure you'll want to pay me something.'

So I went to work for the ESPN. My first broadcast, in November 1987, was a road race at St Petersburg, Florida working with Bob Varsha. Sadly, it was the weekend Jim Fitzgerald, team-mate to actor and racer Paul Newman, was killed in the Trans-Am event. Soon I was doing a lot of work for ESPN, broadening first into IMSA Camel GT and Barber Saab, then Trans-Am and Atlantics.

That same year ESPN parted company with Jackie Stewart, who had been handling their Formula 1 coverage with John Bisignano and Chris Economaki. So for 1988 I was asked to join John and Chris travelling the world with the Formula 1 circus. We went to the opening race, the Brazilian Grand Prix in Rio de Janeiro, working out of a booth made of balsa wood and corrugated iron on top of a grandstand.

Chris, who was 67 at the time, looked at the long flight of stairs to get to our booth and said, 'If I want to go for a piss I'm not walking up and down those goddamn stairs. I need an empty bottle to piss in.' So our producer, Conrad Piccirillo, went off looking for a suitable receptacle. Meanwhile, there was trouble getting an audio signal through to headquarters in Bristol, Connecticut and some poor Brazilian sound engineer was ferreting around on the floor trying to fix it. Of course he could not speak a word of English so Conrad, now back from his menial mission, fell back on the old method of making foreigners understand, screaming more and more loudly, 'Get that effing thing fixed! We're on air in 45 effing seconds!' It came good with about 20 seconds to go but I thought Conrad was going to have a heart attack.

Chris was a great travelling companion that year. He had so many stories, although you did tend to hear the same ones over and over, even if it did take time for them to come round again. Wherever we went he knew all the best restaurants. Before the San Marino Grand Prix

at Imola, Mags and I drove down early from England to visit Venice for a few days before heading onwards to Bologna, where we had dinner with Chris. He told us he had been to the place before with his wife Tommie and recommended a couple of dishes. During the course of the meal I asked when he and Tommie had last visited the restaurant. It was 20 years earlier — and Chris could remember what he had eaten for dinner.

Chris's lifetime in motor racing left him with a common racer's complaint in later years — poor hearing. At the Italian Grand Prix at Monza, Conrad shouted over our headsets that we were going to a break in one minute… going to a break in 30… 20… break in ten, nine, eight... Chris just kept going on and on until finally I realised that

ABOVE **Chris Economaki: commentator, publisher, raconteur — and a huge influence on my broadcasting career.**
David Hobbs collection

he had not heard Conrad's commands. With the combined sound of his own voice and the cars racing past our open booth at Monza, he could not hear anything else. So I jumped in.

'We'll take a quick break and come back with more of the Italian Grand Prix in just a minute.'

'What? What are you doing?'

'They've been counting us to break for the last minute.'

'They have? I didn't hear any of that.'

After one year Chris was replaced by Bob Varsha and together we did more Formula 1 and lots of sports car racing.

I had a rather disappointing experience with ESPN in 1991. They dropped me from their Formula 1 coverage in favour of Derek Daly because a Vice President named John Wildhack considered Derek to be, in his words, 'one of the best announcers I've ever heard'. In fact it was not only Formula 1 that ceased for me — I lost the lot. That provoked me to do something very out of character: I got proactive and climbed on a plane to visit Wildhack.

'I don't know why you don't want me,' I said, 'because you guys get nothing but compliments about my performance. But if you don't want me for Formula 1, what about everything else?'

Wildhack said he had just assumed that I would not want to work for them on anything other than Formula 1. So, he agreed to my suggestion, and after my visit I wound up doing a lot of other series for them — Trans-Am, Formula Atlantic, IMSA. Wildhack is now ESPN's Executive President, Programming and Production, so sacking me from Formula 1 did no harm to him, and nor me that matter.

My last CBS broadcast was the 1995 Daytona 500. Some years earlier my role had changed because CBS wanted to put Neil Bonnett, who had just retired as a NASCAR driver, in the commentary booth instead of me, so I became pitlane reporter. That felt like a demotion and did not suit me. In due course Neil decided to go back to racing and in February 1994 he was killed in a Daytona 500 practice accident, which was most distressing for all of us on the CBS team. A year later Eric Mann, who is still at CBS Sports and has now won 18 Emmy Awards, said they did not need me any more. 'We don't think you're right for the part and anyway NASCAR coverage needs NASCAR guys.'

He was right. In the booth I was fine, but in the pits I was hopeless. I was not a reporter and I disliked having to ask a load of questions. As a racer myself, I never felt comfortable interrogating other drivers about their errors or mechanical failures. The very worst aspect was that when someone got hurt the producer would urge you to find out what had happened and interview the poor man's wife or girlfriend while he was being carried off in an ambulance — not my scene at all.

Enter Speedvision

It was at about this time that I received a call from an ex-ESPN producer called Bob Scanlon. It was well timed. He told me he was part of a new television network that was being set up by Roger Werner, another ex-ESPN guy. Based in Stanford, Connecticut, it was called Speedvision and it would be true to its name — all forms of racing from cars and bikes to airplanes and boats. They wanted Sam Posey and me to be part of it. When I went to see them they offered me more money than I had ever been paid by a television network.

Speedvision was launched on 31 December 1995 and almost immediately upended ESPN's cosy arrangement with Formula 1, which Werner and Scanlon had negotiated in the first place. At first we only had secondary rights, with Speedvision airing the Grands Prix on a Monday with commentary by Sam Posey and me. But within a couple of years Speedvision took the whole thing from ESPN.

Derek Daly's ugly head briefly reared itself again. Roger Werner thought that Sam and I were not sufficiently upbeat and too conversational, so he brought in Derek 'to help'. That did not last long as I think viewers quickly tired of him. Then Bob Varsha joined our group and we even tried a flowery talk show together, with Bob putting questions to Sam and me. It was a complete flop.

LEFT On my 60th birthday, on 9 June 1999, the Speedvision team — Andrew Marriott (left), Alain de Cadenet and me — sneaked away from yet another Le Mans briefing meeting and hit the red wine.
David Hobbs collection

BELOW Steve Matchett gives me a hug in his early days in the Speedvision studio, while Sam Posey looks over his glasses and Bob Varsha is ready for action.
David Hobbs collection

Invariably there was a calendar clash every June between the Canadian Grand Prix and Le Mans. Roger had added Le Mans to Speedvision's programme line-up and he wanted me to do it, since I had been there so many times both as a driver and as a broadcaster. But we needed back-up and so our new producer, Frank Wilson, asked what I thought of Steve Matchett.

'Who's Steve Matchett?'

'He's written that book *Life In The Fast Lane*.'

'I don't read racing books.'

'Oh, it's not a racing book. It's about the life of a mechanic, from a mechanic's point of view. A mechanic who worked for Michael Schumacher.'

'Honestly, I don't know him. I've never read the book. I don't know anything about him.'

Frank had read the book and was very taken with it, so he contacted Steve. The rest, as they say, is history. Like me, Steve has now been a television commentator for longer than he was involved in racing.

In 2000 one of Speedvision's early investors, Fox Sports, took over most of the company and

Roger Werner walked away with many millions. Very soon it became apparent that NASCAR was going to get a much bigger slice of the airtime. Some of the other programming dropped away but they retained Formula 1, Le Mans and the two rival sports car championships, the American Le Mans Series (ALMS) and Grand-Am. The name changed twice, first to the Speed Channel and then just Speed.

Five years with NBC

Halfway through 2012 Speed lost the Formula 1 rights for the following year to NBC, who had set up a new sports channel. Coincidentally, at about the same time we heard that Speed and the Velocity Channel were going to be merged into a new Fox Sports channel. Steve Matchett and I thought we were doomed because we were certain that a new broom would bring in different talent, but to our amazement Sam Flood, Vice President of NBC Sports, asked us to attend a meeting in New York and there we were offered a four-year agreement — and in

BELOW **What the viewers see — introducing NBC's coverage of the Mexican Grand Prix from the studio.**
NBC

LEFT With the great
Mario Andretti at Circuit
of The Americas, Austin,
Texas, for the Formula 1
Grand Prix in 2014.
LAT Images

RIGHT A jolly photo with
my Australian-born NBC
co-commentator Leigh
Diffey. His background
was in motorcycle racing
but more recently he
has also covered the
Olympics, golf and rugby.
Jamey Price Photography

RIGHT AND BELOW

I love this cartoon by well-known Australian 'Stoney' showing me flanked by Leigh Diffey (left) and Steve Matchett at the NBC desk. It was used to promote the stage shows that Leigh runs. These have proved to be very popular, giving us a great chance to interact with the public.
Stoney

the race, but that changed with NBC. At Speed the only Formula 1 Grand Prix we had attended was the one at Indianapolis, but with NBC we did travel to Monaco, Montréal and Austin. That was refreshing because you would always meet a lot of people and there is no substitute for talking face to face. Of course, sitting down with drivers for any length of time has become impossible and they always seem to have a fleet of PR girls controlling them minute by minute.

When we were in the studio back in the US we had the full timing and scoring with all the split times, just like the guys in the booths at the track. Of course, we had no control over the on-site director so we never had any warning if he suddenly decided to pick up that exciting battle for 15th place or show some pretty girl in the pits. You had to be on your guard for that. With both Speed and NBC, there was always a pits reporter at the track for us. Until 2014 this was Peter Windsor and thereafter Will Buxton — both terrific and knowledgeable guys.

I think the chemistry in our NBC commentary

fact I worked for NBC until they in turn lost the Formula 1 rights, to ESPN, at the end of 2017. Unfortunately no call came for Bob Varsha, but there was a place for Leigh Diffey, Bob's occasional Formula 1 'relief' who had worked for Speed for some years.

NBC gave me a whole new lease of broadcasting life with a major network, although the job was busier and more intense. In ESPN days, when we were travelling to races, we never did commentary on practice and qualifying, just

LEFT British readers may wonder why I was being 'roasted' but it is an American expression for a celebration dinner. With me at this charity function in Milwaukee are (from left) Russ Lake (the organiser), Bob Varsha, Tom Anderson, Judy Stropus, Dave Despain, Derek Bell and Kevin Olsen.
David Hobbs collection

team of Steve, Leigh and me was probably second to none. We not only always got on well in the studio but also out of it and had a lot of fun off the set. Steve, of course, has always been very good at laughing at my sillier comments, which always helps. I have had lots of super emails and tweets from fans about the jokes and banter between the three of us.

I love commentating and always found doing television a big vicarious thrill, almost like being in a race except that you do not get hot, sweaty and tired, nor do you get shaken about like a pea in a pod with your neck stretched every which way. There is a buzz doing it, particularly when the lights go out, with a tremendous feeling of anticipation, and I never lost that sense of excitement throughout my 40 years at the microphone.

Public speaking

I have found myself in demand for public speaking, hosting occasions such as banquets and charity events. I think it has always been

LEFT I have always enjoyed the Amelia Island Concours d'Elegance near Jacksonville, Florida, run by the redoubtable Bill Warner. This is the front cover of the programme from 2009 when I was the guest of honour.
David Hobbs collection

Milwaukee Mile and also did a lot of work at Indy. His son had a life-threatening disease so he decided to raise some money for families in a similar position and founded the Wisconsin Motor Sports Charity for children with serious childhood diseases. At its fund-raiser in 1992 I was one of the honorees and the master of ceremonies was Chris Economaki.

The following year Russ asked me to take over from Chris — and I carried on doing it for 16 years. This annual function was big, with as many as 500 guests, and took a lot of hard work and planning. Over the years we raised over half a million dollars for Ranch Community Services, which gave the kids the chance to go to a horse ranch, a treat they always loved. A lot of the big NASCAR names attended and so did stars from other disciplines like drag racing's Don 'The Snake' Prudhomme and the renowned midget and sprint car champion Mel Kenyon.

In 2009 I was inducted into the American Motorsports Hall of Fame and after my acceptance speech, Ron Watson, the General Secretary, asked if I would be master of ceremonies the following year — and I still do that great event to this day.

That same year I was also honoured at the big Amelia Island Concours d'Elegance, just up the road from our home in Florida, and I seem to return every year on one panel or another.

In 2014 I was the Grand Marshal for the Rolex 24 at Daytona and that was a great event. Mags and all the family were there and my speech and question-and-answer session with Murray Smith went down well. In fact I discovered that weekend that being a Grand Marshal is one of the best jobs in motorsports.

I enjoy the banter of these occasions and have always been more than happy to do them, although there are many drivers who prefer to avoid standing up and singing for their supper. Along the way we have done our bit for charity and entertained people at functions of all kinds, not just the events I have mentioned but others involving car clubs or connected with my Honda dealership.

ABOVE I was proud to be inducted into the Motorsports Hall of Fame of America in 2009. I have since become master of ceremonies at this annual event.
David Hobbs collection

in my DNA to entertain: when I was at school I thought about becoming an actor, and my sometimes reluctant audiences were first my parents, then my school mates and later the apprentices at Daimler and Jaguar.

Soon after Mags and I moved across the Atlantic, from Upper Boddington to Milwaukee in 1994, a guy called Russ Lake contacted me. He was the official photographer for the

ABOVE I attend a lot of vintage gatherings and sometimes, as here at Pebble Beach, one of my old race cars shows up. This is the Ford GT40 that I drove to third place at Le Mans in 1969.
David Hobbs collection

LEFT Now we have all written books! From left, Brian Redman, John Fitzpatrick and me with journalist and broadcaster Andrew Marriott, who helped get mine to the finish line. Andrew reported my early races in the Lotus Elite and can still be found in the pitlane at Le Mans.
David Hobbs collection

CHAPTER 16
HOME, FAMILY AND BUSINESS

As you will have gathered, for the best part of two decades, really from around 1969 to the end of my driving career, I raced — and in due course commentated — mainly in America but continued to live in England, where my sons Greg and Guy grew up. Gradually, as more and more of my life revolved around America, it became overwhelmingly logical to make the move and since 1994 Mags and I have lived very happily in the US, and Greg and Guy have made their careers here too.

I have managed to maintain my English accent, which television viewers have always seemed to like. I still miss a few things about England — the pubs, the beautiful countryside, the pretty villages — but now when Mags and I return every six months or so I find the traffic on the major routes absolutely daunting, any time of day or night. Many things about the US suit me: travel is easier, I like the space, the bigger houses and the lifestyle, and the cost of living is so much lower than in Europe.

Our houses

Mags and I set up home together in Warwick in 1961 when we bought our first house with a deposit provided by an inheritance from my grandmother in Australia. It was a modest detached house on the new Percy estate on the north-east side of Warwick, adjoining Guy's

LEFT This is my 50th birthday party at the wonderful Hôtel de France in La Chartre-sur-le-Loir. Among friends and family centre stage with Mags and me are Bill Postins (with arm round Mags) and his wife Joan. My friendship with Bill goes back to my very first year of racing.
David Hobbs collection

ABOVE Cricket in the summer of 1971 on the village green, adjoining our house in Upper Boddington. With our sons Greg and Guy at the wicket, Mags umpires in her trendy Carnaby Street outfit.

David Hobbs collection

Cliffe, ancient home of the Guy family — and a factor in our choice of name for our second son.

In 1966, when I was starting to earn some decent money from racing, we moved into Hill Farm House on Frog Lane, Upper Boddington, in the countryside about halfway between the towns of Banbury and Daventry. As I explained in Chapter 5, Mags gamely had to take care of removals on her own while looking after Greg and Guy, aged four and two, because I was racing in the Spa 1,000Km. When I arrived back on the Monday afternoon, the removal men were shutting up the tail lift on their lorry and about to drive off.

Hill Farm House was about 350 years old and originally its roof had been thatched, but that had been replaced with ugly corrugated asbestos. We always wanted to get rid of this, but despite considerable restoration work over the years it was the one job that never got done. One major improvement was to buy the attached next-door cottage, almost doubling the size of the house, turning the whole thing into a lovely home,

even if it became rather long from end to end.

The next-door cottage was occupied when we moved in. One evening these neighbours had us over for dinner and at the table were Bob Driver and his wife Sarah. Mags and I were astonished — Bob had been with us when we partied in Monaco after the Formula Junior race four years earlier. Talk about a small world. We four have remained friends ever since.

Hill Farm House sat in an acre, a field really, which we developed over the years into quite a nice garden. About a mile down the road was a seven-acre wood that was available as a £750 optional extra, having been part of the original farm. As the vendor of this land offered to lend the necessary funds with no interest over 10 years, we bought that too.

Across the road in a thatched cottage lived a family with children of similar ages to ours and we became firm friends. Percy Taylor was a farmer and lay preacher, a real fire-and-brimstone man, but away from the pulpit he became a very different Percy. His wife Rhiannon was a lovely girl and she and Mags had a great friendship until Rhiannon's tragic death from a brain tumour in 2012. Their two children, Jeremy and Miranda, have played a big part in our lives too. Our Guy and their Jeremy were Best Man at each other's weddings and remain great friends.

In 1971 we considered upgrading when the Manor House and its nine acres came up for sale in Lower Boddington, about a mile away. Luckily for us, before we made any decision a young entrepreneur and his wife stepped in to buy it. John and Helen Sadiq also had a couple of boys of the same ages as our two and we all took to each other immediately. We have spent 40 very happy years as close friends, taken many trips together, and found our lives intertwined in most unexpected ways. Sometimes the Sadiqs joined the Hobbs family on our idyllic summer vacations at Siebkens on the shore of Elkhart Lake, Wisconsin, from where I would go off racing at weekends. In due course both of these Sadiq boys married Siebken daughters and moved there for good. To add to the immigration, a few years later the Sadiqs' third son, Daniel, my godson, married

another totally unconnected American, Kelley, and they wound up in Elkhart Lake as well. John and Helen, wanting to be close to their offspring, built a house at Elkhart Lake and spend a lot of time there. Weird story!

After 18 years in our little cottage, we decided to move to a bigger house in the same area. After looking at a couple of places, our minds were made up for us. Mags and I were having lunch in the Butchers Arms — of which more anon — when we were approached by a lady whom we had both known for a very long time, having been to her house a couple of times for parties when we were teenagers. When we told her we were thinking of moving, she said that her house was on the market and was very insistent that we should look at it as soon as we had finished our lunch. We duly bought Hardwick Hill in 1984 and stayed there for 10 wonderful years. Some foundations of the house went back 500 years but the main part of it was built in the 19th century. I will always remember the marvellous views: you could see for miles over the truly magnificent Warwickshire countryside and there were spectacular sunsets. The house came with 40 acres of land that we rented to our neighbouring farmer.

In 1994, a few years after I had retired from driving, we moved to America, prompted by the need for me to take over the direct running of my Honda dealership in Milwaukee, as you will learn later in this chapter. We kept a foot in the English countryside by buying a brand-new house in the grounds of our old Hill Farm House, built by the bloke who had bought the place from us.

In Milwaukee we lived for eight years in an apartment in a big old house overlooking Lake Michigan. One day in 2002, as I set off for work at the dealership, I noticed a 'For Sale' sign had gone up on a house just a few doors down the street. I did a smart U-turn back to our apartment to give Mags the news and we were immediately in agreement. Just three days later the house was ours — we drivers never hang about!

Our new home was a lovely period piece. It had been built in 1902 for a grocer and fancy

goods storekeeper and had been little touched since. An executive from Allis Chalmers, a manufacturer of agricultural machinery and one of Milwaukee's biggest employers for many years, had lived there for over 40 years and did nothing to it. We, on the other hand, carried out a major but sympathetic restoration and in the end Mags must have had one of the biggest and best kitchens in Milwaukee. As with our apartment just down the road, the location was wonderful, with fabulous views of Lake Michigan and the harbour and marina. Much as we loved that house, in the end we decided to relocate one more time, mainly because Wisconsin winters are so bitterly cold.

We went to Vero Beach, Florida, where our friends Brian and Marion Redman have lived for years. Here we have a much smaller home, but again we seem to be spending vast amounts of money completely rebuilding this one too. It is very convenient for town, on a boat canal with dock and boat lift, although we have no boat. It looks good and it is warm. You cannot beat it.

We still have a house in Elkhart Lake where we spend a few months in the summer, seeing old friends, including the Sadiq family. Daniel and Kelley Sadiq now run the best coffee shop for miles around, 'Off the Rail', frequented by many racers, Oliver Gavin being a big fan.

Racing in the blood

Our older son Greg, born on 3 May 1962, wanted to follow in my footsteps and tried valiantly, on a shoestring. He did a year of Formula 3 in England in 1985 with a very old race car towed around on a two-wheel trailer by an even older van, and he was the mechanic too. Reality struck hard when Derek Warwick's brother, Paul, turned up with a brand-new car, a full race transporter, a couple of ex-Formula 1 mechanics and plenty of spares; Mark Blundell had a similar entourage.

Like me, Greg also came across to the US and raced a BMW 320 with some success. In 1987, as mentioned in Chapter 14, he and I drove together in the Sebring 12 Hours in a BMW-engined Gebhardt, but did not last the distance.

Eventually it became apparent that we were never going to be able to raise sufficient funds for Greg to make a real go of it. Instead he has done a great job running our Honda dealership in Milwaukee for nearly 20 years.

Our younger son Guy, born on 14 May 1964, went into racing but not as a driver. After doing a two-year media course he got opportunities with ESPN, particularly with their international wing, and then worked for Speed at Le Mans and a lot of Indycar races. Unfortunately, some health setbacks have put a stop to this and it has been quite a challenging time for Guy, but he still follows the sport closely and hopefully he can get back into it, because he was good. People still talk about his call at Le Mans when Audi changed the whole rear end of an R8 in about four minutes as a classic example of outstanding commentary.

Now we are onto the third generation with Greg's son Andrew. He started racing go-karts at a place called Kettle Bottom in Elkhart Lake when he was about eight and then competed for some years with the Badger Kart Club at

ABOVE Greg and Guy wearing suitable headgear for a trip on the water, aged about nine and seven. When I was racing in America, we all spent very happy summer holidays together at Elkhart Lake.
David Hobbs collection

LEFT Our son Guy followed me into TV work. Here he is interviewing Emerson Fittipaldi for ESPN International at a 1989 round of the PPG Indy Car World Series.
David Hobbs collection

RIGHT Third-generation
racer: grandson Andrew
in his karting days at
the Briggs & Stratton
Motorplex kart circuit at
Road America.
David Hobbs collection

BELOW When grandson
Andrew was competing
at Road America in
2016, driving an Aston
Martin Vantage in
the IMSA Continental
Championship, Fox
Sports interviewed
both of us.
David Hobbs collection

Dousman, another great Wisconsin venue. He got into cars at the age of 17 in the Skip Barber series and has raced in many different classes and cars, and at some interesting places including in New Zealand. But Andrew, too, has run into that implacable wall of huge expense because it costs so much money to move up to the next stage. He is definitely good and many of the people he has raced against, and beaten, have gone onto bigger things, but, equally, plenty of them reach the next rung and then disappear off the scene as the hideous cost catches up with them too.

Car dealerships

The idea of having a car dealership business goes all the way back to 1978, when I was driving for BMW. I realised my days of earning money as a racing driver were numbered, not thinking that I would carry on pretty seriously for another 10 years. Although I also had my television work, I had no idea how long that might last and so I thought I needed another string to my bow. A car dealership seemed the obvious way to go.

I knew a reasonable amount about day-to-day cars and had been involved with them ever since childhood, first with my father in the little garage at home and then through my apprenticeship at Jaguar. As I was driving for BMW, it seemed the obvious manufacturer and I spoke to the

ABOVE This is David Hobbs Honda in Glendale, Milwaukee. We ran this newspaper advert in 2003 when my sister Barbara and her husband Alan came to visit us. With Mags and Greg in the picture too, the message is that we are a family-run business.

David Hobbs Honda

President of BMW North America. He introduced me to a successful BMW dealer who was based in San Francisco but had other dealerships elsewhere, including a newly acquired one in Houston, Texas that was not performing very well. We called it David Hobbs BMW and in return I received a 10 per cent stake. He changed the management team and immediately our sales went through the roof. Remember, at this time I was still racing the factory-supported BMW 320i Turbo very successfully and that got a lot of exposure. Although I was the silent partner and not involved with the running of David Hobbs

BMW, I used to visit quite often to show my face, talk to customers and sign autographs.

Towards the end of 1980 this fellow took over a Porsche dealership in Monterey, California and put my name on that too. That Christmas he came over to England with his wife and son and they spent a few days with us at home. On New Year's Eve we all stayed at the Lygon Arms in the picturesque village of Broadway in the Cotswolds and had a very good time.

The following summer two of his financial people came to visit me at the IMSA race in Portland and told me of their considerable misgivings about business malpractice in the two operations carrying my name. One of the more serious concerns was that the same assets had been pledged as collateral at different banks — not only dodgy but illegal. Needless to say, this came as a shock and it was obvious that I had to pull out. My ex-friend, to be fair, did pay a very reasonable sum for my 10 per cent.

In 1981, while covering the Talladega 500 for CBS, I was chatting with Brock Yates, our pit reporter and one of America's leading automotive journalists. Brock was enthusing about the new Honda Prelude, saying it was a terrific car made by a well-managed company with a focus on engineering quality. Although Honda at this time was still primarily a motorcycle manufacturer, the company's automotive side was growing rapidly and Brock felt that it would become a major player. Briefly, of course, I had tested and raced for Honda, in 1968, when they were running their Formula 1 programme. Some of the engineers from that race team moved on to senior engineering and management roles.

After that conversation with Brock, I strolled down pitlane to Junie Donlavey's garage. This NASCAR stalwart, for whom I had driven in the 1976 Michigan 400, was still running his trusty Ford, for Dick Brooks. One of Junie's partners was Jack Billmyer, who had been part of Ford's successes at Le Mans but was now a Vice President at Honda in charge of dealer development in the US. We talked and eventually I asked him if a dealership would be a possibility if I were to invest. He was extremely enthusiastic as Honda was already underway with the notion of having well-known racing names as dealer principals. Dick Brooks and Cale Yarborough were owners and Darrell Waltrip and Bobby Rahal soon joined them.

The following year, 1982, I started to drive for John Fitzpatrick and put out feelers. Among Fitz's backers were two real enthusiasts, Ron McIntyre and Gary Wassell, and they agreed to invest with me. One of the people who had warned me of the problems with the BMW dealership, Doug O'Connor, agreed to run the place. We were all set to press the button when the US government, after lobbying from Chrysler President Lee Iaccoca among others, came to an agreement with Japan to limit the number of vehicles imported from that country. So Honda put our dealership on hold. Nearly six years passed before we finally got it up and running but very quickly I found another opportunity.

I was at a BMW car club gathering for a talk to the assembled members when someone told me that the BMW dealership in Columbus, Ohio was for sale. Doug and I went to visit this establishment and felt that it seemed modestly priced considering its potential. The existing ownership had run the place badly, with very mediocre sales and terrible customer relations. With our Honda plans on hold, we decided to buy it, and BMW became quite excited about the prospect of improvement. With Doug in charge, we started to sell a lot more cars, and we found a young service manager, Brian Davis, who was magic on the technical side and also very good with customers. Things really started to hum and turnover tripled within about 18 months.

Then we made a big mistake. The BMW buy/sell agreement between us and the previous owner stipulated that, when the time was right, we would move from the existing downtown location to one of the affluent suburbs and build new, larger premises — and BMW now thought the time was right. We should have resisted because we were not ready and needed to make more money in order to fund this venture. However, we went ahead and built a new place in Dublin, a few miles north-west of Colombus.

By this time BMW's sales in America were starting to decline after a boom period. The peak came in 1986, when BMW sold nearly 97,000 cars in the US, but thereafter volumes fell every year until 1991, when they bottomed out at just over 53,000. With the new premises, we had expected to increase our sales from 300 cars a year to 500 but in fact we carried on at about 300.

Just as the difficulties were setting in with our BMW business, Honda gave the go-ahead. Of three possible locations offered by Honda, the

BELOW **We make the most of my racing connections at David Hobbs Honda and some of my trophies and racing memorabilia are displayed there.**
David Hobbs Honda

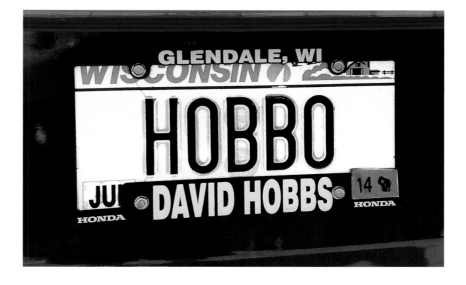

RIGHT Displayed at
David Hobbs Honda
with three generations
of Hobbs racers — Greg,
Andrew and me — is the
Boraxo-liveried Formula
5000 Lola T332 that Brian
Redman drove in 1975.
David Hobbs Honda

biggest and best was in Glendale, Milwaukee,
with projected annual sales of 800 cars. I had
been to Milwaukee many times when racing at
Road America, just 50 miles up the road, and this
prospect seemed a natural fit for me personally.
I got together with my existing backers, Ron
McIntyre and Gary Wassell, because land had
to be bought and built on. At first they were
a little uneasy because we were now going to
have a second dealership at a time when the first
was faltering, but in the end we sold the BMW
business to a guy whose father had prospered as
the US VW importer but had just got divorced.
Our purchaser's mother, I reckon, gave him
the dollars to buy our store for probably more
than it was worth, as a poke in the eye for her
ex-husband. It got us off the hook! When BMW's
turn-around eventually got underway in the
1990s, sales sky-rocketed and a BMW dealership
virtually became a licence to print money.

We opened the Honda dealership in May 1987
and immediately did very well, soon becoming
the number one Honda outlet in Milwaukee. As
before, Doug was going to run the place but then
his wife was offered a big opportunity in Seattle
and they moved there, leaving me and a manager,
whom I will name simply as Judy, to do the job.
Judy had warned me about certain excesses that
went on in the trade but then proceeded to fall
right into those very traps. One example was
advertising — our first TV commercial cost a
ridiculous $25,000 to produce but nowadays we
get a similar result for about $3,000. She just kept
on over-spending and Honda warned that we
were eating into our working capital. We ended
up with an accumulated loss of about $2 million.

Meanwhile, back home in England with Mags,
I had been enjoying the arrival of my monthly
revenue from the dealership until suddenly,
some time in 1990, it stopped coming. I flew to
Milwaukee for a crunch meeting with the bank.
I was told to get rid of my manager and start
running the business myself, even though I
really did not know how to go about that — but
the bank insisted. It all worked out better than I
expected and became relatively successful.

After two years on my own running the dealership, I realised I needed help. Bringing in my son Greg was the ideal solution. Greg had already done spells in the BMW and Honda dealerships before returning to England to work in insurance, initially with motorsports specialist T.L. Clowes. During this period he married his long-time American girlfriend, Kristen, in Priors Hardwick church, from where a 1926 4½-litre Bentley conveyed them the few hundred yards to our home for a wonderful reception in a big marquee on our lawn — all in all one of the best days ever. In 1992 Greg returned to Milwaukee with Kris to rejoin the dealership in charge of the parts department. In due course, as my television career gathered momentum, he became general manager and over time he has taken more and more control. Meanwhile I was able to buy out my partners so now it is a wholly family-owned business. Greg is the voice of the dealership in all TV and radio advertising and in turn his son, Andrew, shows interest in joining the business.

When we first considered the Milwaukee site we had the choice of buying one four-acre plot or two plots totalling eight acres. As I am English and at that time was not a US resident, I was unable to borrow the money for the extra land, so a friendly nearby dealer bought it and built on it, and we rented these premises from him. Of course, he must have been thinking that these boys were going to go bust and then he could take over their very desirable Honda dealership. In fact after 10 years we bought the land and the building from him and expanded further into the area that we could have acquired in the first place. Now we have 1,200 feet of frontage, which is big for a dealership, and our staff numbers around 50 people.

Watering holes

During all my globetrotting I have been lucky enough to stay in some splendid hotels and dine in some fine restaurants, in France, Britain and the United States in particular. Over the years a few have become real favourites.

Top of my list is the Hôtel de France in La

LEFT Not a French car in sight! This is the Hôtel de France in La Chartre-sur-le-Loir on the occasion of my first stay, in 1964 as a works Triumph driver. The noses of two of our team's Triumph 2000 saloons are just visible at left and a couple of British-registered Ford Cortinas are prominent.
David Hobbs collection

Chartre-sur-le-Loir, south of Le Mans. Not only is it a cute little place, although the rooms are small and it can be a little noisy, but the restaurant is always absolutely fabulous. I first went there with the works Triumph team in 1964, and when I signed for the Gulf Ford GT40 team in 1968 I learned that the boss, John Wyer, had discovered this hotel long before and based his works Aston Martin team there during visits in the 1950s.

In fact lots of teams used the Hôtel de France over the years. Steve McQueen based himself there when he first started filming *Le Mans*, in 1970, and two American Presidents have stayed there too. As well as the food, in its favour was a rough old Renault garage nearby where the race cars used to be prepared. The mechanics used to drive the race cars, even the Porsche 917s, on the road the 25 miles to the track.

I have had my 40th, 50th and 60th birthday parties at the Hôtel de France. The 60th was arranged secretly by Mags, although she was not actually present and managed to organise

it, with the help of our friend Peter Pires, by remote control. That year I was commentating at Le Mans for Speedvision and they had put us in a bland hotel in the city. On the day of my birthday, however, Peter and my son Greg turned up and seemed most anxious that I should go down to the Hôtel de France with them. Some Speedvision meetings overran and in the end I said we had better forget it, but they were insistent. By the time we arrived, of course, loads of friends were waiting there, getting pretty hungry. It was a super occasion.

The aforementioned Peter Pires was a family friend who tragically died only recently after a battle with cancer, aged just 50. Our becoming friends is a story in itself. When we were living at Hill Farm House in Upper Boddington, there was a very basic little pub in the next village, Priors Hardwick, a tiny place with about 15 houses set in the beautiful Warwickshire countryside, not far from Stratford-upon-Avon. This pub, the Butchers Arms, was not at all hospitable and very few people went there. Meanwhile, one of the most thriving restaurants in the Midlands was in Warwick and a big part of its success was its barman, Lino Pires from Portugal, one of the most personable people I have ever met. Its customers were generally quite affluent and Lino managed to get some of them to help him invest in his own place. So, in 1971, he bought this dreadful old pub in Priors Hardwick.

After the deal was done, Lino took his wife, Augusta, to check out the place and she burst into tears because it looked so grim, but soon they transformed it into one of the best restaurants in the area, complete with really lovely gardens. Augusta used to do the cooking, Lino was the smooth and urbane front man, and their son Peter in due course became mine host. Mags and I quickly became real regulars. After we moved to Hardwick Hill we were only a short walk from the Butchers Arms and went there even more often.

For decades my favourite watering hole in America has been Siebkens, the famous establishment on the shore of Elkhart Lake,

BELOW The long-time French owners of the Hôtel de France, Noël and Raymonde Pasteau, always welcomed Mr and Mrs Hobbs very warmly. *David Hobbs collection*

close to Road America. It was started in 1916 by Laura and Herman Siebken and remains in the ownership of their descendants four generations later. Although I first went to Road America in 1964, driving a Lotus Cortina, we stayed miles away in Madison, and when I returned in 1969 for Formula 5000 I stayed at Sharp's Summer Resort, which is still there. It was only in 1970 that I discovered Siebkens and soon it became almost a second home in America not only for me but also the family, as Mags and the boys used to come out to stay for the duration of the school summer holidays.

Doug and Pam Lueck, who ran Siebkens at that time, were the ideal hosts and could not do enough for all the drivers and team personnel who chose to go there when racing at Road America. The rooms were nothing special — no air conditioning, no telephones — but still everyone wanted to stay there. Pam did all the excellent cooking and the location, right on the lake, is idyllic. The bar, called the Tavern, has more signed photographs and posters on the walls than anywhere I know. If your face is not there somewhere, you have not made it in racing. I had some most pleasurable nights in this fine bar with people like Brian Redman, Dario Franchitti and Greg Moore, to name just three.

One story concerns the aforementioned Redman. One time during the 1980s we had been at Mid-Ohio having dinner with our respective teams after the race. Brian stopped by to say goodnight and had some sort of mental blackout. Close at hand was a parked dessert trolley and, without thinking, he picked up a piece of chocolate gateau and slapped it in my face before continuing on his way out.

The opportunity to get my own back arose a few weeks later in the main dining room at Siebkens. Brian was with his team at a large table, sitting at the end of it next to the opening into the inner dining room. I crept through this inner dining room and obtained a nice slice of chocolate and cherry tort *en route*. I merely had to reach around the corner and place it squarely in his mush!

All hell broke out and almost the entire room

chose sides. Mayhem. Doug and Pam slowed things down enough to ask everyone to repair to the Tavern bar to continue, which we did for two hours. A vivid memory is of Pam rushing to replenish our supply of aerosol cream topping, which, along with beer and other beverages, was about an inch deep on the floor by the time it was over. Now that's a proper hotel owner!

After we moved to Milwaukee we soon discovered the Lake Park Bistro, another place overlooking a lake with excellent food and very friendly people. As with the Butchers Arms in Warwickshire, it was so close to home that we could easily stagger back after a good meal and a modicum of wine — and in fact we started calling it the 'Butchers Arms West'. The chef, Adam Segal, was so good that sometimes we asked him and his team to cater for dinner parties at home. When Greg had his 40th birthday, Peter Pires from the Butchers Arms came over as a surprise guest, so now we are waiting for someone from the 'Butchers Arms West' to visit the 'Butchers Arms East'.

ABOVE The Tavern bar at Siebkens, my adored haunt at Elkhart Lake, is a homage to race drivers past and present.
Siebkens/Hannah Kaiser

AFTERWORD

A comic tale By Margaret Hobbs

Many people over the years have asked me what attracted me to Dave in the first place and my response has always been the same: 'He's so funny.'

He's a mad comedian, a great mimic and a joke-teller rather along the lines of that famous and crazy comedian Tommy Cooper.

He has always been a very happy person to be with and we spent most of our youth laughing and having so much fun year after year that it seemed we were both very lucky — and these things haven't changed even today.

Dave and I met when I was 14 and he was 15. He was at Feldon School for Boys along with my brother Paul. After school they came back to our house to hang out and play cricket. Sometimes I was allowed to join in, but being a girl only as 'the fielder'!

That was the cricket. But then we began to see another attraction looming large at the house. It was my brother's weekly comic, a comic called the *Eagle*, in which the main character was Dan Dare, Pilot of the Future. He was every schoolboy's hero at the time, and now he seemed to cast his spell on Dave.

At Dave's own home he wasn't allowed the *Eagle* comic (only another benign one called the *Beano*) as his parents considered Dan Dare a rather unsavoury character whose influence on a nice young man's mind was thought undesirable, or something like that. But like all teenagers, when the object of your desires is denied you, you crave it more. It was the thrilling exploits of Dan Dare that really excited Dave and he seemed to immerse himself into that character.

Wednesdays. That was the day the *Eagle* landed through our letter box. And we had started dating and going to the movies on

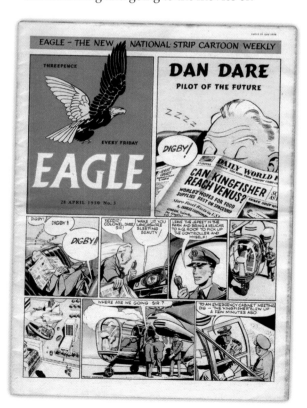

OPPOSITE **Mags at a Mid-Ohio race in the mid-1970s. For many years while I was racing in America, she and the boys came over in the school summer holidays. We based ourselves at Elkhart Lake and had lovely times together as a family.**
David Hobbs collection

LEFT **As Mags recalls, my early interest when visiting her home as a 15-year-old was to read her brother's copy of my favourite comic.**
Private collection

hadn't been delivered that day. 'WHAT? It must be here,' he'd say, and with my brother Paul and sister Pam smirking in the background I'd tell him 'No, it didn't come', and we would be on time for the movie. That tactic worked well a few times but he was so disappointed to miss Dan Dare that I couldn't keep it up. I was beginning to realise how strongly Dave was drawn to this adventure thing. And so it began.

I believe a lot in the 'path of fate or destiny' and I still find it intriguing to think back on how a matter as simple as 'loving parents banning their child's comic' could set others on their destiny.

When I was still only 14, Dave turned 16 and was able to apply for his motorcycle licence. Although he did not get his longed-for motorbike, his parents did buy him a Lambretta scooter. This was a wonderful thing for us, very exciting, fun times; with me hanging on from the pillion seat we felt like a couple of Italian teenagers in a movie.

Dave was a very happy and popular boy at school, if not the most achieving of scholars. This was perhaps his first arena, a stage where he could enjoy the humorous interaction with other boys, a place where he spent most of his time at the back of the class joking with his great pal Tony Barrett, who was, and still is, what every comedian longs for — a helpless giggler. School was all too much fun for Dave what with Tony as the perfect foil for his humour and laughter to be enjoyed. Schoolwork held little charm for him as he was too busy enjoying life.

He had an extraordinary upbringing and his mother just adored him. He was not spoiled, just totally loved, and I think that is what gave him his considerable confidence in himself. He never questions himself and is always happy with who and what he is.

In 1955 his family took a trip around the world, stopping off in Australia for six weeks to visit 'the rellies'. I turned 15 while he was away and when they returned his mother told me that she knew there was 'someone special' as she saw Dave going to the back of the plane, usually a Lockheed Constellation, to write what she knew were love letters.

Wednesdays. Prophetically, the first movie we saw was a motor racing film called *The Racers* starring Kirk Douglas.

But Dan Dare still loomed large in Dave's life and in fact going to the cinema on a Wednesday evening turned into a bit of a 'comic' situation. Always arriving late, he would rush in to settle down and read the latest Dan Dare exploits. Hence, late for the film. So, I began to hide the comic under the sofa cushions and tell him it

When the family returned, Dave persuaded his parents to let him have the family car to drive at Staverton. He became myopic about motor racing. The longed-for motorbike, a Triumph 500, came and went, and his mother's green Morris Oxford, called by its licence plate 'Mol' was the new thing. The bike was replaced by the car, the tweed cap by the helmet, the *Eagle* comic by *Autosport,* and the schoolboy into his version of Dan Dare.

Next came his father's pale blue Jaguar XK140. With lots of club racing success, plus a crash or two, he was fast heading, unaware though I was, towards his next goal.

In November 1960 at the Earls Court Motor Show in London, where every year his father's company Hobbs Transmission would show the Hobbs automatic gearbox, he urged me to come and see what he was going to race the following year. There, sparkling like a diamond under the powerful spotlights of the stand, was a stunning, glossy, scarlet Lotus Elite. I can still see it. It was a car to die for, a car to fulfil every 21-year-old's dream, and a machine straight out of the *Eagle*.

With my modest background I thought there was no chance of Dave being able to own something like that and I remember telling him not to be so silly. I truly believed that it was a fantasy that would end in disappointment. But I was wrong. I had not yet fully understood the intensity of Dave's determination to get what he wanted — to be Dan Dare the racing driver.

Dave's father was always good to him and together they planned to install the Hobbs automatic gearbox in the Lotus Elite for Dave to race the coming season. That, as you will have read earlier, launched us into a lifetime of international motor racing and now it became our whole life. Although I was at Art School studying painting and calligraphy, I spent most of my spare time going to the races with Dave.

After a few years my head was somewhat reeling with so many developments. We got married, set up home, produced two sons, Greg and Guy, and all the while remained very happy for Dave as his new racing career advanced. Of course, there were negative aspects. His long absences were tough to deal with and at times I resented the racing game, but I never wanted him to stop. It was his goal realised.

I remember other women talking about not allowing one's partner to race because it was such a dangerous pursuit, but not me. I had always felt strongly that if one partner dislikes the other's passion, then it must be their place to leave. I could never ask him to abandon his goals for me. After all, I thought, what would you be left with? Someone who is living your life and has lost his own. I had no desire for that and would never have discouraged the ambition that meant so much to him.

Back then Dave would have said that racing was ALL he was capable of, but I knew that was

BELOW This is a publicity shot of Mags when her book *Better to Journey* was published in 1991. It describes her exploits on trekking trips in the Himalayas. She reached Everest base camp at 18,000 feet.
Margaret Hobbs collection

ABOVE LEFT Mags has become an accomplished artist in recent years and her paintings sell well. Here, at home in Vero Beach, she is putting the finishing touches to a landscape.
Andrew Marriott

ABOVE RIGHT This painting by Mags depicts the Ford GT40 that Mike Hailwood and I brought home in third place at Le Mans in 1969. She painted it for the silent auction at the Amelia Island Concours d'Elegance in 2017.
Margaret Hobbs

untrue, I knew that racing was THE ONLY thing he could think about. It was an obsession.

Like his Dad, cars and everything to do with them was his life. He grew up in a car sitting on his Dad's knee learning to study the instruments at all times. Because of that he became a fine test driver and was known throughout his career for that — it was in his blood.

Before our boys were born, I went to every race and hung over the pit wall like everyone else. I became quite adept at reading a race: I could always tell where Dave was on the track, exactly when he should come into sight, and I could read the flags, the crowd and the stopwatch. I used to watch it all very intently, mainly because I was worried. But I tried not to show these feelings as I knew he would only have worried about me worrying about him — and where does that leave you?

When Dave raced abroad, especially when he was far away for longer periods in America or South Africa, I would wait and wait for the phone to ring after the end of each race. I was not so much interested in hearing the result; I just wanted to know he was all right.

Years later, I looked back and thought about the way I concealed worries, and puzzled why I had not been more emotional and demonstrative when I was younger. Eventually the only reason I could find was that we were so young. When you are a teenage girl it is exciting if your boyfriend starts motor racing or some other risky, dangerous but glamorous activity. With the energy and innocence of youth, you do not dwell on the bad things that can happen and back then no one fully recognised how dangerous the cars and the circuits were.

We had great fun at the tracks in those days. We were a big gang, all friends, helping each other, borrowing tools, assisting a rival by pushing his car to scrutineering or onto a trailer. After a day's racing we all headed off to the pub, where the men dissected and re-enacted every moment of the day's racing, endlessly — the 'I would have won but' conversation! It was fun, a social scene, and Dave's competitors meant a lot to him. If someone was in hospital after a 'moment' on the track, Dave would invariably visit if he could. He valued his pals and his colleagues, and I am happy to say we still remain the best of friends with so many of them.

I had a great deal of faith in Dave's skill. He always drove with a degree of caution and I knew he did not take unnecessary risks. He was a thinking driver. He understood the technicalities of a car and knew instinctively how to look after it. When a car broke, or was not performing correctly, he could describe clearly to his pit crew what was going on. Sometimes they would tell him that he must be wrong, but he never was, and often by the Tuesday after the race they'd call and say, 'David, you were right, it was so and so!'. He would roll his eyes and smile.

Over the years I have learned that racing is a very frustrating business and technical difficulties affect even the best-prepared cars. If you could wish for one thing in racing, I think it would be to have Lady Luck sitting beside you in your car as often as possible. In terms of race results I don't think Dave saw too much of her but perhaps she was present in other ways, and although his concern for the car and thoughtful driving may have cost him a place or two, she may be the reason we still have him.

I was not at all surprised by his move into television. The story he tells in the book about going for an interview with CBS and leaving with his tail between his legs is surprising. But then he follows it up with his story of how, one evening, making everyone laugh on the *Ken Squier Show* in Daytona Beach led to his big break at CBS and a career in TV that lasted 40 years. This story is a perfect fit for Dave. Given a school-like interview, he could not hack it, but let him be his natural self in a comfortable situation and success will follow.

As I have said before, he has always wanted to be on the stage and I think he finally made it, as his entertainment abilities are a core part of him. If he can stand up in front of a crowd of people with a microphone in his hand, he is a happy man.

So now, 60 years on, we are still together. Dave achieved his fame, not fortune, but he has never changed one tiny bit. He is still the same old Dave to me and everyone around him, and very much loved by all our large family and numerous friends. He still makes me laugh and we still have lots of fun. He continues to chase around the world, not yet ready to retire. He is still telling, at the request of many, the very old twenty-quid joke, and he is still enjoying life. He has been quite an asset to motor racing and motor racing has been very good to him.

As for me, after all those years of motor racing, I finally got to follow my artistic heart and do what I was always meant to do — paint.

BELOW Mags and I at Vero Beach, Florida in 2017, 63 happy years after we first got together and 56 years on from our wedding day.
Andrew Marriott

DAVID HOBBS
Acknowledgements

Where do I start? Easy: my wife Margaret, Mags as she likes to be called. We have been together for an amazing 63 years and, reading through the book, you will have understood what a special person she is. But for her, my career would not have developed as well as it did. Whenever I jetted off to the next race, she was always there to look after our boys, who had to put up with me being away so much when they were young, missing all those school and sports events. Mags coped with everything a happy family needs to hold it together — and even moved house without my help. She was the catalyst for this book, urging me over the years to get on and write my story, to which we have added her account of how it all began.

Rather like Le Mans, writing *Hobbo* has been a bitter/sweet endurance experience. In fact it has taken almost a decade to complete, but then my career did span five decades.

I would like to thank my dear friend and old broadcasting colleague Bob Varsha for dropping the flag and getting the book off the starting line. For a very long time he listened to me rambling on, patiently recording my haphazard racing memories. By putting them into some sort of order, he created the mainframe of *Hobbo*. After a 'pit stop', Andrew Marriott took over the job. He tweaked it, fine-tuned it and got it to the chequered flag. Andrew has been a pillar of motor racing journalism for nearly 50 years and as a young cub reporter for *Motoring News* he wrote about my early races in the Lotus Elite. Now he is a TV colleague. My admiration for these two guys knows no bounds.

I must thank Eric Verdon-Roe and Mark Hughes at Evro Publishing who took on the book after another publisher ran into problems. They have done a great job. Thanks must also go to the photographers who captured the many fabulous images we have used. Wherever possible they have been credited. Many of these photographs we have treasured over the years and still do.

In my career I have driven for some wonderful teams with some very supportive sponsors. I have lost count of quite how many, but those that stand out are BMW, Penske Racing, McLaren Racing, Team Lotus, JW Automotive, Carl Haas, Neil DeAtley and John Fitzpatrick. Special mention must go to the engineers and mechanics who worked late into the night and so often gave me a winning car. Big thanks to all of you for allowing me to have fabulous fun behind the wheel. Thanks, too, to the many team-mates I have raced with over the years, some sadly now gone, but others remain great friends.

A big thank you also goes to my great mate Sam Posey for providing the foreword. It is written, as ever, in his peerless and elegant prose, although as you can see it did not take him long.

LEFT Mags commissioned this portrait by British artist Paul Oz, who is well known for his Formula 1 subjects. I like it a lot.
Paul Oz

No doubt he was still thinking that the story of my achievements could only be 'a very thin book'.

For my broadcasting career I owe a large debt of gratitude to Ken Squier. He saw my potential and set me on the road to the fascinating world of television. Thanks also to his boss Clarence Cross who, not withstanding his grave doubts about me, gave me my first chance. Since that first show I have had immense pleasure working with some superb television professionals at CBS, ESPN, Speedvision, Speed and most recently NBC, covering the Formula 1 World Championship with Leigh Diffey and Steve Matchett. These colleagues have been in front of camera with me but let us not forget the directors, producers, cameramen and technicians, all of whom make it happen. To all of you, my many, many thanks.

Another big thank you goes to all the fans, both those who cheered me at the side of the track and those who have watched me on television, some of whom are even old enough to have done both.

Thanks also to the customers at David Hobbs Honda. We love you all and hurry back.

I hope this book gives you an insight into my career and illustrates how lucky I have been both in love and in life. With a little help from my friends (as John Lennon said) it has been a great journey. Thank you — all.

APPENDIX
Some favourites

Race cars (in order)

1 Ford GT40
2 Porsche 956/962
3 McLaren M10B (Formula 5000)
4 Lola T330 (Formula 5000)
5 BMW 320i Turbo
6 March-BMW sports prototype (1986 IMSA GTP)
7 Lotus Elite (with Hobbs Mecha-Matic gearbox)
8 Ferrari 512M (prepared by Penske)
9 Jaguar XJ13
10 Lola T70 Spyder

Favourite tracks (in order)

1 Nürburgring (Nordschleife)
2 Le Mans
3 Road America (Elkhart Lake)
4 Watkins Glen
5 Silverstone (1970s configuration)
6 Oulton Park
7 Mosport
8 Sears Point
9 Kyalami (in original configuration)
10 Laguna Seca (with the old Turn 1)

Favourite co-drivers (in alphabetical order)

Richard Attwood   Greg Hobbs
Derek Bell   Sarel van der Merwe
Mark Donohue   Ronnie Peterson
John Fitzpatrick   Sam Posey
Mike Hailwood   Brian Redman
Paul Hawkins   Hans Stuck

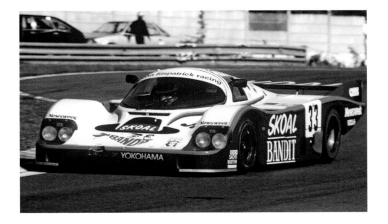

LEFT My favourite car at my favourite track. And it so happens that my driving partner that day, in the 1,000Km race of May 1968, also appears in my list of favourite co-drivers. As well as that, Brian Redman is one of my oldest and best friends in racing.
LAT Images

ABOVE My second favourite car at my second favourite track. On the way to third place at Le Mans in the Skoal Bandit Porsche 956B in 1984, when Sarel van der Merwe, another of my favourite co-drivers, was one of my team-mates.
Bill Warner

Index